Invisible Men

Life in Baseball's

Negro Leagues

by Donn Rogosin

INTRODUCTION BY MONTE IRVIN

University of Nebraska Press
Lincoln and London

∞

First Nebraska paperback printing: 2007

Appendixes are reprinted from *Only the Ball Was White* by Robert
Peterson, published by Prentice-Hall, Inc. Copyright © 1970 by Robert
Peterson; used by permission of the author.

Library of Congress Cataloging-in-Publication Data
Rogosin, Donn.
Invisible men: life in baseball's Negro leagues / Donn Rogosin;
introduction by Monte Irvin.
p. cm.
Includes index.
Originally published: New York: Atheneum, 1983.
ISBN-13: 978-0-8032-5969-0 (pbk.: alk. paper)
ISBN-10: 0-8032-5969-7 (pbk.: alk. paper)
1. Baseball—United States—History. 2. Negro leagues. 3. African
American baseball players. 4. Discrimination in sports—United States.
I. Title.
GV863.A1R585 2007
796.357—dc22   2006029419

EUGENIE AND ROGIE

Introduction

I first met Donn Rogosin when he was a young, dynamic professor of American Studies at the University of Texas. I was very impressed with his knowledge of the Negro leagues, but it was his close contact with Willie Wells, my manager when I was with Newark in the Negro leagues and my dear friend, that made our relationship. Not only was Willie Wells a truly great player and one of the smartest baseball men who ever lived, but his career went back to nearly the beginning of the Negro leagues, and I knew right away that Donn would have access to the whole story.

Over the years with my help and the help of the other fellows, Donn went around the country meeting the old Negro leaguers and interviewing them in their homes. The time was right. Donn had a chance to talk with Satchel, Cool (Papa Bell), Judy (Johnson), Buck (Leonard), and the rest. If he had not had this opportunity, their stories would have been lost.

Much hard work went into this project—both time and energy. Donn has attempted to tell the story of the Negro leagues the way it should be told. He gained a complete perspective by talking to managers, owners, and players. He did an in-depth study and was very thorough. He had adventures "on the road," and he interviewed in some pretty tough parts of this country. Sometimes the fellows would keep up with each other through Donn.

At the time we played in the Negro leagues we were young and we had talent. Negro baseball was very important to us, but it was not important to the other segments of American life—by that I mean white people. We were saying, "Hey, notice us." Now it has become important, and the establishment wants to make amends.

Invisible Men is really much more than a book about sports. I am happy to be in it and to have helped with it. For many of us who played Negro league baseball, this is a book we have long awaited.

MONTE IRVIN

Preface

This book began in Willie Wells's living room, where I first heard the tales of the Negro leagues and learned of segregated baseball. My initial visit to Wells's home was innocent enough. At the time, I was teaching American Studies at the University of Texas and was seeking someone or something that might shake the lethargy which permeated my classes. I felt that maybe a Negro league baseball player discussing segregated baseball could bring home the essence of segregation to students seemingly so insulated from America's past history of racial injustice. So I went to see Wells, to check him out and to discover if he would "work" as a classroom speaker.

I came away from our meeting stunned. I was amazed by his stories and profoundly moved by his spirit and dignity. Needless to say, he was most effective in the classroom.

But I also had found a friend. Many times during the summer of 1977, I returned to visit with Willie Wells. Usually we would listen to ball games on the radio and he would patiently answer questions about

Satchel Paige, Josh Gibson, Oscar Charleston, and the other great ballplayers he had known. (He almost never spoke of himself and I had to get my Willie Wells stories later from his teammates.)

After a while I began to tape our meetings. Then I asked National Public Radio if they would back a documentary series based upon the oral histories of as many Negro leaguers as I could find. They agreed. And so, with a borrowed tape recorder and instructions in the rudiments of radio production, I set out after Negro leaguers. It was a joyous task and one that got easier as one player led to the next, and each impression contributed to a more complete picture.

The completed documentaries were broadcast by National Public Radio first in 1980. I shall always feel grateful to NPR and KUT-FM in Austin, Texas, for making my work on Negro league baseball possible. I remain especially indebted to Bill Grimes, a radio producer and editor of skill and integrity. James Earl Jones's willingness to narrate that series for me was a kind act by a most decent and wonderful man.

Once Negro league baseball had become my passion, I was pleased to find that, without exception, those who had been touched by the Negro leaguers were eager to assist me. Robert Peterson and John Holway, the men who first wrote about the Negro leagues for white audiences, were always helpful. While *Invisible Men* contains my own deeply felt view of the Negro leagues, it is no secret that I follow a path that these men first marked out.

I was fortunate that the Smithsonian Institution asked me to help mount a special exhibit on the Negro leagues for display in April of 1981. Working with curator Carl Scheele, Ellen Rooney Hughes, and Jim

Piper of the National Museum of American History
was an education and a pleasure. It also added a dimension to my work by exposing me to the sensitive
perceptions of the best museum people in the world.

In 1979 in the midst of my researches, the Negro
league reunions began in Ashland, Kentucky, and with
them the push to build a black baseball Hall of History. Without Nancy Dickinson and Harry Wiley of the
Greater Ashland Foundation, the reunions could not
have happened and without the reunions, this book
would be a lesser effort. I have the deepest affection
for Nancy and Gene Dickinson, Lisa Mahood, and
Harry Wylie of Ashland, Kentucky; they have done
much to preserve the story of the Negro leagues. Ashland Oil Company and Schlitz Brewing Company
generously gave corporate funds to make the reunions
possible.

Finally, of overwhelming importance to my work
were my relationships with Craig Davidson, Scott
McPherson, and Steve Schwartz. Craig Davidson had
embarked on a project similar to mine—to capture
the texture of the Negro leagues and their glorious
history. Only, Craig is a talented film maker and, unfortunately, film costs much more than audio tape or
pencils. For years Craig plowed his time and money
into his film. We became dear friends "on the road."
I was invited to join Refocus Productions, and we
shared everything. Many things in this book are a
result of our long and productive collaboration.

Of course, my largest debt is to the Negro leaguers
themselves. They gave everything they had, generously and warmly. Of particular assistance to me were:
Newt Allen, Dave Barnhill, Pepper Bassett, Cool Papa
Bell, Gene Benson, Willard Brown, Roy Campanella,

Jimmie Crutchfield, Ray Dandridge, Leon Day, Rudolpho Fernandez, Wilmur Fields, Bill Harvy, Buster Haywood, Sammy T. Hughes, Connie Johnson, Judy Johnson, Monte Irvin, Walter "Buck" Leonard, Webster McDonald, Jack Marshall, Minnie Minoso, John "Buck" O'Neil, Ted Page, Satchel Paige, Pat Patterson, Andy Porter, Ted Radcliffe, Chico Renfroe, Dick Seay, Harry Solomon, Hilton Smith, Theolic Smith, Paul Stevens, Sam Streeter, Quincy Trouppe, and Willie Wells. In addition, Ric Roberts, Art Carter, and Sam Lacy, talented sportswriters of the black newspapers, provided further information. Dorothy Harris, Effa Manley, and Lahoma Paige added their perceptions of Negro baseball, and they were close enough to it to know what was really going on.

Others who contributed to my research include Bill Veeck, Gov. "Happy" Chandler, Bob Feller, Tom Lasorda, John Welau, Birdie Tebbetts, Bill Harris, Mack Robinson, and Luis Tiant, Jr.

I am proud to call William Goetzmann my mentor. Bill Goetzmann gave me critical, emotional, and intellectual help when my manuscript was a struggling dissertation. Ricardo Romo, Jeff Meikle, and Al Crosby read and commented on it at that time. (The dissertation, "Black Baseball, Life in the Negro Leagues," is available on microfilm, scholarly impedimenta and all, from the University of Michigan.)

Along the way I piled up other intellectual debts. Jules Tygiel let me see a chapter of his work on Branch Rickey; Dick Crepeau showed me his work on the Jake Powell affair; and Janet Bruce allowed me access to her immense research on the Kansas City Monarchs. Stephen Banker's "Black Diamonds" collection of oral histories was of great help.

I appreciate deeply the assistance of Craig David-son, Steve Schwartz, Phil Dixon, and Jim Thompson in preparing the necessary photographs for this book.

I thank Ernie Barnes, Gail Von Halvorsen, and Judge and Mrs. Henry P. Nelson for the use of Ernie's magnificent drawing of Satchel Paige, and Kathy Eckstein for helping type the manuscript more than once.

How can a writer thank those who made his first book possible? Although Julian Bach and Tom Stewart know how much it means to the author that they believed in this book before it was a book, let me again reiterate my lasting gratitude.

Contents

Invisible Men

The World That Negro Baseball Made

In segregated America, great black baseball players were forced to exhibit their talents behind a rigid color barrier—victims of the unwritten law that no black man was allowed in the major leagues. Men of extraordinary athletic ability passed their lives in obscurity, absent from the sport pages of the white newspapers, obliterated from American sports history.

Confronted by an intolerant society, the black athlete and the black community built their own sports world. Black teams were formed and later, black leagues. The better players rose to the top; the very best became genuine heroes. Their names and deeds never did completely die. For the achievements of the great stars of what was then called "Negro baseball" lived on in the folk experience of American black people. The feats of black pitching masters like Smokey Joe Williams—the best pitcher of the teens and twenties—or Satchel Paige—who dominated the thirties—became treasured memories for a people held down by a segregation all too easily accepted by others. The legendary hitting of Josh Gibson and Buck

Leonard, the Ruth and Gehrig of Negro baseball, was something no apologist for white supremacy could take from black people.

But the importance of the Negro leagues transcended the world of sport. A small group of black men, gifted with remarkable skills, reached far above the menial and the mundane. In the process they became worldly, and some became wise. Scuffling to make a living playing the game that they loved, these men became symbols of competence and achievement for all black people. Because they provided joy and excitement in their often dramatic quest for victories and Negro league pennants, they enriched life in black America. When their baseball victories came against white opponents, they undermined segregation itself.

From 1920, when the first Negro National League was founded in Kansas City, until 1946, when Jackie Robinson formally stepped across the color line and into organized white baseball, the Negro leagues grew, matured, overcame hardship, and even flourished.

Black teams, representing black communities, formed a replica of major-league baseball, separate and unequal in everything but athletic ability. Though it was virtually ignored by the dominant white culture, in the black community the Negro league was a cultural institution of the first magnitude.

The heart of the Negro leagues was in the emerging Northern ghettos: New York's Harlem and Chicago's South Side and other major Northern black settlements. Teams grew where there was a rich enough black soil; among them were the Pittsburgh Crawfords, Kansas City Monarchs, Chicago American Giants, New York Black Yankees, Philadelphia Stars, Newark Eagles, and Baltimore Elite Giants. The Deep

South had a smattering of Negro league teams, too: the Memphis Red Sox, Jacksonville Red Caps, Atlanta Black Crackers, and, especially, the Birmingham Black Barons were part of the Negro leagues* at one time or another.

The term "Negro league baseball," strictly speaking, described the big-league black teams of segregated America. It differentiated the Negro major leagues from the white majors, from several Negro minor leagues such as the Texas Negro League, and from the ubiquitous independent black baseball teams that swirled through America in hopes of finding opponents and a dollar.

Although team finances were always precarious, the Negro leagues enjoyed substantial community support. "There wasn't hardly anything else we could do," Satchel Paige's wife Lahoma once remarked. Even in

---

*In their speech, Negro leaguers use "Negro league," "Negro leagues," "The League," and "Negro major leagues" interchangeably when referring to their segregated baseball. Everything prior to 1920 was considered "independent ball" and everything after about 1951 or 1952 didn't really count because by then all the best Negro baseball players were in the white leagues. The first Negro league, called the Negro National League, was founded by Rube Foster in 1920. It was joined in 1923 by the Eastern Colored League, which survived until 1928. That first Negro National League lasted until 1931 and then was reformed by Pittsburgh's Gus Greenlee in 1933. In 1937 a Negro American League was created. The second Negro National League, primarily based on the Eastern Seaboard—"Jackie Robinson country"—died abruptly in 1948, while the Negro American League continued on until 1960, though with only a fraction of its previous support and prestige.

1920, the first year of the Negro National League, a Sunday crowd of five thousand was the norm. At the celebrated four-team doubleheaders in Yankee Stadium in the 1930s, a crowd of twenty thousand paying black fans was not unusual. One year, in the 1940s, the *Chicago Defender*, the city's black newspaper, labeled "disappointing" a crowd over thirty-five thousand for the East-West Classic, which was the black all-star game. Speaking of his first East-West game crowd, Orestes "Minnie" Minoso of the New York Cubans laughed, "I never saw so many Negroes in all my life."

In fact, the Negro Leagues were among the largest black businesses in the United States before the breakdown of segregation; in their prime they were a multi-million-dollar operation. The cafes, beer joints, and rooming houses of the Negro neighborhoods all benefited as black baseball monies sometimes trickled, sometimes rippled through the black community. The management of two leagues with twelve to fifteen teams, each league playing across the entire nation and employing hundreds of people, may rank among the highest achievements of black enterprise during segregation—a sorry comment on segregation, but a tribute to the world that Negro baseball made.

How good were the Negro league teams? Good enough to win over sixty percent of their encounters with white major-league opponents, though the records are incomplete and the meaning of these games difficult to evaluate. Good enough to train Willie Mays, Jackie Robinson, Hank Aaron, Monte Irvin, Roy Campanella, Don Newcombe, Elston Howard, Ernie Banks, and dozens more, though the major leagues pretended that the black teams didn't exist. "They're not organized," charged the baseball authorities led by Commissioner Kenesaw Mountain Landis. "We were organized," retorted Hall of Fame member Buck Leonard. "We just weren't recognized."

The first successful Negro league was the Negro National League, established by Andrew "Rube" Foster in 1920. Foster was a charismatic giant who won the nickname "Rube" for pitching a much-savored victory over major-league ace Rube Waddell at the turn of the century. Born in Calvert, Texas, in 1879, he left home and school after the eighth grade to become a touring ballplayer. Within a few years he was the premier hurler for the Waco Yellow Jackets and well known to the better Northern black teams who came south to gain a jump on the baseball season. Soon enough Foster was with them; a star in New York, Chicago, and Philadelphia, featured in exhibitions against white clubs, and feted throughout urban black America.

Had he remained a mere ballplayer, Foster would be assured a large place in black baseball history. His four victories for the Cuban X Giants in 1903 in a series for the "Colored Championship of the World," or his wins for the Philadelphia Giants in a similar series the following year were all the credentials Rube needed. Indeed, Foster, the submarine pitcher with the original "fade-away" screwball, was the best black pitcher of the twentieth century's first decade.

However, it was as a manager and baseball entrepreneur that Rube Foster earned minor immortality and a very belated spot in the Baseball Hall of Fame. While pitching for the Chicago Leland Giants in 1907, Foster was outraged at the small pay he and his teammates received for weekend games against strong white semi-pro opponents. He succeeded in convincing owner Frank Leland to let him negotiate for more, and thereafter no Rube Foster team ever took less than fifty percent of the gate for playing independent ball. By 1911 Foster had taken some of the Leland Giants' best ballplayers and used them as the nucleus of a new team: the Chicago American Giants, or, as they were known on the street, Foster's Giants. With Charlie Comiskey's son-in-law John Schorling as a business partner, he rebuilt the grandstands at the old White Sox stadium at 39th and Shields. Foster was now in the baseball business.

Foster's helmsmanship was characterized by a daring, energetic, attacking style that put a premium on speed. Rube loved the hit-and-run bunt, the double steal, the squeeze play. One of his protégés, Webster McDonald, recalled, "If you walked a man against Rube, that was a run." Rube often said, "You don't have to get three hits every day for me, you don't have to get even two. But I want that one at the right time."

A fastidious man, Foster sometimes sat up in the stands and managed the game from the box seats as he puffed away on his meerschaum pipe or chomped his favorite Havana cigar. When Foster traveled he rented a Pullman car—a spectacle much talked about and appreciated throughout black America. Above all, he molded the Chicago American Giants into the top black team in the nation: a team so strong they held their own with the Cubs and White Sox in their few meetings. The story still circulates that Connie Mack and John McGraw sought Foster's baseball advice, and that Foster taught the legendary Christy Mathewson the "fade-away".

The Chicago American Giants were at the pinnacle of black baseball throughout the teens. They made decent wages playing white semi-pros or the better black independents, and they sometimes outdrew the Cubs and White Sox. Several times a year Foster took the American Giants on tour, east, south, or into Canada. (It was on a trip to New York City, routed through Hamilton, Ontario, that black heavyweight champion Jack Johnson jumped bail after his conviction for violating the White Slave Fugitive Act. His crime had been to take a [willing] white woman across state lines for an immoral purpose. Johnson, dressed as an American Giant and carrying baseball equipment, had had no problem convincing either police or the customs that he was a professional athlete.)

In 1916 Foster took his team to Cuba, and in the late teens Rube had a contract with the Florida East Coast Railroad to entertain tourists with winter baseball at the Breakers in West Palm Beach. Foster also was one of the first to send a complete black ballclub to California for winter baseball.

Foster quickly became aware of the drawbacks of independent baseball. He was at the mercy of white booking agents, and, in the increasingly hostile racial climate of post-World War I Chicago, that reliance was inherently unsatisfactory. Then too, strong Eastern black independents competed with the American Giants for the best black ballplayers. Relations between Foster and Nat C. Strong, the East's most powerful booking agent, became particularly strained, especially by the battles for shortstop John Henry Lloyd, the "black Honus Wagner."

Foster soon realized that creating a strong league was the best way to set up a schedule without having

to rely on booking agents, and the only way to avoid
self-defeating bidding wars for top players. Further,
Foster was a man of vision; he understood the pro-
motional possibilities built around pennant races and
rivalries between cities. With his outstanding record
in every phase of the game, Foster was ready to campaign for a Negro league.

The idea of a Negro league was not new in 1920.
Beauregard Moseley, the secretary of the Chicago Leland Giants, had attempted to form a National Negro
Baseball League of America in 1910 and 1911. "Blacks
are already forced out of the game from a national
standpoint," Moseley had noted. He urged a self-help
philosophy to stabilize the black man's deteriorating
position in American society. However, Moseley lacked
Foster's leadership abilities and his nationwide contacts with black baseball independents and white
baseball figures of every sort.

In the decade after Moseley's proposal failed, Foster
solidified his relations with other Midwestern independents. Foster conducted preliminary discussions
concerning a Negro league and, in 1919, set up a sat-
ellite operation in Detroit headed by Tenny Blount.
When Foster arrived at the historic founding meeting
of the Negro National League at the Kansas City YMCA
in February 1920, he had no difficulty shaping it the
way he wanted, right down to the league slogan: "We
are the ship, all else the sea."

The Chicago American Giants, the Chicago Giants,
St. Louis Giants, Detroit Stars, Taylor ABC's, Kansas
City Monarchs, and the Cuban Stars made up the First
Negro National League. ("Giants" was the most pop-
ular name for black baseball teams after the 1880s,
when a team of New Yorkers called the Cuban Giants

proved themselves the best team of the era.)

J. L. ("Wilkie") Wilkinson of Kansas City was the only white owner. Foster, well aware that Kansas City was the natural rival for St. Louis and Chicago, somewhat reluctantly settled on Wilkinson in recognition of his previous success with the All-Nations, a touring ballclub composed of Indians, blacks, Japanese, Mexicans, and whites. The All-Nations team was owned and promoted by ex-minor-league pitcher Wilkinson. Although the All-Nations team was a ballplaying international, its black contingent, led by Newt Joseph, Bullet Rogan, and Jose Mendez, was its core. When Wilkinson created the Monarchs to play in the segregated world of the black league, he simply switched his stars to the Negro league team.

To balance his league, Foster authorized several equalizing trades, sending outfielder Oscar Charleston from Chicago to Indianapolis, for example. In 1921 he offered Nat Strong's Lincoln Giants of New York an associate membership to neutralize his main Eastern rival. In 1923 he encouraged the formation of the Eastern Colored League, which gave the Negro leagues the same symmetry as the majors.

This relationship was institutionalized in 1924 with the advent of the Negro World Series, played between Hilldale of Philadelphia and the Kansas City Monarchs. The Monarchs won the nine-game series. They were led by pitching aces Bullet Rogan and Jose Mendez, a "coal-black" Cuban. Hilldale's most valuable player was Julius "Judy" Johnson, a skinny third baseman and a future Hall of Famer.

The first Negro National League and the Eastern Colored League did well during much of the twenties, though Foster's departure from baseball in 1926, allegedly as a result of mental problems, left the league without its leader. (According to Foster's wife, a delirious Rube had a recurring premonition that "he was needed to pitch" a World Series game. The cause of his illness remains conjectural).

Some Negro league stars commanded salaries exceeding four hundred dollars a month—an almost incomprehensible wage by the standards of black wage earners. One year, the lowest-paid American Giant received one hundred seventy-five dollars a month, a sum many times greater than a workingman's pay. The twenties, the Golden Age for white baseball, was probably also the absolute zenith of Negro baseball. The superstars of the decade—Oscar Charleston, John Henry Lloyd, Smokey Joe Williams, Bullet Rogan, and Dick Redding—stand out in black baseball folklore with unsurpassed brilliance.

Who was the greatest Negro league player of all time? A ballot of his peers would undoubtedly choose Oscar Charleston, the left-hand hitting outfielder and later first baseman of the Indianapolis ABCs; the Chicago American Giants, the Pittsburgh Crawfords, and a half-dozen other Negro League teams. From the teens to the thirties, Charleston had no equal as a hitter and fielder. Chicago White Sox pitcher Hollie Thurston, a twenty-game winner, noted acerbically that when he barnstormed against Charleston in the twenties, the latter "hit a home run every night." Second baseman Dick Seay was once asked whether Charleston was really as great as everybody said he was. Seay responded curtly, "He was greater!" Outfielder Bill Evans called Charleston "the franchise." "He'd come to bat with the score tied and they'd walk him," remembered the hard-throwing Connie Johnson. "I wondered why. 'Til one day they pitched to him and he hit it out of the park." Satchel Paige described Charleston's fielding as something that had to be seen to be believed. "He used to play right in back of second base," Paige commented with only slight exaggeration. "He would outrun the ball." Dave Malarcher laughingly observed that "Charleston could play the whole outfield himself."

A 1952 poll of black baseball figures voted Smokey Joe Williams the greatest black pitcher of all time, a single vote ahead of Satchel Paige. A giant of a man, William's fastball seemed to be "coming off a mountain top," as an opponent would later recall it. Jesse Hubbard, another star of the period, was unequivocal. "Joe was the greatest pitcher in baseball, white or black," he claimed. "He'd throw harder and the ball travelled faster than any ball I ever seen."

While Smokey Joe Williams toiled in the East, his Western counterpart was Bullet Rogan of the Kansas City Monarchs. "Rogan could throw the ball by you, and he had one of the greatest curves too," noted Buck O'Neil of the Monarchs. O'Neil's colleague Chet Brewer believed Rogan was the most outstanding of all. "He had a blazing fast ball and a big curve that he could throw harder than most fastballs," remembered Brewer. "Then he was the master of the palm ball— something like a knuckleball if thrown right." Many Monarchs who saw them both rate Rogan above Satchel Paige. After all, as one observer said, "Satchel was strictly fastball."

For much of the twenties, the black leagues did extraordinarily well. The better teams regularly played schedules of from sixty to eighty games and often drew over five thousand fans for weekend games. With their deeds chronicled by the black press, the Negro leagues developed a truly national following. However, despite a wealth of acknowledged stars, the Depression and a lack of sustained leadership destroyed the fortunes of Negro league baseball. As the Depression bottomed, the leagues collapsed, with many of the teams reverting to independent status. Only a massive infusion of gangster capital revitalized the league structure beginning in 1933 under the guidance of Gus Greenlee, Pittsburgh's most prominent black racketeer.

The "numbers," as every Eastern black knew, were a fixture of black community life by the twenties. For as little as a penny, a gambling man picked any three-digit number, and if those digits turned out to be the last numbers of the volume on the stock exchange, or the last numbers of the race-track handle, or the last numbers of any mutually agreeable measure, they paid off—usually at odds of 600 to 1. Six hundred to one was not all that attractive odds, of course, but for blacks without much opportunity to accumulate capital, a 600 to 1 payoff might mean a radio, a new suit, or a memorable night on the town. And six dollars was a lot of money in 1930.

Greenlee's fortune had been built on the pennies of Pittsburgh's black laborers. Morever, Greenlee possessed a strong sense of black boosterism. Thus it wasn't surprising that the domineering Greenlee wanted to own a baseball team. In 1930 he began to sponsor one of Pittsburgh's best semi-pro black teams—the Crawford Colored Giants.

These Crawfords had been organized by Jim Dorsey, the director of the Crawford Recreation Center, located at the corner of Wylie and Crawford Avenue in Pittsburgh's Hill District. Crawford Avenue was the main drag of black Pittsburgh, and the most celebrated "black and tan" in the area was Greenlee's Crawford Bar and Grille. The Grille was a two-story restaurant and dance hall where Duke Ellington, Lena Horne, Count Basie, or the Mills Brothers played and partied when they came to Pittsburgh. It is said to have had the best food in the city.

When Greenlee adopted the "little Crawfords"—just after the first Negro league era had closed—they were clearly of lower caliber than the Homestead Grays, by far Pittsburgh's best and most successful black team. The Grays, led by Smokey Joe Williams on the mound and Vic Harris in the field, and adroitly managed by ex-Penn State basketball star Cumberland Posey, were America's most formidable black independent team. When the Pirates were away, they played in Forbes Field, and they traveled widely to meet the best semi-pros. The Grays were, in fact, a Pennsylvania institution. Pittsburgh, with its raucous semi-pro tradition in both football and baseball, was the ideal location for a strong black independent team, and the Grays thrived. (It was in the twenties that the lifelong friendship between Cum Posey and a young infielder for the Wheeling, West Virginia, Stokies named Art Rooney began.)

Envious of the Grays, Greenlee set out to surpass them and, in the process, created a magnificent if short-lived rivalry in every respect equal to New York's Dodger/Yankee war.

Greenlee's first step was to give the "old bath house gang" a touch of class. This he easily accomplished by sending his assistant, a character with the marvelous nickname of "Woogie," to purchase two seven-

passenger Lincolns for the team. Then in 1931 Greenlee obtained Satchel Paige—already a folk hero in
black America—and in 1932 he added the pride of
Pittsburgh, a young catcher named Josh Gibson. "Gib-
bie," as his friends sometimes called him, was a shy
youngster never totally at home in the fast-paced urban North. But there was nothing shy about Gibson
at the bat, even in the early days. "If you wanted to
see a man who looked like trouble at the bat, look at
Josh," recalled an early friend of the "Bronze Sultan
of Swat."

Satchel Paige had burst upon the Negro league scene
in 1926 with the Birmingham Black Barons. "He struck
out eighteen of us at three o'clock in the afternoon,"
Newt Allen remembered. "His arms were so long, he'd
raise up that big foot and the next thing you'd know
the ball was by ya." Paige fluttered from team to team,
and when the Cleveland Cubs folded in 1931, Greenlee
bought him for the Crawfords.

In 1932 Greenlee also built the first entirely black-
owned baseball stadium with $100,000 of his money.
The new stadium, which, appropriately, he named
Greenlee Field, was located on Bedford Avenue.
"Mountain" Jesse Hubbard ruined the stadium debut
when the Black Yankees beat Satchel Paige 1-0,
with Clint Thomas scoring the winning run and making a spectacular game-saving catch in deep center
field. "Clint could chase that ball into another world,"
said Ted Page of the Crawfords with admiration.

Were the numbers lucrative? A black man spending
$100,000 on a baseball stadium in the midst of the
Depression clearly could afford the best black baseball talent. Soon Greenlee had assembled a team Bob

Feller admiringly called "the Yankees of Negro baseball." During the early 1930s, five future Hall of Fame members cavorted on the Crawfords: Satchel Paige, Josh Gibson, Oscar Charleston, Judy Johnson, and Cool Papa Bell.

In his rebuilt Pittsburgh Crawfords, Greenlee had a team with extraordinary drawing power throughout black America. With the Crawford-Gray rivalry as the centerpiece, it was not difficult, even in 1933, to see a future in a new Negro league. And with Greenlee's wallet, not to mention his well-developed underworld contacts with sources of black money throughout the East, the Negro leagues were soon on their feet. In this second phase of Negro league baseball, the numbers men played a dominating role. They were the small-time, and not-so-small-time, gangsters of the black ghettos, and they were almost the only blacks with the money and inclination necessary to subsidize black baseball.

The Manleys in Newark, Alex Pompez of the New York Cubans, Ed Bolden of the Philadelphia Stars, Tom Wilson of Nashville and later the Baltimore Elite Giants, Ed "Soldier Boy" Semler of the Black Yankees, and Sonny "Man" Jackson, who bankrolled the Homestead Grays—all were numbers bankers, personal friends of Gus Greenlee, and charter members of the second Negro National League.

The Negro American League, established in the Midwest and South in 1937, was less strongly influenced by the numbers bankers, primarily because the impeccable J. L. Wilkinson of Kansas City was the backbone of the league, and his team the league's principal draw. The Monarchs had weathered the collapse of the first Negro National League and had struggled along as an independent; the reputation of Wilkinson's teams, established over three decades, gave the Monarchs a base from which to carry on. With the white House of David team—a bewhiskered bunch of ballplayer/zealot/entertainers—as their main opponent, the Monarchs booked games throughout the entire Midwest, from Waco to Winnipeg. Though times were tough, in 1934 Wilkinson mortgaged his home to pay his ballplayers, and the Monarchs were paid working salaries throughout the Depression.

As the Depression slowly receded, the Negro leagues re-formed and then gained strength. The Negro American League was created out of perennially important Negro baseball towns like Kansas City, St. Louis, and Chicago. Memphis, Atlanta, Jacksonville, and Birmingham also became part of the new Negro American League—a reflection of growing Southern urbanization and strengthening North-South black community relationships.

During World War II Negro baseball entered its flush period. The black population in the Northern Negro baseball heartland had grown steadily. By the 1940s crowds in the tens of thousands were commonplace throughout the North, and special events such as the Negro World Series, the East-West Classic, exhibitions against Bob Feller's or Dizzy Dean's All Stars, four-team doubleheaders, or even a regular league game with Satchel Paige pitching might fill a big-league park.

This success of Negro baseball was not lost on the major-league establishment. White baseball owners rented the Negro league teams their parks, their better players barnstormed with the Negro leaguers after the World Series, and their best players played against and with Negro leaguers in the Caribbean during the winter. After 1940 white and black sportswriters pressed increasingly the cause of baseball integration in the mass-circulation white newspapers. Their pleas were epitomized by the wartime slogan, "If he's good enough for the navy, he's good enough for the majors."

Finally, in 1945, at the very height of Negro league success, Kansas City Monarch rookie shortstop Jackie Robinson reported to his teammates his meeting with Dodger general manager Branch Rickey. He told them that the Dodgers were interested in him and that something might come up. It certainly did. In 1946 Robinson became the first black man to participate openly in "organized" baseball in the twentieth century, playing with Montreal of the International League.

In every way, 1946 was a banner year for Negro baseball. Attendance was up throughout the Negro leagues, and over forty-five thousand attended the All-Star Game at Comiskey Park. The Newark Eagles defeated the Kansas City Monarchs in a thrilling seven-game Negro World Series. Larry Doby and Monte Irvin scored the tying and winning runs in a 3-2 victory for Newark in the climactic game. How could the Negro league have realized that the beginning of the end was at hand?

The year 1947 was different. As Wilkinson watched in stunned disbelief, many Monarch fans rode the train five hours to St. Louis to sit in segregated bleachers and cheer for Jackie Robinson, a ballplayer who had broken into the Monarch lineup only because Jesse Williams, the regular shortstop, had injured his arm. The black fan voted with his feet and supported integration; and every Negro league team near a National League city was badly hurt.

Rather than a disheartening spectacle, however, the integration of baseball was the Negro leagues' finest moment; it represented all that the Negro leagues stood for, all they believed in. Only because they had grown powerful was baseball integration possible.

Of course, at the time the owners did not see it that way. They were sad because their young players deserted them, frustrated because the white press ignored them, and bitter because their franchises were in ruins. Most of the teams quickly and quietly disappeared. In their decline, the Negro leagues were a vast source of cheap baseball talent. The Mays, Campanellas, Dobies, and Aarons played in that twilight, came out of baseball's shadow, and then changed major-league baseball forever.

Yet baseball integration was not swift. Only the Dodgers and Bill Veeck's Cleveland Indians integrated with any speed. It took twelve years for the Red Sox to get "Pumpsie" Green in 1959, a few months behind the Phillies, who also hired their first black player that same year. Some of the greatest players of all time finished their careers in the Negro league, cheering on the youngsters they trained, never tasting what they most coveted.

Buck Leonard, the greatest first baseman of black baseball history, was one such figure. "I felt worse for Buck than anybody," said Monte Irvin. "I wish people could have seen what a marvelous athlete he was."

Ray Dandridge was the top third baseman in black baseball for most of his sixteen-year career, which began in 1933. In 1949 the strongest Giant farm team, the Minneapolis Millers, took Dandridge as a forty-year-old rookie. He was the Rookie of the Year. In 1950, Dandridge hit .311 and was the farm league's Most Valuable Player. But he never reached the majors. Horace Stoneham, owner of the Giants, refused to sell Dandridge's contract to Philadelphia. "You were the drawing power of Minneapolis," the tightwad Stoneham had the nerve to tell Dandridge. "I just wanted to put my left foot in there," said Dandridge (a righthanded batter). "I just would have liked to have been up there one day, even if it was only to get a cup of coffee."

Willie Wells was Jackie Robinson's counterpart for the East in the 1945 East-West Classic. While that game was Robinson's only appearance in the most celebrated black sports event, it was Wells's eighth. Wells, the greatest living player not in the Hall of Fame according to Monte Irvin, and the Negro leagues' greatest shortstop, never "went up."

The life of the Negro leagues was woven firmly into the fabric of the black experience. The season began in the Deep South in February where, after a few days of spring training in Florida, Texas, Arkansas, North Carolina, or wherever a suitable arrangement was made, barnstorming began. Some teams, Jackie Robbinson once complained, "are playing the first day of spring training." But most took a week or so and then went on the road: the economic situation was tenuous enough so that those first barnstorming dollars were very important indeed.

From February to April, most of the better Negro league teams were in the South catering to the baseball fever of the Southern baseball fan. In the large Southern cities, such as Atlanta, Jacksonville, and Birmingham, the Negro leaguer was a celebrity, performing before large, though almost exclusively black crowds. The Negro league teams played each other, or a local Southern black team, or even a Negro college nine, perhaps Clark University or Tuskeegee.

In smaller Southern towns the only difference was the level of play and the size of the crowds. Enthusiastic receptions for the Negro leaguers were, if anything, more fervent the smaller the town.

The pre-season Southern foray was critical for Negro league baseball. Here the Negro league teams, predominantly Northern teams, renewed their connection to the mass of black folks. Much of the recruiting was done then, for even in the forties the vast majority of Negro leaguers were Southerners.

Usually by the end of April, but never later than the middle of May, the Negro League teams had worked their way north preparing for the season opener. A liberal politician such as New York mayor Fiorello LaGuardia, a Negro celebrity such as Lena Horne, or a Negro politician such as Chicago Congressman William Dawson threw out the first ball and the season began.

Pictures of the period attest to the ritualistic importance of this day in the black community. "Oh boy, did they dress," remembered Effa Manley. "People came out who didn't know the ball from the bat. All the girls got new outfits." The society pages of the black newspapers gushed with baseball stories that suggested opening day's importance for a culture with limited opportunities to partake in American tradition.

As the *Chicago Defender* noted of opening day in 1937, the American Giants were greeted in Kansas City with a parade of "500 decorated cars, the Lincoln

High School Cadets, two fifty-piece bands, a group from the Veterans of Foreign Wars, and the Kansas City Monarchs Booster Club." Despite its glamorous accoutrements, the life of a Negro league player was an extremely difficult one. For economic reasons, the Negro league teams played every day if possible and frequently more often. Roy Campanella, who played ten years in the Negro league and ten years in the majors, recalls that on more than one occasion he caught four games in a single day for the Baltimore Elite Giants. "I didn't know what it meant to be tired," he related with a smile and a shake of the head, "as long as I got my turn at bat." A four-game day was a rarity, reserved for special occasions such as the Fourth of July, when the nation's appetite for baseball was insatiable; however, many if not most Negro leaguers played three games every Sunday.

That third game was a "twilight game." Twilight ball flourished prior to the widespread use of electric lights for night baseball—a technological advance pioneered by the Kansas City Monarchs in 1929. A twilight game began just after the day shift ended, and players gratefully noted that when the sun went down, the game was over. It was another six, seven innings, particularly tough on the outfielders, but it was also another payday.

Negro league games were held wherever the team owners and the booking agents could make a profit. At first that meant renting as a home field a second-rate park which had accommodated a minor-league team or even city teams. Bugle Field in Baltimore, Sprague Field in Newark, Ammon Field in Pittsburgh, and Shibe Park in Philadelphia were examples of these stadiums at the lower end of the spectrum. In Shibe

Field the right-field line was sloped, giving the Philadelphia Stars a terrific home-field advantage. Many of the parks were relics of the ill-fated Federal League of the teens.

Gradually, however, as the economic power of the Negro leagues increased, the Negro leagues began to rent major-league stadiums. When their teams were on the road, the major-league owners were eager to do business with the Negro leagues. At rates varying from ten to twenty percent of the gate, Negro league teams used Yankee Stadium, Sportsman's Park in St. Louis, Griffith Stadium in Washington—in fact, every single major-league stadium.

Invariably the white owners insisted that the Negro league teams use their concessionaires, too. It was while working the concessions at Comiskey Park that a young Bill Veeck saw Josh Gibson hit two home runs into the upper deck in one game. "They went off like nickel rockets," Veeck reported. "Gibson was the greatest hitter I ever saw."

The routine use of major-league parks made comparison easy for knowledgeable baseball people. Clark Griffith, owner of the Senators, watched one year as Josh Gibson of the Homestead Grays hit more home runs into Griffith Stadium's left-field seats than did the entire American League, excluding the Washington Senators themselves. Griffith frequently asked *Afro-American* sports reporter Art Carter to tell him "when those little bowlegged men are coming to town," by whom he meant Newark Eagle shortstop Willie Wells and third baseman Ray Dandridge, for Griffith loved the way they fielded. In black baseball lore, Wells and Dandridge were the left side of the "million-dollar infield," so called because it was said that they

would be worth a million dollars if they were white.
Dick Seay at second and Mule Suttles at first completed the infield. Prior to Gibson's ascendency, Suttles was sometimes called the "Negro Babe Ruth."

Once the Negro leagues began playing regularly in
major-league stadiums, it was easier for white sports-
writers and baseball officials to observe the Negro
league players. Damon Runyon and Heywood Broun
were particularly known for their sports slumming at
Yankee Stadium Negro league doubleheaders. In 1932
Runyon saw Pittsburgh Crawford Ted Radcliffe catch
Satchel Paige in an easy 4-0 victory over the Black
Yankees. Then to his amazement, Radcliffe went out
and pitched the nightcap, winning 5-0. The next day
Runyon immortalized Radcliffe in print as "Double
Duty" Radcliffe, a nickname he carried proudly for
the rest of his life.

The high point of the Negro league season, without
question, was the East-West game. This was the black
all-star game begun in 1933 by Gus Greenlee and his
secretary, Roy Sparrow. Immediately the game became the single most important black sports event in
America, attracting twenty thousand fans in its first
year and over fifty thousand by the late forties.

The teams were chosen through voting in the two
largest black newspapers, the *Chicago Defender* and
the *Pittsburgh Courier*. Both papers were national
weeklies that probably owed their circulation as much
to their sports coverage as their reportage of black
news. The *Courier* in the forties had a circulation of
over 277,000 at a time when Pittsburgh's black population was less than eighty thousand. Vote totals were
enormous. Willie Wells was selected 1934 West shortstop with over 48,000 votes. Willie Foster edged Chet

Brewer for the starting shot in that 1934 game by only 601 votes out of a quarter million cast.

For the Negro league players, the East-West game was the high point of the season. "That was the glory part of our baseball," sighed Sammy T. Hughes. "It was an honor to be picked even if you were just gonna sit on the bench." With the Grand Hotel in Chicago as their headquarters, a group gathered who, if they had been white, would have rewritten every record in baseball. However, the quality of this particular game was so outstanding that even many white sportwriters attended. It was hard to ignore a sporting event that attracted thirty to forty thousand people to a big-league stadium at big-league ticket prices.

The East-West game was popular with black fans of every status. It was a "highlight in the affairs of the elite," as the *Defender* proudly observed, and the motive for many more middle-class fans to take their summer vacations in Chicago. In fact, the Union Pacific added additional cars on the trains going to Chicago for the East-West Classic. Chicago was the mecca for blacks from Arkansas, Tennessee, Louisiana, and Missouri anyway, and this was another event to reinforce that cultural importance to all black communities in the middle part of the nation.

The Negro World Series, which brought the official Negro league season to a close, never captured the imagination of the black public like the East-West game—despite strenuous efforts by the Negro leagues. The reason for this failure can be traced to Negro baseball's structural problems. The black population was unable to support a seven- or nine-game series over a short period. The black population was not big enough, the black fan's discretionary income was not large enough, nor his leisure time extensive enough. The Negro league tried to overcome this problem by shifting the site of Negro World Series games among the bigger black cities, but even this strategy failed to raise the Negro World Series to a "spectacle."

In fact, the structural problems of Negro baseball prevented the introduction of a full major-league schedule of 152 games. In 1921 the Chicago American Giants won the Negro National League pennant with a 41-21 record. In 1946, the year of integration, the schedule had not expanded: Newark won a pennant with a 47-16 record. Some years fewer games were played, and within the league, some teams played more games than others.

But the Negro league teams were not unhappy with incomplete schedules, for this arrangement allowed their owners to book exhibitions wherever a dollar beckoned. In fact, the Negro league teams may have made a majority of their money in exhibitions in which they played against each other, minor-league teams, or the semipros that populated the American baseball landscape.

The Negro league season ended in September with the conclusion of the Negro World Series, but baseball did not. "None of us made enough that we didn't have to work in the winter, not even Satchel Paige," said Buck Leonard. And the easiest, best, and often only money to be made was as a ballplayer.

Prior to the establishment of the Negro leagues, black baseball players had discovered how to earn winter income playing ball in Florida. The better Negro players joined local teams, which were special aggregations created to entertain the winter tourists.

In the late teens Foster's Chicago American Giants and Nat C. Strong's Lincoln Giants represented the Royal Poinciana and Breakers, respectively. The players slept in barracks, worked as bellhops and cooks for extra money, and played games whenever they could, reserving Saturdays for a highly competitive game between themselves. Mayor John "Honey Fitz" Fitzgerald of Boston was so delighted with the Breakers team that he participated himself in their pre-game amusements of egg tosses and gunnysack races.

Even earlier Mayor Henry Bacharach of Atlantic City was impressed enough with a group of Jacksonville lads playing winter baseball to invite them to Atlantic City, put them on the city payroll, and christen them the Bacharach Giants—a team which, after several permutations, ended up in the Eastern Colored League.

Florida independents like the Jacksonville Red Caps and the Miami Giants also strengthened themselves considerably by hiring a few Northern stars for the winter. In the 1920s the Red Caps obtained ace shortstop Dick Lundy for the winters by guaranteeing him a job redcapping at the Jacksonville train station. Needless to say, Lundy did little redcapping.

At a slightly later date, California competed with Florida for winter baseball talent, drawn from a pool of Negro leaguers, major leaguers, and the best Pacific Coast League talent. Several promoters advanced fare for an entire Negro league team to play in California for a percentage of the gate. Tom Baird, who was Wilkinson's partner with the Monarchs, became perhaps the most important California winter baseball impresario, arranging for Monarch personnel to earn additional salaries in the Golden State.

The California baseball business was particularly lucrative. It was supported by the growing population of the state and enjoyed a special drawing power because at the time, major-league baseball was played only in the northeast quarter of the country. Thousands of Angelenos took the old "S" cars to Wrigley Field, Los Angeles, to see the best baseball available on the coast. Called the "California Winter League," teams of black all-stars, major-league all-stars, the better minor-league players, and even a select group of Mexican all-star baseball players journeyed up and down the Pacific Coast playing each other. They were all based in Los Angeles. Since salaries were low for white players at that time too, most of the white players did not hesitate to play against blacks.

Racial incidents were rare, although when Ty Cobb saw the Lincoln Giants enter a San Diego stadium in 1920, "he just changed and sat up in the stands and looked at the ball game," remembered Jesse Hubbard bitterly. "He was a mean man."

Ironically, Cobb was barnstorming that year on Chief Meyers's team, and Meyers was a full-blooded Indian.

In 1934 Lonnie Goodwine, a black promoter, sent a black all-star team, built around Kansas City Monarch personnel, to the Orient for 13 months on a baseball extravaganza that took the team to Hawaii, the Philippines, Hong Kong, and Japan. They sailed on the S.S. *President Lincoln*. Many of the players considered the trip the high point of their lives. "You'd pay your money and get in that rickshaw, and ride wherever you wanted to go," recalled Newt Allen about Kobe, Japan. "It was fun."

In the 1940s Chet Brewer invested his savings in

the creation of a Kansas City Royal team which he helped sponsor in the California winter league, drawing on his fellow Monarchs for much of the team. It was at one such game in 1944 that Pasadena's Jackie Robinson approached the Royals' bullpen for advice on joining the Negro league. Pitcher Hilton Smith, who knew Robinson's football record, called Wilkinson and told him that Jackie Robinson, the well-known UCLA football player, was looking for a baseball job. Wilkinson asked Robinson to report to spring training in Houston in 1945.

The final, and by far the most important, wintering spot for American black players was Latin America. Near the turn of the century, American blacks discovered Cuba as a place to play ball. By 1910 the Cuban leagues openly sought American players, blacks as well as whites. At the same time Cubans began to arrive in the States, and the darker among them were forced into the world of Negro baseball.

In the teens, Rube Foster and C. I. Taylor took the American Giants and the Indianapolis ABCs to Cuba on tour, following the major-league pattern. In the Caribbean, American blacks tested themselves against Cuban players and the white American players who also supplemented their income with Latin American paychecks. In Cuba, Negro leaguers and major leaguers competed on the same teams for similar salaries. No better measure of their comparative baseball ability exists than their records in the Cuban leagues.

Then, following Cuban leadership, the rest of the Caribbean basin adopted baseball and began to provide opportunities for American black players. Puerto Rico and the Dominican Republic were important in the 1930s, particularly after the Dominican dictator

Rafael Trujillo began sponsoring the Ciudad Trujillo team. In the 1940s Panama, Venezuela, and Mexico competed for the best Negro leaguers.

In all these countries the Negro leaguers tasted a life denied them in the United States. "Not only do I get more money playing here [in Mexico]," Willie Wells told a *Courier* reporter in 1942, but "I am not faced with the racial problem....When I travel with Vera Cruz we live in the best hotels, we eat in the best restaurants and can go anyplace we care to. I've found freedom and democracy here."

When U.S. baseball integrated in the years 1945 to 1947, American black players were already playing integrated baseball all over the Caribbean. Although the American assumption was that integration was a new and difficult experience for American black ball-players, in the Caribbean basin, integration had long been the norm. Roy Campanella recalled Branch Rickey's intense nervousness about how Campanella would "handle" white pitchers. "I told Mr. Rickey I handled white pitchers in Spanish down in Mexico!" remembered Campanella.

Like Rickey, American sports fans never fully appreciated the depth of this Latin American-North American sports exchange. In the first half of the twentieth century, jockeys, fighters, and above all, baseball players engaged in sports exchanges of such significant proportion that it is perhaps appropriate to speak of a North American sports environment stretching from the Panama Canal to the Canadian prairies.

In a typical year, white players would play white players in the summer and blacks would play blacks, but in the winter the situation was different. Then the best black and white players competed in special-attraction games throughout the land, and in Latin America they were often teammates. Choosing to fraternize was always an individual decision, given the prevailing mores. Certainly the best players of both races knew each other reasonably well, well enough to consider one another acquaintances and to have strong opinions about one another's professional abilities.

Most of the recent interest in Negro league baseball has been devoted to the admirable task of setting the record straight: rehabilitating Negro leaguers from baseball's Gulag Archipelago. Some reputations have been restored. Josh Gibson, Cool Papa Bell, Satchel Paige, Buck Leonard, and Oscar Charleston have earned a comparatively modest celebrity by entering the Hall of Fame. The case for Willie Wells, Ray Dandridge, Biz Mackey, Smokey Joe Williams, Bullet Rogan, Hilton Smith, Dick Redding, and others continues to be made—though unfortunately each day brings fewer eyewitnesses to their baseball magic.

However, there is more reason to pay attention to the Negro leagues than merely to correct the injustices of an inherently unjust era. To examine the world that Negro baseball made is to open a window on black life during segregation. Scrutiny of the life of the Negro leagues provides a texture, a context, necessary for grasping segregation's workings and plumbing its irrationality. Negro baseball operated in a segregated world. But the walls of segregation were porous and, in the final analysis, Negro league baseball attacked those walls ideologically, economically, and emotionally.

The Negro leagues were at the forefront of virtually

every important development taking place in black America. The Negro leagues were the objective correlative of Booker T. Washington's image of interracial relations: "In all things purely social we can be as separate as the fingers, yet one as the hand in all things essential to mutual progress." When blacks had been thrust out of organized baseball in the nineteenth century, as Jim Crow was being institutionalized nationwide, segregated black baseball retreated to Washington's model. The Negro league developed explicitly from the self-help strategy that Washington believed to be the only practical avenue of advancement.

Foster, when he founded the Negro National League in 1920, expressly desired to "keep Colored baseball from the control of whites." "In keeping with the times," Foster argued in a significant phrase, he intended to "do something concrete for the loyalty of the Race." But Foster and nearly all the other Negro league team owners felt that if they proved that the Negro leagues were viable economically and competitive athletically, white America would eventually accept them. Indeed, shortly before he left black baseball in 1926, Foster was planning to put a white player on the American Giants as a strategy to advance the ultimate goal.

While the Negro leagues were, by definition, an accommodation to segregation, their leadership remained outspokenly in favor of integration. Foster, described by the *Defender* as the "militant fighting head of an organization that was a direct slap at the inferiority complex," emerged, according to Webster McDonald, as "the most famous black man in Chicago," because he expressed prevailing black opinion while remaining rooted in the popular culture of his era.

Foster did not live to see Jackie Robinson succeed. He died on December 9, 1930, after four years of exile from the game he loved. Yet the spontaneous outpouring of grief at his passing measured not only his personal reputation but also the impact of the Negro leagues.

Foster's body lay in state in Chicago for three days. During the services three thousand mourners stood outside an already packed funeral parlor at 47th and Lawrence in a pitiless rain that turned to snow as the refrain of "Rock of Ages" wafted through the chill, dark, winter day. The casket was closed at "the usual hour a ballgame ends," reported the *Defender*, and then a long solemn procession carried him to the graveyard. The American Giants Booster Association presented a huge wreath with a green baseball diamond with white carnations for the path between bases. The assessment of the black press, represented here by the *Defender*, was that he "had died a martyr to the game, the most commanding figure baseball had ever known."

The great question for black Americans after the turn of the century was how to deal with the imposition of segregation by white America. The response in general had been accommodation without acquiescence. The realities of mood and raw power allowed no frontal assault on segregation. If many black leaders turned from the ideological struggle to build black institutions, they never relinquished a belief in a better, integrated future. The Negro leagues were created in this process, and because of the importance of sports in the psychological life of a people, they became a particularly important community institution. Besides providing enormous emotional satisfaction and entertainment, the black players realized an essential goal of black culture, namely, to prove that blacks and whites were equal, and they proved it in a way that common people understood. No other group of black Americans so regularly challenged the assumptions of segregation. As the *Kansas City Call* so pointedly observed: "from a sociological point of view the Monarchs have done more than any other single agent in Kansas City to break the damnable outrage of prejudice that exists in this city."

In the South and much of the North, the Negro leaguers mimicked the etiquette of segregation. With bitterness, but without hesitation, they headed for the back door of the cafe to buy sandwiches to be eaten on the bus, for the dining room was off limits. And yet those same ballplayers ate those same sandwiches in a totally integrated environment when they played the Canadian Pacific Line, barnstorming the prairie provinces. In a few rural American towns the Negro leaguers were the first blacks the whites there had ever seen. Such provincialism shocked the well-traveled black ballplayers. Months later they might be in Cuba, Mexico, or Venezuela, speaking Spanish and, like pushy tourists everywhere, waving that Yankee dollar and cursing the spicy food.

The Negro leaguers sometimes played baseball against whites who were clearly inferior. At other times they played against whites who were their equals and against whom they could accurately measure themselves. They played on all-black teams in the all-black Negro league, they played on all-black teams against whites, and in Latin America, they played on integrated teams. They suffered through racial encounters they knew they could not win, and they watched as some whites reached out across the color line to them. The game they loved and the life they endured taught much. Some became genuine heroes, always in the spotlight of black life. Despite the many hardships, they were not bitter men.

"Baseball opened doors for me," Quincy Trouppe wrote in his remarkable monograph, *Twenty Years Too Soon*. "When I felt low and disgusted it gave me a lift. When I was riding high and the wind of glory was caressing my ears, it brought me down to earth. Because of this great National game, I have lived a life comparable to the wealthiest man in the United States."

Unlike their friends and fellow vagabonds, the great black musicians, black ballplayers left no discographies. Monographs were rare, pictures faded in old scrapbooks, film was virtually nonexistent. Thus an oral testimony of extraordinary eloquence became the main source of Negro baseball information, though an outline of the phenomenon was traceable in the black press. That oral history of black baseball grows more powerful with time. The only explanation is the strength of the story itself; it grew into a legend that transcended history because of its intense meaning for black Americans in search of their true identity.

2

Up from Obscurity

On a crisp, late April day a baseball game began at a small local stadium in Portsmouth, Virginia. The scene was vintage Americana circa 1933: a local team challenging the barnstorming professionals, a crowd in the hundreds, impromptu concessionaires selling barbecue and soft drinks, and cigar-box promoters taking the money as children saved seats for momma and daddy. A sense of community permeated the lush Southern landscape. There was only one anomaly in this Rockwellian scene: the crowd and players were all black. The professionals were the Detroit Stars, a Negro league team working their way north from spring training. The locals were the Portsmouth Fire Fighters, captained by nineteen-year-old Ray Dandridge. Dandridge, who went on to become perhaps the most popular American ballplayer ever to play in Cuba and Mexico, could not have known the importance that day would have in his life.

The Detroit Stars were glamorous intruders in the eyes of Portsmouth's black community; they were glamorous intruders wherever they went. Their lives contrasted sharply with those of most Portsmouth blacks, for whom textile mills, cigarette plants, and the docks were the reality. Dandridge, whose father was an invalid as a result of a textile-mill accident, expected to work in a textile mill himself.

Yet that day Dandridge had one of the greatest days of his life. He hit a home run, he fielded splendidly, and he made an impression even in defeat. Of course the Detroit Stars won; they were expected to win. But Detroit manager "Candy Jim" Taylor, so nicknamed for his candy concession in Chicago's Brookmont Hotel, saw greatness in Dandridge. Taylor, who began as a third sacker himself in 1904, implored Dandridge to join the Stars.

Taylor found out where Dandridge lived. He brought the bus and met "Danny's" father. He pleaded with Dandridge, explaining that this was the opportunity of a lifetime, and that he needed another infielder immediately. "Man, where is Detroit?" Dandridge asked Taylor. He thought it was on the other side of the world. But Dandridge's father wanted him to go, for he had been a catcher himself years before, and he loved baseball. "Why don't you go ahead on, go ahead on," his father urged. And then they sat down and talked. Dandridge fearfully asked his father, "Do you really think I can make it?" And his father answered, "Why don't you go there and try?" So the next morning, Dandridge packed a straw suitcase and became a traveling ballplayer. "When I went to Detroit," Dandridge reported, "I didn't have enough to come back."

Dandridge's entrance into Negro league baseball was typical. For the mass of black baseball players, their coming up and their separation from their roots was the result of an outstanding day and the right audience. Many a Negro league player got his chance because an injury, sudden slump, or romance forced the traveling team to give a local hero an instant tryout.

Connie Johnson, for example, was an apprentice granite cutter working Stone Mountain in Georgia when the Kansas City Monarchs and the Toledo Crawfords (the remnant of the Pittsburgh team) came through in 1939. The Crawfords needed a pitcher in a hurry. Hearing that Johnson was the best pitching prospect in the area, player-manager Oscar Charleston and part-owner Jesse Owens traced Johnson to the quarry. "We want you to pitch," said the ex-Olympian. "I never played no professional ball," replied the gangling adolescent. "They say you can throw hard, that's all we want," continued Charleston. They gave the 6' 2", 165-pound youngster a size-48 uniform. He had to pin his cap in back. But he threw hard, won the game, and proved that he was Negro league material. After the congratulations, the Crawfords said, "Hey, you did good today, beat Monarchs, one of the best teams," and they invited him to eat with them. Johnson thought they were trying to pay him off in food, rather than cash, so he quickly devoured a whole chicken. Then Jesse Owens asked, "How'd you like to play with us?" Johnson reflected. Then he answered, "You'll have to ask my mother." So Owens made the obligatory call on the lady of the house and asked for her son. Johnson's mother looked Owens right in the eye, hands on her hips, and said, "It's no use my asking him if he want to go, 'cause I know he want to go, but will you take care of my son?" And after Jesse Owens said yes, Connie Johnson was on his way.

Most Southern parents did not want their children

to become ballplayers. "They didn't want me to be a ballplayer," acknowledged Jesse Hubbard, "[they] wanted me to be a railroad man, a brakesman." In 1916 Rube Foster returned from a Cuban tour and began playing his way back to Chicago. In Shreveport, Hubbard defeated the American Giants. Foster immediately offered Hubbard a contract. "You'll play with the great Rube Foster," he boasted. "You'll travel in a Pullman car, be in Chicago." A sorely tempted Hubbard declined. But Foster's shortstop, the justly famous John Henry Lloyd, was impressed enough to continue the negotiation. He took Hubbard aside and confided, "I'm gonna jump Rube. I'm going to New York to the Brooklyn Royal Giants. When I get there I'll have Nat C. Strong send for you."

When Strong wired money for Hubbard to come to New York, there was no further hesitation. The arrangement called for the Southern innocent to live with his mentor, Lloyd. With a bag of clothes and Lloyd's address, Hubbard pulled into New York City. He told the railroad porter he was going to Lenox Avenue, and the porter suggested he get off at the 125th street station and walk the rest of the way. "You're liable to get down to Grand Central Station and never get out," the porter advised. And Hubbard agreed. "I was a country boy then."

Willie Wells was the premier shortstop of Negro baseball from the late twenties to the mid-forties. He too was discovered during spring training while playing on Southern sandlots. The St. Louis Stars and the Chicago American Giants trained in Central Texas during the twenties. Wells was selected to lead a local all-star group that challenged the Negro league teams in spring exhibitions. Both Rube Foster and St. Louis'

Bill Wallace saw that Wells had extraordinary reflexes, and they traced him to the South Austin shack of his birth.

Wells's mother insisted that her son, a graduate of Anderson High School, the only Negro high school in the area, was going to college. Both Wallace and Foster offered money, a salary in the hundreds of dollars a month. Wells's previous work history had consisted of shucking corn and delivering papers. Still, Wells's mother was firm until both men promised her son could attend college after baseball season; Foster pointed to Aubrey Owen, who was attending Meharry Medical College in the off-season.

Foster and Wallace knew, of course, that if Wells was a success, his life would soon be too full for much thought of college; they knew that once a man experienced the life of the Negro leagues, he changed. Finally, Wells's mother decided. Much to Foster's dismay, she told Willie to go with St. Louis because it was overnight by train from Austin. Wells did not shine immediately. He batted eighth and could not hit the curveball. During the season opponents teased him unmercifully. "Hey Wells," they yelled as he approached the plate, "here comes that curveball." He retreated abruptly to Austin when the season ended and entered Huston College—a small, central Texas Negro college.

But Wells was a studious and likeable player, and when shortstop Dick Riggins was injured playing winter baseball in California, the Negro leaguers, who had ribbed him harshly during the season, thought again about the promising rookie. They wired money, enticing him westward. "My mother said, 'nah, nah, you got to finish college,'" remembered Wells. "But I looked at her taking in washing and ironing. 'Now I can help her,' I thought. I didn't tell my mother, got my clothes, and almost slipped out of here." Wells spent that winter at the Dunbar Hotel on Central Avenue in Los Angeles.

Dave Malarcher was the grand old man of the Negro leagues. He was a charter member of Rube Foster's 1920 Chicago American Giants, and he outlived all his teammates. Born in Whitehall, Louisiana, in 1894, he was reared within throwing distance of the Mississippi, the youngest of eleven children. His mother was born a slave and raised her family to stress education above all else: she was a product of the missionary teachers who had come south to educate black people after the Civil War. Malarcher's older sister sent him as a child to New Orleans to obtain a better education. His summers were spent working the cane and cotton in rural Louisiana; his winters in the grade school and high school departments of New Orleans University.

But like all the Negro leaguers, "Gentleman" Dave felt baseball was everything. He became the star player for the New Orleans University Eagles while still in high school. "Why were you such a great athlete?" he was asked late in his life. "Because I led a good clean life, because I swam the Mississippi, ran through the woods looking for rattlesnakes, worked in the cotton fields, and I was really strong," he responded with a smile. When the Indianapolis ABCs returned from Cuba in 1916 they played the Eagles. Malarcher showed so much potential that the ABCs invited him along, offering him fifty dollars a month. Since Malarcher was making two dollars and fifty cents a week plus room and board as a house boy, he gladly accepted. He managed to save enough of his salary to send his mother twenty-five dollars a month.

Rube Foster coveted the talented infielder the moment he spied him in independent games in 1916, and Foster followed his development carefully for the next two years. In 1918, with World War I in progress, Malarcher joined the 309th Pioneer Infantry Unit and was sent to France. Laying in a bunker at St. Luce, France, he received a personal letter from Foster; it contained the request that upon his return he become an American Giant.

Yet discovery was neither always quick nor inevitable. Rumors of unrecognized talents still percolate through the tales of the old Negro league players. Buck Leonard, Hall of Fame member and consensus choice as the all-time greatest first baseman in Negro baseball, spent twelve years on the sandlots of Rocky Mount, North Carolina, and it took a Depression and a series of fortuitous events to send him north toward stardom.

Born in Rocky Mount in 1907, Leonard was forced to enter the railroad yards in 1919 when his father died in the great influenza epidemic. His break occurred in 1933 when, playing in Virginia, a Baltimore team saw him and invited him along. "I decided to go with them; they had a better team," he reported matter-of-factly. From Baltimore he advanced to New York and the Brooklyn Royal Giants. That same year, he began to hang around a Harlem bar where the recently retired Smokey Joe Williams was bartending. Williams saw Leonard play and said, "Look son, why don't you get with a good team?" He recommended Leonard to the Homestead Grays. Solely on Williams's word, Cum Posey sent bus fare, and Leonard became a Gray. Once in Pittsburgh, Buck Leonard evolved into the Gehrig of Negro baseball, starring in Pittsburgh and Washington, D.C., for seventeen years, and then playing five more in Mexico.

A way station on the road north was often a Southern Negro league team. Motivated by the model of Foster's Negro National League, the stronger Southern independents formed a Southern Negro League within weeks of the creation of the first Negro National League in 1920.

This Southern Negro League was a very strong league indeed, due to its proximity to the main black population centers. No Negro National League team took a Southern Negro League team lightly, and no Negro league team emerged from Southern barnstorming trips unscathed.

Yet because the Southern Negro teams were denied white opponents, they lacked the financial capabilities of the Negro league, and, as a matter of course, their better players were scooped up into the Northern league. Such was the case of the master of the mound, Leroy "Satchel" Paige. Satchel Paige first demonstrated promise with his hometown Mobile (Alabama) Tigers. The Tigers made money by passing the hat among the spectators at their games. Reputedly, Paige sometimes received lemonade in return for his stint on the mound. Nonetheless, Paige's fastball was self-evident—in Paige's phrase, "thoughtful stuff"—and soon he was carried to Gulfport, Mississippi, every Saturday for a slightly higher-level game. It was in Gulfport that the Chattanooga Black Lookouts, a weak team in the Southern Negro League, spotted Paige and paid him fifty dollars a month to become their ace. "Fifty dollars was what we was calling money

then," said Paige, "and the thing about it is I would
have played for nothing if you want me to tell you the
truth, that's how much we loved baseball." From
Chattanooga, Paige jumped to the New Orleans Black
Pelicans, also a Southern Negro League team, and
then to Birmingham, the jewel of Southern black
baseball. In 1927 when Birmingham entered the Negro National League, Paige suddenly found himself a
national figure. Creeping into the national Negro press
as "Satchelfoot" Paige, or "Satchell" Paige, Paige's
natural showmanship found a welcome audience. (Although the term Satchelfoot implied that his name
referred to his enormous feet, in fact, Satchel was
nicknamed for his long arms. At a temporary job at
the Mobile train station, he had attracted notice as a
result of the number of satchels he could manage.) It
was in the Southern Negro League that Paige began
to emphasize his precise control by disdaining a regular home plate and placing a gum wrapper down
instead. "This is my base," he'd chortle, or he'd place
two bats about six inches apart and zap the ball between them into the catcher's mitt.

However, Birmingham could not hold Satchel Paige
or any of the other better players in the twenties because the Black Barons were not able to play white
teams in their home territory and therefore they could
not make as much money as a Northern Negro League
team. (Birmingham lost Solomon, Streeter, Crutchfield, and Paige to the Crawfords!) Thus Birmingham,
and later the Atlanta Black Crackers, the Jacksonville
Red Caps, and the Nashville Elite Giants remained
Negro league baseball's poor relations. Paige bounced
as a baseball commodity from team to team and finally in 1931 reached the well-bankrolled Pittsburgh

Crawfords. From the shotgun shack of his birth, Paige, more colorful than a carnival of butterflies, had made his way to the Crawford Bar and Grille; soon he was a regular performer in Yankee Stadium. (Nonetheless, Paige remained at lifelong odds with his mother over his chosen career. "She believed in the old-time way," he recalled with remorse. "Said it was a sin to play baseball for money, never did see me play.")

In a development parallel to the creation of the Southern Negro League, a Texas Negro League took life during the 1920s. Hilton Smith, the "money pitcher" of the Kansas City Monarchs even during Paige's tenure with the team, came up through Texas's version of Negro baseball's minor leagues.

Smith was born in Giddings, a little German Texas town. As a child, Smith spoke some German. Having made a local reputation, he was called upon to pitch for Brenham against the Austin Black Senators in an exhibition game. When Smith shut Austin down, the Austin manager, DeWitt Owens, was impressed and spread the word. Later, when the American Giants came through Austin, the Black Senators induced Smith to pitch a game for them. "I pitched for Austin and beat them," recalled Hilton Smith fondly. "I remember the score: 4-3. And so they [the Senators] said, come up next spring."

Coming up in the Texas Negro League was slightly easier than in the Southern Negro League because race relations in Texas were slightly better than in the rest of the Deep South. In Central and West Texas, black teams played white teams on occasion. (This was also true in Kentucky, Missouri, and anywhere near the Mason-Dixon line.) And in Texas there was that important third layer of race differentiation: Mexican and Mexican-American teams.

Hispanic teams did not hesitate to play blacks, and the natural rivalry in San Antonio and the Rio Grande Valley improved team finances in general. In 1933 the Austin Black Senators with Hilton Smith barnstormed to Mexico City and back. This trip only whet the appetites of Negro players for Mexico. Following the initiative of the Texas black teams, American black ballplayers found a haven in Mexico after 1930.

Hilton Smith eventually joined Satchel Paige on the Kansas City Monarchs. In Black Kansas City, Smith was given the nickname "Satchel's Caddy" because he invariably finished games that Paige started. Yet in black baseball there was a large group who felt Smith was at least the equal of Paige. One of those was Quincy Trouppe, who claimed that Paige wasn't as versatile as Smith. "Hilton Smith was probably the greatest pitcher in the world in 1942," added Buck O'Neil, referring to a year in which both Smith and Paige were O'Neil's teammates. "It's not fair," some of the better Homestead Grays kept telling Smith, "he [Satchel] gets all the credit." But the almost scholarly Smith paid it no mind. One time Paige even came to Smith and said, "You're always relieving and relieving and relieving me, let me relieve you tonight."

Another path into the Negro leagues led through the black college. The black colleges had a lusty and thriving baseball tradition. Important rivalries such as Howard-Lincoln, Fiske-Tuskeegee, and Wiley-Prairie View not only attracted local fans but also received extensive Northern Negro newspaper coverage. A symbiotic relationship between the colleges and the pros developed because, of course, when the Negro league teams barnstormed against a black college team, they both shared a payday. In addition, the college was another reservoir of talent to be exploited, and in fact, a young Negro leaguer, if he was insufficiently seasoned to merit a Caribbean salary, still might spend the winter months in school.

Indeed, the black colleges vigorously recruited athletes, aware that athletic victories were the easy route to their alumni pocketbooks. Pat Patterson of East Chicago attended Wiley College in Texas because of the cheap tuition and the chance to play serious baseball there. He passed up opportunities to play college football and basketball (at NYU). Patterson's decision was an indication of baseball's general preeminence at the time.

J. D. Hardy of Piney Woods, Mississippi, plaintively addressed all young black men in a 1933 advertisement in the *Pittsburgh Courier:* "If you are a real good baseball player and want grammar school, high school, or college education in exchange for playing baseball in Northern states with a college baseball club during the summer job [,] write."

The flexible (and usually ignored) rules of the Colored Intercollegiate Athletic Association allowed high school athletes to compete on college teams. For the gifted, it meant early recruitment and superior training. Since most black colleges were centers of teacher education, they frequently had on-campus primary and secondary schools, and they catered to high school athletes.

Also, the CIAA imposed no prohibition on making extra money by playing on barnstorming teams. A significant number of the better black college athletes earned their expenses through a summer of barn-storming baseball, particularly in the thirties, when the harshness of the Depression encouraged school administrators to loosen the rules even more.

For John "Buck" O'Neil, a future manager of the Kansas City Monarchs, entering a Negro college's high school department was the decisive event of his life. Raised in Sarasota, Florida, he anticipated ending school in the eighth grade, like the rest of his generation. "I walked by that white high school many a day," he recalled, "but I couldn't go in that school." So after the eighth grade he went to work on a Sarasota celery farm, in the black-dirt muck of rural Northwest Florida. One day as he sat behind some packing boxes in the fields, he said, "Damn, got to be something better than this." His father heard him, and, on the way home, said to his son, "J., you said there's got to be something better, and there is something better, but you can't get it here. You know you can't get it here." They talked on, and O'Neil's father insisted that the only route out of the fields was as an athlete. "I haven't got any money to send you to college," he told his son, "but you're a pretty good athlete. Why don't you talk to your friend Lloyd Hasley about an athletic scholarship?"

With the assistance of his friend, O'Neil entered Edward Waters College in Jacksonville, in the ninth grade—he was part of their high school department. But he was also a college varsity baseball player. Much, much later O'Neil became the Monarch manager. After integration, O'Neil joined the Chicago Cubs organization as a scout and coach. Finally in the late 1960s, when the Cubs experimented with nine rotating coaches at the helm, O'Neil was one of them—the first black man to direct a big-league team.

For the segregated high schools on Dixie's fringes, baseball was no less significant. In St. Louis, where Vashon High School and Sumner High School met annually for the unofficial black championship of St. Louis, black community interest was total, and even members of the St. Louis Stars, the St. Louis Negro League team, attended the contests. The Stars' park was across the street from Vashon High. Thus a truly outstanding player from Vashon, such as Quincy Trouppe, was automatically on the periphery of professional Negro baseball. Quincy Trouppe volunteered to be the Stars' third-string catcher and began to work out with the team regularly—a training which proved priceless.

A final source of Southern talent for the Negro leagues were the industrial baseball teams of the South. Centered in the growing cities of Atlanta, Nashville, and especially Birmingham, in industries such as mining and saw mills, industrial baseball had a flourishing life of its own in the South. Nowhere was this baseball more competitive than around Birmingham, where ACIPCO and Stockham were fabled throughout the region. (ACIPCO stood for American Cast Iron Pipe Company, and Stockham was short for Stockham Valve and Fitting Company.)

Industrial ballplayers received special privileges. Lorenzo "Piper" Davis began with a coal-mining team in Piper, Alabama (whence the nickname "Piper.") When Davis joined ACIPCO he received no money for playing baseball, only a guaranteed job paying $3.36

a day. But $3.36 a day and time off for baseball was terrific in Birmingham in 1938. Still, when the Birmingham Black Barons offered five dollars a game, Piper Davis moved up and into the upper echelons of the Negro baseball pipeline. Only a few years later, Davis became the first black signed by the Boston Red Sox organization. (Ironically, as he was growing up, Davis listened to Birmingham (white) Barons games on the radio. The announcer was Bull Conners, who became notorious in the 1960s as the segregationist sheriff of Birmingham, Alabama.)

Harry Solomon, the star hurler for the Birmingham Black Barons the year Satchel Paige joined them in 1926, began on a mining team, too. Solomon worked all winter driving a mule team into the pits at Soloko, and then played for Soloko in the summertime. Ball games were festive occasions for the workers and their families in sooty Birmingham labor pits, but the ball games were especially appreciated by men like Solomon who received a full day's pay for a half day's work on game day. Willie Mays, Sr., was another mining-camp ballplayer; he eventually went to the Birmingham Black Barons and into the Negro league.

The technology for night baseball reached the camps in the late 1930s. "Every mining camp and cotton mill had a field and put lights in it," according to Elmer Knox, a nephew of one of Rube Foster's founding members of the first Negro league. "Now some of the lights out there looked like a candle at the end of the tunnel," chuckled Knox. "But there was a place where you could play baseball and they could draw twenty-five hundred to five thousand to see the game." Knox recalls that during the spring, when the Negro league teams came to play the industrial teams, "you'd think it was the major leagues playing, they got double the take."

Naturally, Negro baseball had a Southern feeling. Almost everything in black culture from 1920 to 1946 had that tone. Whether it was the gospel singing which punctuated the long night-rides to the next ball game, or the Southernisms of language that punctuated their speech, the Negro leaguers were never far from their spiritual homeland, even when they were in Quebec City or Seattle. However, two groups moderated the Southernness of the Negro leagues, namely the increasingly important Northerners and the Latin Americans. Many of the Northerners, of course, were Southern-born participants in the great migration which sent almost two million blacks north between the World Wars. Josh Gibson was the prototype Southern-born, Northern-raised Negro leaguer. His father gladly left Buena Vista, Georgia, for the smokestacks of "Iron City" and a job in Pittsburgh's Carnegie-Illinois Steel plant. Like Quincy Trouppe and Ted Page, Josh spent several fatherless years while Mark Gibson accumulated the money and self-confidence necessary to send for his family. Educated only through the fifth grade in Georgia, essentially illiterate, Josh Gibson attended a vocational school on Pittsburgh's north side until he was sixteen. He then apprenticed in a manufacturing plant and did a stint in a steel mill.

Yet athletics and especially baseball pulled him forward. In 1927 he was playing for a sandlot team called the Pleasant Valley Red Sox and, the following year, was an early member of the Crawford Colored Giants. Gibson's hitting was already legendary even though he was still in his teens, and Cum Posey, the cagey owner of the Homestead team, was already measuring Gibson for a spot on the Grays, one of black baseball's best teams. In a baseball-crazed city like the Pittsburgh of the late 1920s and 1930s, it was impossible to hide a player of Gibson's ability.

According to a famous story, Gibson's entry into the top echelon of Negro baseball occurred when the Grays' regular catcher, Buck Ewell, split a finger in a 1930 game against the Kansas City Monarchs. Gibson, supposedly a paying fan, dropped everything, changed, and finished out the game. (Actually, as Bill Brashler discovered, the catcher's name was Buck Ewing; the opposing team was a white semipro team called Dormont, and Gibson had to come from across town to catch the nightcap of a doubleheader.)

Josh Gibson had a marvelous year in 1931 with the Homestead Grays. He was called "Sampson" and was fast overshadowing such luminaries as Smokey Joe Williams and Oscar Charleston in the fans' affection, though Satchel Paige's appearance in a Pittsburgh Crawford uniform in late 1931 inevitably pushed Gibson one step down the ladder in Pittsburgh.

In 1932 Greenlee of the Crawfords raided the Grays. He obtained Judy Johnson, Oscar Charleston, and Gibson in a nasty assault on Cum Posey's entire operation. Gibson, who "signed" to play with both the Grays and Crawfords, settled on the Crawfords as a result of peer pressure. Greenlee wisely signed Gibson's closest friend, Harry Kincannon, and gave Gibson an offer slightly higher than the Grays'.

The arrival of Gibson in a Crawford uniform diminished a host of other home-run hitters. Turkey Stearns, Mule Suttles, Louis Santop, and—even earlier—Bruce Petaway had all been called the "black Babe Ruth," prior to Gibson's entrance into the Negro leagues.

With a natural swing, the quickest of reflexes, and an eye that was almost never deceived by a bad ball, Gibson was the kind of hitter to whom "you threw the ball and prayed," recalled pitcher Andrew "Pullman" Porter. Once, Gibson was trailed by a little boy who begged, "Give me your broken bat, Mr. Gibson, please, give me your broken bat." Gibson looked at the boy and said, "Son, I don't break bats, I wear them out." In an important game, pitcher Bill Harvey quickly got two strikes on Gibson and then Gibson tagged him for a tremendous home run. As he trotted the bases Gibson was heard laughing, "Ole Josh hit another one."

The Southern children raised in the North were of course deeply influenced by their parents and their parents' world. Collard greens and the African Methodist Church were as common in Homestead, Pennsylvania, Compton Hill, St. Louis, or on 18th Street in Kansas City as in Starkville, Mississippi. Yet there was a critical difference for many of these Southern-born, Northern-raised children; they interacted in the white world. Negro leaguers Joe Black, Monte Irvin, Roy Campanella, Larry Doby, Pat Patterson, Dick Seay, and Jackie Robinson all started on integrated high school teams before economic necessity and a love of baseball sent them into the segregated Negro leagues.

Some of these Northerners came to exercise cultural leadership in the league. They initiated their Southern brothers into the ways of Northern city life, and because they tended to disparage the South, they helped the Southerners sever their psychological connections to Dixie.

Chet Brewer was one of the natural leaders of Negro baseball—one of its major figures on the field and off. His grandparents, Louisianians, had joined the exodus to Kansas in the nineteenth century seeking land and freedom. Brewer was born in Leavenworth, Kansas, in 1907. But Kansas was "just like the South" to Brewer's father, and because he didn't see any progress there, he moved to Des Moines, Iowa, where his oldest boy Chet went to integrated schools from the third grade on.

As a youngster Brewer watched the independent black teams that passed through Iowa each summer. He would climb a big tree that stood behind the leftfield fence to watch as the Kansas City Monarchs or the All-Nations entertained below. His idol was Bullet Rogan. He never dreamed that one day he would replace him.

Brewer was a big, strong, young pitcher when Brown's Tennessee Rats, a touring team that was the model for Brashler's Bingo Long's Traveling All-Stars, passed through Des Moines in the early twenties and saw Brewer pitch. "They wanted to know if I wanted to go out with them," recalled Brewer. When he asked his mother, it turned out she knew Brown and so she said yes. As Georgia Dwight, wife of Brewer's teammate on the Rats, Eddie Dwight, recalled, "the Rats had a kind of Chatauqua—little skits, and musicians and singers too."

From the Tennessee Rats Brewer and Dwight then joined the Gilkerson Union Giants of Joliet, Illinois. "That was a little better baseball and a little better conditions for the ballplayers, but not much," remembered Brewer. When Brewer and Dwight performed well for Gilkerson against Wilkinson's All-Nations team they were invited to join the Monarchs/All-Nations operation of Wilkinson.

Brewer's incredible career in Negro baseball lasted twenty-two years, most of them with the Monarchs. Brewer suffered the agony of losing more close pitching duels to Satchel Paige than anyone else. His most bitter loss was the 2-1 defeat in 1934 at the Denver Post Tournament; his greatest victory was a no-hitter against Satchel in the Dominican League in 1937.

Brewer also lost the "Battle of the Butchered Balls," in 1930 to Smokey Joe Williams. Playing under the lights at Muehlebach Stadium, Brewer and Williams unleashed emery balls, "goo" balls—Williams sometimes applied a black, tarry substance to the ball— or even sandpapered pitches. The result was devastating. In twelve innings Williams struck out 27 while Brewer got 19 in the Homestead Grays' 1-0 victory over the Monarchs.

Yet Brewer's greatest contribution to Negro baseball was his assumption of some organizational responsibility for the Negro team in the California winter league in the 1940s. It was against Brewer's Kansas City Royals that Bob Feller's All-Stars played during the war, and it was through the Kansas City Royals that Jackie Robinson was introduced to Negro baseball.

Even in the North, with the fame of the Negro league teams and their all-pervasive presence, parents sent their children to the baseball world with reluctance. Seventeen-year-old Leon Day was playing on a local team near Baltimore called the Silver Moons when his blazing fastball was spotted by the Baltimore Black Sox's Rap Dixon. One look at Day was all Dixon needed. He told Day to be prepared to leave the next weekend. "I asked my father if I could go," remembered Day. He asked, "Is that what you really want to do?" Leon Day thought a moment and said, "It's the only thing I want to do." "Well, if that's what you want go ahead." In the late years of Negro baseball, Day became the league's number-two pitcher, just a step behind Satchel Paige—and a real nemesis to Paige in their personal encounters. Day's greatest moment, however, came in Europe. Like over fifty other Negro leaguers, Day volunteered for the army and waded ashore at D-Day plus 6 "scared to death." Once ashore, Leon Day became ace pitcher for the European Theater team—an integrated team—and, before fifty thousand appreciative G.I.s in France, defeated the Mediterranean Theater by a run. Another Negro leaguer, Willard Brown, struck the decisive blow. What kind of pitcher was Leon Day? Monte Irvin stated unequivocally, "He was like Bob Gibson. In fact, I think he was a better pitcher than Bob Gibson."

When barnstorming, the Northerners simply refused to accept their inferiority in the South; they railed against petty segregation. Feisty, tiny Dick Seay, raised in upstate New York, never heard the word "nigger" until the fifth grade. He had to ask his mother what it meant. A naive Southerner like Satchel Paige found Seay a font of information about the Northern world. Seay was sickened to see his teammates call fifteen-year-old white lads "Mister." Seay ultimately turned his back on the entire United States and settled in Puerto Rico.

Roy Campanella had an Italian father and black

mother. American race casting made him black, though he always attended integrated schools. Born and raised in Philadelphia, his playground ability was so outstanding that the Negro leaguers of Philadelphia and nearby Baltimore quickly adopted him. In the late 1930s, Philadelphia Stars manager Webster McDonald, already a heroic figure in black baseball because of his record against white major leaguers was 16-4, took a liking to Campanella. As Bill Cash said, "Roy was cute and round and fat. Mac took him along for just that reason, because he fell in love with him." Later McDonald, to the future detriment of his team, encouraged the teenager catcher to play with the Baltimore Elite Giants, who were at that time under the tutelage of Biz Mackey, the best receiver (defensive catcher) in black baseball history.

Campanella at first played in the Negro leagues only on weekends. He'd leave school at two o'clock on Fridays, play the Friday-night game and then on Saturday and Sunday, and be back in high school the following Monday. His parents—not Campanella himself—received the thirty-five-dollars-a-weekend Negro league salary. "I felt proud then and now I feel prouder," Campanella beamed years afterwards.

Campanella's Italian father invariably sat directly behind home plate at Negro league games, his white skin glistening in the sun as he yelled encouragement to his "Negro" son. For the Campanellas of Negro baseball, integration was no tremendous psychological barrier. (In Campanella's first year of integrated ball he was so obviously the veteran at Nashua that manager Walter Alston appointed him acting manager when Alston was ejected from games.)

The odds-on Negro league choice for the historic

task of integrating baseball was Monte Irvin. Born in Dothan, Alabama, Irvin's parents brought him as a youngster to Orange, New Jersey. Irvin was a youthful knothole-gang supporter of the Newark Bears, the white International League team. But he also followed the independent baseball of the area, as the semi-professional Orange BBCs challenged Negro league teams at the Grove Street Oval almost every Saturday. There he saw the Lincoln Giants, the Newark Eagles, and the Homestead Grays. In 1937, he joined the Negro National League.

While Irvin was playing for the Orange Triangles in the mid-thirties, the word spread that he was "a kid who looked a little like Josh Gibson at the plate." The Black Yankees, the Homestead Grays, the Elite Giants, and the Newark Eagles all wanted him. Abe Manley, the Newark owner, formally contacted Irvin first and asked if he'd like to play for the Eagles. Shyly Irvin tried to negotiate by mentioning the Black Yanks, Grays, and Elite Giants. "Well," said Manley, "since you've got good friends on the Eagles you ought to sign with us. Furthermore, you won't have the expense of paying room rent when you're at home." Irvin, who was attending Lincoln University at the time, was swayed by this argument. He asked about salary, and was offered $150 a month. Irvin asked for a bonus. "We don't give bonuses," Manley said. "Bonuses tend to spoil players; if you work yourself up to a good salary you'll appreciate it more!" Monte Irvin came to the Eagles as a shortstop when Willie Wells played short and managed too. Early in the first season Wells took Irvin aside and said, "Young man, you're a wonderful athlete, you can hit and you're strong. But I'm the shortstop here. You should play outfield." And in

Negro league ball, Irvin was both an infielder and an outfielder.

Exactly the same thing happened to another New Jersey athlete named Larry Doby. As a senior at Eastside High in Paterson, New Jersey, he was as well known for his ability as a running back on a mostly white football team as he was for baseball, which he played semiprofessionally under an assumed name. From high school football workouts at Baurlie Field to professional baseball games at the Grove Street Oval, Doby's exploits were followed by most sports fans in northeastern New Jersey, including the Eastside High administration. Once Doby had joined the Eagles as an infielder, he was tutored by Willie Wells, who strongly suggested to him, as he had already to Irvin, that he was a natural outfielder.

Jackie Robinson also fit the profile of the Northern Negro leaguer. He too had played against whites, and he too had been raised in an integrated setting. However, in terms of education, cultural style, and even region, Jackie Robinson was most unusual. Robinson was the first Californian (he was raised in Pasadena) to achieve success in the Negro leagues. He attended Pasadena Junior College for two years. There he was their most outstanding athlete by far, a four-letter man in track, football, basketball, and baseball. He went on to UCLA, and thus became the only important Negro league player to be educated at a major white university. However, as a teetotaler of strong views, Robinson did not relate very well to the Southerners, many of whom he considered "country," or the Easterners, most of whom were too brassy for his taste.

Adding to the meld of Negro baseball were the Latin Americans, spearheaded by the Cubans. Ironically, the first professional black team, in a vague attempt to confuse its players' blackness with the uncertainties of Caribbean race mixing, had called itself the Cuban Giants. This charade was unconvincing on Long Island. Among other things, the gibberish the "Cubans" pretended to speak bore no resemblance to Spanish! Nonetheless, from then on, "Cuban" had a widely understood connotation in black baseball. It stood for high-quality ball and suggested an exotic land where better race relations existed. The name Cuban developed such box-office appeal that promoters "created" Cuban teams to capitalize on the demand. When necessary, they fleshed out their team with Americans. (In the 1940s about half of Alessandro Pompez's New York Cubans were American.)

Shortly after the turn of the century, following the Spanish-American War, when Cuba ceased being a colony of Spain, real Cubans began to arrive in the United States, and the black ones played in a black sports world. When two very light-skinned Cubans, Rafael Almeida and Armando Marsans, broke the Cuban barrier with the Cincinnati Reds in 1911, blacks seriously thought integration might quickly follow. Black newspapers covered Marsans and Almeida at a time when they ignored most everything else in white baseball.

To the truly dark-skinned Cubans, however, organized baseball was as tightly barred as to any black American. Routinely the best dark Cubans after 1920 joined the Negro league. Bill Yancey remembered the black Cuban Julio Rojo saying "byemby, s'thousands of dollars," as he watched whites playing ball; he was painfully aware of his inferior caste. In every decade there were Cuban superstars in black baseball, and there was always an all-Cuban team, and sometimes more than one. In the mid-twenties there was a Cuban team in the Negro National League, another in the Eastern Colored League, and a third in the Southern Negro League as well as Cuban players with great reputations who played for Negro league teams. Cristobel Torrienti was so outstanding that Foster kept him for the Chicago American Giants, and Wilkinson was not about to lose Jose Mendez, star pitcher of his All-Nations team and later of the Kansas City Monarchs. Torrienti was scouted by the majors in 1922 and 1923 even though his Negroid features clearly indicated his African ancestry.

While to the black mind, the Cubans added cosmopolitanism to the Negro leagues, Cuban ballplayers were in fact often as parochial as the most "country" black from the South Carolina lowlands, and, just as in the United States, the majority of the players were from the countryside. Orestes "Minnie" Minoso was typical.

Minoso was born in El Parrico, a small town about sixty miles from Havana. He played in the streets and on the ranches; Minoso never saw a professional game until he was in one. As a talented player he was quickly spotted by a scout in Oriente province, where an American-owned company called Cuban Mining sponsored the team. From there, it was a short jump to Marianao of the Cuban League. As a star in the Cuban League, Minoso knew that he could play anywhere, and when his manager Jose Fernandez offered him a job on the New York Cubans in 1944, he was overjoyed. His pay was $150 a month plus a boat ticket to Key West and a train ticket to New York. At exactly the same moment, multimillionaire Jorge Pasqual was trying to lure him to Mexico. But America was a promised land.

Adding international flavor to the Negro baseball world was a smattering of Cuban-Americans, Puerto Ricans, Panamanians, and even a Jamaican or two. Pitcher Janelo Mirabal was born in Key West, but was raised a Cuban. He played on Cuban teams in the United States and then entered winter ball in Cuba, just like any other American. Perucho Cepeda, the father of Orlando Cepeda, was the best known of the Puerto Rican players. As would later his son, the elder Cepeda won the admiration of all the Negro leaguers with his towering home runs. In the 1930s famed Negro league shortstop Bill Yancey was hired to teach baseball in Panama and prepare a Panamanian team for the 1936 Olympics. Yancey was so outstanding as a coach, and Panamanian baseball caught on with such intensity, that almost a dozen Panamanians entered the Negro leagues, including Pat Scantlebury— proud possessor of one of the most feared spitballs in the league. Bob Feller, who barnstormed against Scantlebury, described his spitter as looking like "a pigeon coming out of a barn."

There were thus many roads to the Negro leagues; players came from the North and South, cities and farms, sandlots and industrial teams, and from the entire Caribbean basin. In every part of America where blacks lived in any numbers, there were black teams, and everywhere baseball was the number-one sports spectacle. In schools, factories, church leagues, and on the sandlots, baseball was "it." Therefore, making it into the Negro leagues was an extraordinary accomplishment. The players who negotiated that journey represented the tip of a black sports pyramid which reached into every black community in the nation.

Baseball was also the only athletic vocation which promised a living. Of course, a few black boxers, among them Joe Louis, Henry Armstrong, and John Henry Lewis (managed by Gus Greenlee) made a go of it, but only Louis was a sustained success. It was simply too easy to draw the color line against most black fighters. Not until World War II did boxing promoters believe that whites would pay to see two blacks fight.

Negro league baseball, on the other hand, was profitable from its inception. Although wages fluctuated with national economic trends, even the lowest wages on the poorest teams—say Birmingham's sixty dollars a month and expenses at the pit of the Depression—represented a living wage. Indeed, Negro leaguers supported extended families throughout much of the Depression. In 1934, Buck Leonard recalled that players "were getting sixty cents a day to eat, and you could really eat a couple of meals for sixty cents. But not good meals, and not steaks. When they raised it to a dollar, I started saving a little money."

The exalted position of baseball in the black sports hierarchy is seen in the pull baseball exerted on the better athletes in other sports. Heavyweight champion Jack Johnson earned money as an umpire in black baseball after his boxing career ended. Johnson in fact enjoyed playing and umpiring in the teens while still champion. Jesse Owens, fresh from his Olympic triumphs in 1936, discovered that his greatest value was as a sideshow to the Negro league games and black barnstorming. Some of the greatest black basketball players of the thirties and forties—Fats Jenkins, Dick Seay, Goose Tatum—made the majority of their money in the Negro leagues. When UCLA football star Jackie Robinson needed to make a living in 1944, he turned to baseball.

There were only about two hundred jobs in the big Negro leagues, perhaps twice as many on other black teams nationwide. Teams tried to get by with as few players as possible and, to keep salaries and expenses down, the league limited the number of players per team—in 1937, the limit was only fifteen. Pitchers doubled in the outfield or even at second or third. "I was the damnest third baseman," Satchel Paige liked to say. Leon Day was an outstanding second baseman as well as pitcher. Josh Gibson often ended up in right field on Negro league all-star teams because Biz Mackey was catching, and, of course, Josh's bat was wanted in the line-up.

As a consequence, pitchers didn't get much relief. Dick Redding and Smokey Joe Williams were heralded for their ability to pitch both ends of a doubleheader. A pitcher who was clobbered, was clobbered. It was thought better to lose a 13-1 game than carry an extra player—though any pitcher that lost many 13-1 games was soon no longer a Negro leaguer, as there were hundreds clamoring to take his place.

And because the money was good, because decent jobs for blacks were few, and, finally, because many players had few other skills, Negro leaguers tried to stay on and on. Second baseman Newt Allen began in 1918 and played steadily until 1950. Rookies on the Newark Eagles called the old-timers "the syndicate," and Andrew "Pullman" Porter remembered when, early in his career, he went to the Baltimore Elite Giant bullpen and a recalcitrant catcher refused to warm him up—a crude and nearly successful attempt to save a friend's job. To reach the Negro leagues in the teeth of the stubborn opposition of veteran players was an achievement of real substance, a cause for enormous pride.

This black baseball meritocracy must be understood if the psychology of the Negro league player is to be understood. In his terms, and in the terms of his culture, the Negro league player was a great success. The Negro leaguer had more money, more attention, more lasting fame, and a richer life than almost all the rest of his contemporaries. The result was that Negro leaguers, in general, were not bitter men. Even in the face of racism and the certain knowledge that, had they been white, they would have been major leaguers, these players achieved more than enough to be satisfied. As Kansas City Monarch John "Buck" O'Neil emphasized, "Don't feel sorry for me, I had a beautiful life. I played with the greatest ballplayers in the world, and I played against the best ballplayers in the world. I saw this country and a lot of other countries and I met some wonderful people." Judy Johnson in his eighties once remarked, "They were my happy days, and I don't regret one minute."

The Cult of Professionalism

3

Robert Peterson, the first historian of black baseball, to whom all who study the Negro leagues owe an enormous debt, described charting the history of Negro baseball teams as "like trying to follow a single black strand through a ton of spaghetti." Many of the weaker teams joined the leagues in an instant, and bad management killed them almost as quickly. For every Cool Papa Bell, Newt Allen, or Satchel Paige with a four-or-five-decade career there was a "Goo Goo" Livingston or "Moocha" Harris whose only notoriety was a catchy nickname. Anecdotes are countless, and the best have countless variations. But because the story of Negro league baseball is so compelling, people were found to tell it. Robert Peterson wrote *Only the Ball Was White*, a comprehensive look at a century of blacks in baseball. John Holway, like John Lomax before him, collected numerous oral histories so that "great voices" might be heard. Bill Brashler created the fictional Bingo Long and his traveling all-stars, a barnstorming tale, and also wrote a brief biography of Josh Gibson. Art Rust, Jr., paid homage to the players of his youth in *Get that Nigger Off the Field*.

Yet in the struggle to rescue the exploits of magnificent athletes for baseball's history, to tell the world about Satchel and Rube and Josh, it was easy for historians to overlook the larger picture: black people, crushed by segregation, desperately needed models to emulate; and they required men and women who cast large shadows, large enough to make known the truth of black talent. Gunnar Myrdal, in his famous study of American race relations, *An American Dilemma*, observed that, "Negroes who have accomplished something extraordinary, particularly in competition with whites," automatically were accorded great "power and glamour." And the Negro league players revelled in that power and glamour while in the main accepting its responsibilities, too. The Negro leaguers were a part of that "missing" coterie of professionals, the invisible men of American history: black men of substance.

Players, managers, owners, Negro newspaper men, and even Negro league fans infused black baseball with an ethos that stressed discipline, hard work, competency, sacrifice, and the pursuit of on-the-field excellence. "They had standards you had to live up to," insisted the lanky second-base standout Sammy T. Hughes. Negro leaguers were expected to represent their town, Negro baseball, and the black race.

The demand that players act as role models was carried to extremes. When Paul Jake Stevens came up with Hilldale his nickname was "Country Jake"— "country" being a term of derision. Stevens was on probation his first weeks. The diminutive shortstop with the golden glove learned that he had made the team when owner Eddie Bolden took him downtown and bought him "two suits, one banker's gray and the other one blue, and two stetson hats."

The Chicago American Giants under Foster's leadership had not only a dress code, which conformed to Foster's essentially conservative taste, but also a curfew. (The curfew was not appreciated. To enforce it himself, Foster often sat up late in hotel lobbies, regaling fans and passersby alike with tales of the mayhem he was preparing for the next game.) Of Negro league curfews, Sammy T. Hughes commented, "They were like all curfews: if you win, OK; if you lose, you better be in." Bill Drake, a sometimes undisciplined pitcher, once joined his manager Bingo DeMoss for a night of carousing that did not end until six the next morning. As Drake told John Holway, "One o'clock come along and I'll be doggone, that son of a bitch tossed the ball to me." After giving up four runs in the first inning, Drake met DeMoss at the coach's box where all the smiling DeMoss said was, "Nine innings, win or lose."

Management was always concerned with the appearance of the Negro leaguers. J. L. Wilkinson even schooled his players in proper "hotel behavior," to the extent of forbidding house slippers in hotel lobbies. The *Kansas City Call* observed with some exaggeration that the Monarchs' "deportment on and off the field would do honor to the most exacting conventions of an English family." Enforcing a dress code was easy, for the players thrived on their role as professional ballplayers. They were proud of their appearance and they worked at it. Quincy Trouppe still recalls the commotion when Cool Papa Bell promenaded through Compton Hill in St. Louis. "When Bell walked past, sometimes with his pretty wife, Clara, he was always tagged after by two or three kids," Trouppe said, "and one of those kids was bound to be me."

Monte Irvin found the look of the Negro leaguers compelling. "What impressed me was how the athletes looked," he said, recalling his days as a staunch fan of the Newark Eagles. "They looked like ballplayers. I liked the way their uniform fit, the way they wore their cap, the fact that they showed a style in almost everything they did. It impressed me to want to become a professional baseball player."

When New York Black Yankee centerfielder Clint Thomas received his Black Yankee uniform, he was told, "You look like them, you dress like them, and you act like them." It was a lesson "the Hawk" never forgot. Willie Wells, nearly blind from glaucoma, leads friend and visitor alike to a jammed closet, overflowing with once-elegant clothes. Pulling a white suit from the closet he proudly recalls, "I always tried to dress my best."

If black people loved their ballplayers, and if some whites felt relief at the conventionality of their aspirations, for hard-core racists the Negro leaguers were a threatening sight indeed. Once when Judy Johnson, Ted Page, and Jimmy Crutchfield strolled into downtown Nashville dressed to the nines, they were greeted by a Southern policeman who told them, "Don't you come uptown looking this a-way." Thinking back over the incident, Hall of Famer Judy Johnson shuddered, "He'd have cut the suits off our backs."

The concern for style was best symbolized by the use of Pullman cars by Negro league teams of the twenties. Both the Chicago American Giants under Rube Foster and Wilkinson's Monarchs usually hitched a private Pullman parlor car to the train for long-distance travel. Nothing was as imposing as the sight of the Pullman, fully loaded with the nattily attired young men, pulling into a Deep South city. "These are gala days in the Southern metropolis," a Negro newspaperman wrote of Foster's arrival in 1920 in Birmingham for some exhibitions. "Folks from miles around came to see Rube Foster's club." Foster kept the car as his personal office while the team made do in the city; then the American Giants received the traditional exuberant train-station send-off, an episode subject to countless retellings.

Pullman cars, of course, had symbolic importance for all black people in the twenties. Not only was the Pullman Company the largest employer of black workers in the nation, but the Brotherhood of Pullman Porters, under the leadership of A. Philip Randolph, was the only black union of any influence whatsoever. Pullman meant wages; but it also meant being a servant. Blacks thrilled to see other blacks as passengers on a Pullman car.

To some degree, the cult of professionalism simply meant mimicking the major leagues whenever possible. The Negro leaguers fought to use major-league ballparks and unabashedly copied everything from the New York Yankee pin stripes to special-order Louisville Slugger bats. When Bill Robinson, the dancing wizard known as "Mr. Bojangles," took over the New York Black Yankees, almost his first act was to purchase year-old Yankee uniforms. Little-known Black Yankee infielder Al Fennar loudly boasted that he wore Lou Gehrig's pants.

Whenever the Negro leaguers visited Chicago, the Spalding store and factory was an obligatory stop.

Spalding treated the Negro leaguers as valued customers, and a few of the Negro leaguer old-timers such as Willie Wells were accorded the ultimate in sports status, the privilege of picking their own wood and having a bat made to their specifications. Wells, who wanted only hickory for his bats, observed that "the ball just came flying off that hickory bat. I didn't want no ash." When the Homestead Grays became regular tenants of Griffith Stadium in Washington, Clark Griffith arranged for the Grays to buy their equipment in the same purchase order as the Senators. "Grays" was stenciled on the uniform instead of "Senators." Under this set-up each Gray found a Senator whose equipment closely matched his own needs and ordered additional quantities of that item under the name of that Senator player. Buck Leonard, a lifetime .355 hitter in the Negro league, used Len Okrie's bat. Okrie batted a lifetime .218.

Invariably the Negro leaguers' taste gravitated toward the best. Shoes, gloves, sliding pads, sanitary hose—they had to be the same as used in the major leagues. The players bitterly ridiculed the inferior 150cc Wilson baseball which cost twenty-three dollars a dozen and saved the league fifty cents over a major league ball. Chet Brewer discovered a unique way to doctor that ball. "I liked to pitch when [Oscar] Charleston was playing first base," he said. "He was so strong, when you threw him a new ball to rub up he could just take his hands and open up the seam on it." Rarely was a ball thrown out of a Negro league game, with the obvious result that, as the game progressed, each pitch looked more and more like a knuckler. If a ball was hit out of the park it often only meant that a youngster finally had himself an admission ticket. (And if the hitters did not have enough to worry about, spitballs and emery balls were an accepted part of the game. "Lefty" Sam Streeter was generally acknowledged the spitter king of the Negro leagues, while for an emery ball—a ball sanded down with an emery cloth—none surpassed Smokey Joe Williams.)

The Negro leaguers added a few items to the artifacts of baseball history as well. Pepper Bassett, a huge catcher who played with a host of Negro league teams, found that the 1930-style catcher's mitt with its pillow-like design was unsatisfactory, particularly when a quick release was needed to get the runner stealing second. Experimenting, he gradually removed more and more of the padding, toughening his hand in the process. Unknown to history, he helped create the "squeezer" style of catcher's mitt. Willie Wells took the idea a step further, cutting a hole in the center of his glove. With a palm that looked like a slab of worn leather, Wells found he could field significantly better than he could with the lumpy gloves of his day.

Even the umpires got into the act. In general, Negro league umpiring was poor. The league couldn't afford a stable of traveling umpires, and so each team provided its own, with mixed results. When asked about the quality of Negro league umpiring Pepper Bassett was bemused. "There was no umpiring, only guesses," he replied. However, a few umpires gradually earned reputations for accurate calls, and several, led by John Craig and Fred McQuery, invariably were selected for key games such as the Negro World Series or the East-West Classic. To get a closer look at the strike zone, Craig one day in Pittsburgh experimented with a chest protector worn inside his jacket. As Bill Harris, another Negro league umpire and the brother of Homestead Gray manager Vic Harris watched, Craig prepared an inside protector of two flattened cardboard boxes with sponges inside. This inside protector later became standard in the National League.

In 1942 Baltimore Elite Giant pitcher Bill Byrd knocked Willie Wells unconscious in Newark, and he was carried from the stadium. A week later Wells's Eagles journeyed to Baltimore to meet Byrd and the Elite Giants again. Against the advice of everyone, Wells decided to play. He visited a Jersey City construction site, picked up a workingman's hardhat, and became the first professional baseball player to use a batting helmet. "We thought he was crazy," said teammate Dick Seay.*

In a frankly capitalistic age, the cult of professionalism meant making money and using money to evaluate achievement. Rube Foster said his goal in

---

*There was another, probably apocryphal, version of the beaning that lead to Wells's first use of a helmet. Effa Manley, the Newark owner, was a beautiful woman who loved baseball, and who began to think that she managed pretty well, too. On occasion she insisted on picking the starting line-up and even telling the players when to bunt or steal. Mule Suttles claimed, as retold by Jimmie Crutchfield, that Effa, "who was very beautiful, would cross her legs for a hit and run. Or she'd cross them back for a bunt." One day, Wells was supposed to be getting the signs and "she hesitated and [Wells] was looking, the pitcher threw, and before he could duck [Wells] was hit in the head." This tale was passed quickly into Negro league folklore, for among other things it played upon the Negro leaguers' profound ambivalence toward this femme fatale of their game.

Philadelphia Giants, ca. 1902.
Rube Foster is second from left,
back row; Charley Grant (known
as Chief Tokohoma) is at back
right. *(Courtesy National Baseball Hall of Fame Library,
Cooperstown, NY)*

Rube Foster, founder of the Negro
National League, 1910. *(Courtesy
Robert Peterson and Craig
Davidson)*

Rube Foster (in suit) and his Chicago American Giants, ca. 1918. Oscar Charleston is on Foster's right. *(Courtesy National Baseball Hall of Fame Library, Cooperstown, NY)*

Kansas City Monarchs night game, 1933. The Negro leagues pioneered night baseball, predating the major leagues by several years. *(Courtesy Janet Bruce)*

ST. LOUIS CARDINALS vs. KANSAS CITY MONARCHS
Six Thousand People Attended this Game at Oxford, Nebraska, October 4, 1933

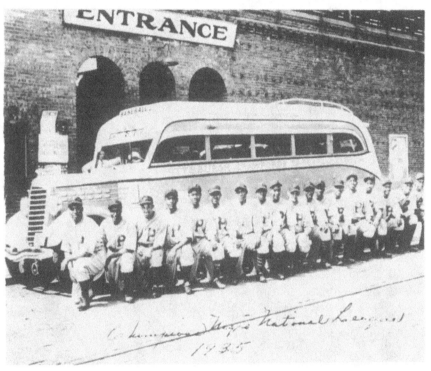

Pittsburgh Crawfords baseball club, 1935. *(Courtesy Jimmy Crutchfield)*

Pittsburgh Crawfords Oscar Charleston, Josh Gibson, Ted Page, and Judy Johnson, 1933.
(Courtesy National Baseball Hall of Fame Library, Cooperstown, NY)

Top left: Josh Gibson at bat, ca. 1942.
(Courtesy Robert Peterson)

Top right: Satchel Paige, ca. 1942. *(Courtesy Craig Davidson)*

Left: Cool Papa Bell, ca. 1930. *(Courtesy Robert Peterson)*

Integrated Bismarck 1935 Championship team. *(Courtesy Craig Davidson)*

Kansas City Monarchs on the road with some House of David players, early 1930s. Chet Brewer is standing at left; L. L. Wilkinson is second from left (in suit). *(Courtesy National Baseball Hall of Fame Library, Cooperstown, NY)*

Ciudad Trujillo, R.D.
Junio 28 de 1937.

Don't be vague — ask for
Haig

Sitio: Café Lindbergh.
Hora: 7.30 p.m.
Umpire: Meng.
Motivo: Partido amistoso de maní contra mandíbula
como homenaje a los dragones victoriosos.

Por café Lindbergh:

Meng & Hoy Chez.

Line-up

1.- Abre un cocktail "Cool Papa".
2.- Sacrifice de entremés Silvio García.
3.- Lázaro empujando ensalada de camarones.
4.- Plato de home-run: Pavo relleno Jhosúa.
5.- Doble robo de legumbres Williams/Bankhead.
6.- Triple play de puding Castaños/Sonlly/Vargas.
7.- Foul fly de café a lo Perkins.
8.- Vinos pitching staff first class.
9.- Tous café frente unido.
10.- Tabacos emergentes Cepeda/Ninín.

CAMPEONATO REELECCION PRESIDENTE TRUJILLO!

(Un día después de Griffith haber dejado en
un anémico hit a la máquina cibaeña.)

Invitation to dinner party celebrating both the Trujillo re-election and the Ciudad Trujillo baseball team victory, 1937. Note (1) Cocktail "Cool Papa," (2) Hors d'oeuvres Silvio Garcia (famous Cuban shortstop), (4) Home-run plate: stuffed turkey Joshua (Josh Gibson), and (5) Tobacco Cepeda (Perucho Cepeda, father of Orlando Cepeda). *(Courtesy Craig Davidson)*

The Negro leagues' greatest home-run hitter: Josh Gibson. *(Courtesy National Baseball Hall of Fame Library, Cooperstown, NY)*

Vol. 1 - No. 1   NEW YORK, SEPTEMBER 1, 1934   Price 15c

COLORED
BASEBALL & SPORTS
~ MONTHLY ~

C. THOMAS, C. JENKINS, C. SPEARMAN
Three Shining Lights in Colored Baseball.

THE ONLY PUBLICATION OF ITS KIND IN THE WORLD

Black baseball became a distinct cultural phenomenon, as evidenced by this early baseball magazine, 1934. *(Courtesy Clint Thomas)*

Players from the House of David baseball team, 1930. *(Courtesy Craig Davidson)*

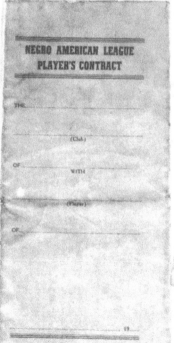

Tickets to East-West Classic (1935), Black World Series (1934), and a Negro American League player's contract. *(Courtesy Jimmy Crutchfield)*

Jimmy Crutchfield played winter ball during the late 1930s for San Juan in the Puerto Rican League. *(Courtesy Jimmy Crutchfield)*

East-West Classic, Comiskey Park, 1939. Note the teeming grandstands at rear. *(Courtesy National Baseball Hall of Fame Library, Cooperstown, NY)*

BILL'S AND JAMES' RESTAURANT

Newark Eagles Baseball Club

Newark Eagles' bus, 1940s. *(Courtesy Craig Davidson)*

Happy Flight of the Eagles

Opening Day - 1942

By Alan D. Levitt

"I used to see the Newark all the time and thought really good. Then one d— see this team called the expecting much. I cove— during how the Bears cou— selves a ball club."

"The man who said this been following sports in nearly two generations, observed with such awe is that well-known to even m— area residents, much less s— ers born since the war. T— Bears went on the road used their park, and, wh— played in Sprague Field o— Avenue, the East Orange Irvington. They also used

Effa Manley, second from left, and Jim Hawk G. Hoffman, second from right, attended opening day ceremonies.

Newark Eagles' opening day, 1942. *(Courtesy Craig Davidson)*

Buck O'Neil and Dizzy Dismukes, a former player who became road secretary to the Kansas City Monarchs upon retirement, late 1940s. *(Courtesy Phil Dixon)*

Cool Papa Bell (far right) fishing in Cuba, early 1930s. *(Courtesy Craig Davidson)*

Cool Papa Bell (front) and Satchel Paige (rear) clowning with Leroy Madlock in the Dominican Republic, 1937. *(Courtesy Craig Davidson)*

Chet Brewer in Panama, early 1940s. *(Courtesy Chet Brewer)*

establishing the league was "to create a profession that would equal the earning capacity of any other profession." Later Negro leaguers took perverse pride in Satchel Paige's 1942 claim that the "majors couldn't pay me enough" to induce him to join. Paige's $37,000 a year was at least four times the major league average, and, in fact, when Hank Greenberg entered the military that year Paige became the highest paid ballplayer in America.

Contract or no, Negro leaguers sold their services to the highest bidder, firm in the conviction that professionals measured their worth in dollars. There was no stigma attached to jumping teams, indeed, no stigma attached to jumping from one country to the next.

At the core of the Negro league folklore were the tales of players' hardiness; it demonstrated their total commitment to the profession. "If you're gonna make baseball your profession, you'll have less privilege, not more," announced one Negro league manager during spring training. Three games every Sunday was simply something to endure. "I said a lot of bad things before we had to play that first [Sunday] game," admitted Judy Johnson. "Everybody [had] their mouths hanging to the floor. But as soon as we put the uniform on, we were just a different team. We'd forget the last game we played and we'd go out and win this one." There were times when they played a game in the morning, then a doubleheader, and then went elsewhere for a night game. "Never took my uniform off," Bill Cash acknowledged. "We didn't even take batting practice, the people were already in the ballpark." Buddy Burbage summed it all up: "You loved baseball. Then you played it, and talked about it, and you dreamed it. Sometimes when you're in bed asleep you have to duck from the ball hitting you. Sometimes you'd duck right into your bedsheets."

Negro leaguers stoically absorbed hardships, playing in conditions where major-league games were called off. "We almost never cancelled," remarked Buck Leonard. Sometimes this policy meant "a fire at first base and fire at third." Buck Leonard still bares spiking scars because once the Grays' doctor refused him time off to let his stitches heal properly. Since the Negro league owner did not control his stadium, rainouts were financially disastrous, and many a game continued in a driving downpour.

The players played rough, too. "If your mother's playing second base they'd tell ya, run over her," remembered Dick Seay. Negro leaguers recall with wide-eyed amazement how the otherwise friendly Crush Holloway filed his spikes in the dugout "just to put a little something on your mind." "They'd throw at you," Newt Allen reported. "They wanted to see if you had guts enough to get back in there." Connie Johnson of the Monarchs, and later the Chicago White Sox, declared, "Out on that mound you were my enemy.... After the game we go out together, eat together, laugh together, have a good time, but not out on that mound, the smiling's gone." Many a Negro league rookie experienced his moment of truth guessing at a curveball that wasn't a curve at all. Willie Mays, who began with the Birmingham Black Barons, called it "combat training." Once Chet Brewer knocked him down and Mays lay there about a minute. Nobody moved. Finally Piper Davis, his manager, approached. "Can you stand up?" he asked. "Yes, I can stand up," Mays replied weakly. "Can you see first base?" Davis continued. "Yeah, I can see first base," Mays responded, again weakly. "Then you get up and you go down to first base," finished Piper Davis and headed back to the dugout.

The one player with the reputation for never throwing at a man was Satchel Paige. "I don't call that no baseball if I got to cave your ribs to get you out," he said to the relief of generations of baseball players.

Tough as Negro baseball was played, pressures rarely spilled over into outright fighting. As an ineffectual Negro league commissioner, Rollo Wilson, declared, "We have to be more careful than white baseball. The wrong construction would be put on our fights. To put it in the vernacular, they'd be saying colored people don't know how to behave themselves." (But baseball, Negro or otherwise, would not be baseball without an occasional celebrated brawl, of which the Negro leagues had a few.)

If there was one thing which tested to the limit the players' professionalism, it was the grueling travel. In the thirties, much to the players' anguish, buses became more flexible and economical than trains. To eke out more Depression money, teams also ventured further afield. The first Negro league buses were little more than big cars with benches in them, nice for short trips but murder to sleep in. Eventually the rule hardened: the classier the team, the classier the bus. Gus Greenlee's 1935 GM special was without question the snazziest team bus of the thirties. When Effa and Abe Manley traded in the "Gray Goose" for a top-of-the-line $16,000 bus in 1946, it was one of her happiest moments.

Yet most of the buses were awful. For the players who had tasted the halcyon days of Pullman cars and no night baseball, making the adjustment often proved too tough. Dave Malarcher and Judy Johnson both were driven from the league when they could no longer accept the endless hours of riding dilapidated buses through a countryside not always benign. Exhausted from years on the road and twenty in the game, one veteran explained his leaving succinctly: "The nights weren't long enough. You were just as tired the next day as when you went to bed the night before."

And of course, there was no such thing as a rest during a slump, or even plentiful reserves. A team might travel all night only to arrive just in time for a doubleheader. Nine men entered the fray while the lucky five or six slept. In the nightcap, three or four pulled double duty. One of the most heralded pitching duels of Negro baseball history, between Dick Redding and Smokey Joe Williams in the early twenties, is illustrative. Redding beat Williams in the first game of a double header 1-0 and then, after a short rest, Williams came back and beat Redding to win the second by an identical score. Many of the greatest Negro league pitchers thought nothing of twirling both ends of a doubleheader.

Wendell Smith argued that Satchel Paige's greatest days came in July of 1934. Pitching for the Pittsburgh Crawfords, Paige mowed through the Homestead Grays' lineup at Forbes Field. Paige had such extraordinary stuff that day, he'd shout to the batter, "You'll get nothing today," while an appreciative crowd howled with laughter. Finally Buck Leonard, to slow Paige up, complained that Paige was tampering with the ball, and, in an unusual concession, several were thrown from the game. Paige scornfully approached Leonard and yelled, "You might as well throw them all out, 'cause they're all jumping today." Then, after his victory, the incredible Paige hopped into his roadster and drove straight to Chicago; there he outdueled the American Giant ace Ted Trent 1-0 in a twelve-inning ballgame!

Martin Dihigo and Oscar Charleston sometimes played all nine positions during a game to demonstrate their versatility and to hold the crowd. Like doctors on call, the Negro leaguers were ready at a moment's notice to play and make a payday. In fact, in the patois of the Negro league, just about the highest compliment was, simply, "That man can play."

The Negro league players performed under enormous pressures. They had the usual expectation of any athletic competitor, namely, winning. But they also were in a profession so clearly superior to other black occupations in earning power that they knew that there were dozens waiting to take their places. This circumstance focused their attention on baseball to a remarkable degree and resulted in one of the profound ironies of baseball history: Negro league baseball was a more thoughtful game than was white baseball.

As Ted Page explained, "When we lost a game we'd sit up practically all night discussing it. Why did we do that? This is the way I had to keep from washing windows in a downtown store or sweeping the floor." Page wanted no part of the twelve to fifteen dollars a week he'd command as an adult window washer. "Well, if [you're] gonna play on these teams, you got to win," he added. Webster McDonald noted that, "If we lost a ballgame we'd go talk it over. Why we lost. Instead of rushing into the street." "We didn't just use muscle," Quincy Trouppe observed emphatically, "we

used our heads." According to Bill Evans, Oscar
Charleston, his manager with the Crawfords, emphasized fundamentals. "Everything he did, he did well,"
said Evans. "And games that we won or lost Charleston would take to bed with him and go through everything in the game." Shortly before he died, Satchel
Paige reflected, "The thing I don't understand even
now [is], if one of my players [while in the Negro
league] made a mistake, the manager would tell him
how he got beat. But when I got to the majors, it
wasn't nothing like that."

Gradually Negro leaguers realized that they possessed a distinctive style of baseball. The central difference stemmed from the Negro league's emphasis
on speed and its rejection of the Babe Ruth-inspired
long-ball game. "I wasn't after no home-run hitter,"
declared Satchel Paige in explaining how he chose his
barnstorming companions. "I only wanted a fellow
who'd get a piece of the ball." Paige always claimed
that his success in the majors, at age forty-two with
the Cleveland Indians, was due primarily to the fact
everyone tried to homer off him. "That was like cool
water to me," said Paige, who went 6-1 in 1948 and
was Rookie of the Year.

Negro leaguers raised the bunt to a high art; they
bunted to advance runners and they bunted to get on
base. "I was death on a man [who couldn't sacrifice],
when I managed," reported Webster McDonald of the
Philadelphia Stars. "If you want to make an attack on
the other fellow you got to keep a man in scoring
position." Rube Foster ordered his players to bunt into
a strategically placed hat during practice, and once
clobbered a future Negro league all-star with his
Meerschaum pipe for hitting away on a bunt sign.

Stealing bases in the Negro league was much more common than in the majors. One of the league's better stealers, Buddy Burbage, observed, "I could do some things they couldn't do. They didn't know how. Running bases, stealing, and when to get by watching the pitcher close." The Negro league's most feared base stealer was Cool Papa Bell. Bell was so fast he frequently went from first to third on a bunt. "If he was playing on Astroturf like they got now," remarked Judy Johnson, "they'd never get him out." Rudolpho Fernandez saw Bell hit three inside-the-park home runs in the same game in the Cuban league. A measure of Bell's speed is the fact that Olympic champion Jesse Owens, who traveled with Negro league teams, refused to race Bell around the bases—a match numerous Negro leaguers tried to promote and, failing to, argued about anyway.

The quintessential Cool Papa Bell story came from Satchel Paige, who claimed that Bell was so fast "he could flip the switch and get into bed before the room went dark" (a tale to be chalked up to Paige's lovely sense of hyperbole). Years later Bell remembered that in a flea-bitten hotel, while rooming with Paige, he noticed a short in a light switch. He flipped the switch and after a moment's hesitation, the light went off. Bell tried again with the same result. "Oh boy, I'm gonna tell Satchel something tonight," thought Bell. When Satchel Paige came in exhausted Bell asked, "you all right?" "I'm tired," responded Paige as he slumped into bed. "You know, Satchel," said Bell, "I'm so fast I can beat the light out." And he did.

Black players' proficiency in stealing bases embarrassed the white major leaguers on numerous occasions. Most noteworthy perhaps were the two

successive days in 1929 when Willie Wells stole home
with winning runs against a major-league all-star
team. Jackie Robinson, trained in the Negro leagues,
found easy going on the base paths his first years in
the majors. Neither Monte Irvin nor Roy Campanella
ever stole home in a Negro league game, but they both
did it in the majors. "They invented many things in
baseball that caught on," said Birdie Tebbetts, who
ultimately managed the Cincinnati Reds and barnstormed his native New England with Negro leaguers.

While Negro leaguers were frequent paying customers at major-league games, white major leaguers
almost never saw Negro league games. Moreover, they
tended to dismiss the results of their barnstorming
encounters with black players. Consequently only the
Negro leaguers were in the habit of assessing the quality of both styles of play; and only the Negro leaguers
tended to profit from the lessons learned on both playing fields. The white major-league players were brain-
washed; many believed that no Negro leaguer, or only
a few, could make it in the majors. The Negro leaguers
knew otherwise. "In my heart I knew I could play as
good and better than a lot of them," one player wistfully explained. But the Negro leaguers' only recourse
was to take it out on the playing field in October
exhibitions.

The group most responsible for implementing the
cult of professionalism, the group that stamped its
character on the Negro league, was a "talented tenth"
of former black players who became the managerial
class of the league. Rube Foster, Sol White, Dizzy Dismukes, Willie Wells, Vic Harris, Dave Malarcher, Biz
Mackey, Webster McDonald, Candy Jim Taylor, Judy
Johnson, Newt Joseph, Buck O'Neil, Oscar Charles-

ton, and a dozen more made up this remarkable group of black men.

Again, Rube Foster was the catalyst of it all. Dave Malarcher, who replaced Foster as the American Giants' manager, acknowledged, "After I became manager I used to win so many ball games the fans would say to me, 'you're a greater manager than Rube.' You know what I said? 'I'm just doing what the master taught me.'" Webster McDonald, another Foster protégé, claimed the turning point of his life was when Foster took him under his wing. Foster, who placed great importance on intelligence, had no place on the American Giants for a fellow who could not follow instructions or understand why a certain strategy was applied. "You go out and play with the boys," was the stern disciplinarian's instruction to those unwilling to accept his coaching. However, for those wanting to learn, Foster had infinite patience.

Indeed, a sign of Foster's greatness was his constant effort to spread his hard-earned baseball knowledge throughout the league. Even though the St. Louis Stars had obtained Willie Wells in a haggle with the American Giants, Foster extended Wells an open invitation to visit him while in Chicago. Wells would camp spellbound at Foster's office at Indiana and Wentworth as Foster passed generations of black baseball lore to the youth he dubbed "Little Ranger." Foster exhibited a partiality for his fellow Texans; Wells, Biz Mackey, Newt Joseph, and Newt Allen all spent hours at the foot of the master prior to assuming managerial positions.

It was almost as if the traditional southern black commitment to education, epitomized by the creation of the Negro colleges, and the missionary role of ed-

ucation in the black community had spilled over into
baseball, an arena where such aims could prosper and
pay dividends. When Willie Wells was a young boy
hanging around Dobbs Field in Austin, Texas, he recalled how Biz Mackey, then a rising star from San
Antonio, would allow him to carry the San Antonio
Aces' equipment into the rickety ballpark and sit on
the team bench. It was perhaps the most vivid and
happy memory of Wells's childhood. Years later in
Florida, Wells returned the favor to Othello "Chico"
Renfroe. When the Newark Eagles went to Jacksonville to train, young Chico would "rush the bus before
the doors were open." He was the Eagles' mascot, and
the players taught him fundamentals and gave him
encouragement, for he was a darling in manager
Wells's eyes. When Renfroe matured he too became
a Negro leaguer; an East-West Classic player, and, in
fact, Jackie Robinson's replacement as the Kansas City
Monarch shortstop. Much later, as the most respected
black sports broadcaster in the South, he continued
working with young people, a tireless proselytizer for
the Florida A & M Rattlers, and a voice for reason in
college athletics.

Teaching ability and a fierce commitment to
spreading baseball information were the qualities
which bound the talented tenth of Negro baseball together. Of Dizzy Dismukes it was said, "He could tell
you more about baseball in a few minutes than a
youngster could ever remember." Willie Mays, as
he reminisced about his days as a Birmingham
Black Baron, remarked, "The major leagues were easy
for me. I learned baseball the hard way; the Negro
leagues made me."

Working with the material they had, the Negro

league managers had to indoctrinate the Negro leaguer into the world of Negro baseball. For a few native intellects such as college-bound Monte Irvin or Joe Black, the task was relatively straightforward. On the other hand, more than one manager learned it was possible to want too much. "You got to evaluate your personnel first," was Willie Wells's cardinal rule. "Don't go tampering with a ballplayer that's mechanical, don't put too much into his head."

When Kansas City Monarch Jackie Robinson first met Branch Rickey in August of 1945, all the Negro leaguers immediately knew that Robinson might be chosen to integrate the game. This filled them with great anxiety because Robinson was a rookie in the Negro league, relatively inexperienced. Quickly, the old-time baseball men pulled together in an effort to teach Robinson the trade in as short a time as possible. Playing for the Homestead Grays in the twilight of his career, Cool Papa Bell was approached by Dizzy Dismukes of the Monarchs, who informed Bell that Robinson was on the verge of signing with the Dodger organization. "He wants to play shortstop," Dismukes told Bell, but Dismukes and everybody else on the Monarchs knew that Robinson would not be able to play major-league shortstop. Bell's concern was strong. "If he missed his chance, I didn't know how long we'd go before we'd get another" he recalled. Dismukes requested Bell to hit into the hole and test Robinson's move to the right, and he asked Bell to give Robinson a base-stealing exhibition because the Negro leaguers were not impressed with Robinson's tagging ability. Bell, who "ran like he stole something," easily beat out two infield hits that went to Robinson's right, and he stole four bases that night. Coming into second just under Robinson's tag he said, "See that? They got a lot of guys in the major leagues slide like that. You can't get those guys out like that."

Later that winter Robinson joined a Negro league all-star group in Venezuela. On his team were Roy Campanella, Quincy Trouppe, Parnell Woods, Roy Welamaker, Buck Leonard, Gene Benson, Sam Jethroe, and Felton Snow—all considered better ballplayers than Robinson at that time. But with the full expectation that if Robinson succeeded, there would be room for many more, they worked hard to improve Robinson's play. Ironically, Robinson did not like being tutored by the self-made Negro leaguers. "Jackie's temper was a real problem for his friends," admitted Quincy Trouppe. "One day Felton Snow tried to talk to Jackie about the right way to handle a certain play at shortstop, and Jackie really talked to him bad."

The reason that black baseball put such intense pressure on the players to conform to standards was the fervent belief that, by setting that good example and performing at the maximum of their capabilities, black players would someday win recognition from white America. As Sol White argued in his *History of Colored Baseball,* "Baseball is a legitimate profession. It should be taken seriously by the colored player. An honest effort of his great ability will open the avenue in the near future wherein he may walk hand in hand with the opposite race in the greatest of all American games—baseball." "We have to be ready when the time comes for integration," was how Rube Foster put it.

Reinforcing the cult of professionalism was the dominant means of communication of black culture:

the black newspapers. These papers functioned as the conduit through which black news moved at a time when white America virtually ignored everything of real concern to blacks. Because black problems and interests were remarkably similar nationwide, but access to information from distant communities was extremely difficult to obtain, important black newspapers such as the *Pittsburgh Courier*, the *Chicago Defender*, New York City's *Amsterdam News*, and the Baltimore/Washington-based *Afro-American* carried extensive national news, and the *Defender* and the *Courier* grew into truly national newspapers.

Yet while the Negro newspaper headlined lynchings and campaigns for equal rights, it is likely that, even in the South, the sports section sold more papers than any other. Sports interest was ubiquitous in American culture, but black sports information was almost exclusively the province of the black newspaper. And because baseball was played year round by the Negro leaguers, their names remained always before the black public and, particularly, the black leaders, who took their cues from the Negro newspapers.

Sociologist E. Franklin Frazier in his well-known *Black Bourgeoisie* bitterly accuses the black press of perpetuating "wish fulfillment." He argues that the papers were alienated from the fundamental concerns of black life and with justification criticizes the hidden agenda of their society pages and all-too-subservient attitude toward white opinion makers. However, in its support of baseball integration and in its treatment of black athletes, the black press was at one with the black population. Never acquiescing to segregation in baseball, the Negro newspapers conducted a sustained campaign for sports integration that gave moral encouragement to the black athlete and the black population. With the box scores of black-vs.-white barnstorming games as their evidence, the black press hammered for equality, and were quick to spot any chinks in the armor of sports segregation.

It was the Negro press which also led the campaign for accurate record-keeping in black baseball. "The local newspapers must guess at hits, runs, errors, doubles, triples, and the many other things which happen in a ballgame," they complained. And their sportswriters argued that "because this phase of the game has gone unrecognized is one of the genuine reasons why the status of Negro players cannot be proved." Of course, given the conditions the players toiled under, it is no wonder that no one wanted to keep an accurate scorebook. Sometimes a reserve pitcher kept the book; often it was ignored.

For short periods the Negro newspapers attempted to send sportswriters with traveling teams, but it became too expensive and the newspapers settled for by-mail submissions of team managers or local baseball enthusiasts. The results were at best mixed, as the following notice in the *Defender* would suggest:

NOTICE TO BASEBALL OWNERS AND MANAGERS

1. Mail special delivery as soon after game as possible
2. Send games whether you win or lose
3. Do not wire games collect
4. In sending telegrams pay for them at your end
5. Do not abbreviate words

6. Do not hold games and send them two or three at once.

Not before Jackie Robinson's first years of integrated baseball did Negro newspapers fully cover a baseball team. Wendell Smith of the *Courier* and Sam Lacy of the *Afro-American* became Robinson's writers, companions, and psychologists. (Smith and Lacy were part of a cadre of extremely talented sportswriters who labored in the separate and unequal world of black sports journalism. Black sports had its Grantland Rice and Damon Runyon, but their names were Faye Young, Wendell Smith, and Ric Roberts. And a white nation that missed seeing Josh Gibson at the plate missed just as much by never reading the imaginative prose of the journalists who chronicled the Negro leagues.)

Despite the failure to record black baseball statistics accurately, the Negro newspapers consistently harped upon the necessity to keep Negro league baseball dignified. When a shirtless spectator was photographed at a Chicago American Giant game, the *Defender* editorialized, "no matter how hot it might be, and it wasn't that warm, men naked to the waist have no place in audiences at our baseball games. Notice the woman sitting next to the man in question," it pointed out. Drinking, gambling, improper dress, foul language, all were periodically condemned in the black press. This editorializing was a strong sign of the symbolism of the baseball spectacle as experienced by black Americans.

For the black fan, the sports pages of the *Defender* or *Courier* were a lifeline to the rest of black America. How else could a black fan learn the name of an aspiring "race fighter," discover that black and white ballplayers did in fact play against each other in the North, or that the Cuban winter league was integrated? There was no such thing as a radio broadcast of a black game, and the white papers, with only the rarest of exceptions, ignored Negro league baseball. Thus that weekly *Courier* or *Defender* delivery made all the difference, as tattered clippings surviving decades in the scrapbooks of loyal fans and fellow townsmen attest.

In the 1930s, for a short period, a Negro sports periodical joined the Negro newspapers in a crusade to upgrade Negro sports. Nat Trammell's *Colored Baseball and Sports Monthly* was a well-edited, historically accurate periodical that not only carried current baseball and sports information but also tried to document the history of black sports. In keeping with the pro-integration views of black sportsmen, Trammell's magazine featured many articles on liberal white sports figures such as Nat Strong, characterized by Trammell as "a very broad minded man of wide experience. He holds dear the friendship of some of the greatest stars that the race has produced."

Ultimately, the quintessential value of the cult of professionalism was the psychological boost it gave the Negro leaguers themselves. It was how they rationalized making a living playing the game that they loved. As Buck Leonard said, "I loved the game and would have played for nothing, and did play some of them for nothing." Baseball thrust them forward into difficult but exciting and distinctive lives.

At the time that Negro league teams toured throughout America, the black professional class was extremely small. In 1940 there were fewer than four thousand black doctors in the entire nation. Businessmen were also few. Only ministers and school teachers contributed any numbers to a professional class. (An indication of the relatively high status of the players was the large number of them who married schoolteachers.)

Yet by calling themselves professionals, and by giving the term meaning through their strenuous efforts, baseball players projected a model of accomplishment and achievement throughout their society. A few entered directly to high status positions. George Sweat used money earned as a Monarch to put himself through medical school; Charlie Ruffin of the Newark Eagles became a minister. The majority, however, simply maintained a strong sense of personal importance on the basis of their on-the-field success.

As Satchel Paige once said, "I used to feel so bad before I got to the clubhouse I didn't know what to do. But when I got that ballsuit on I don't know where I got that spunk to save my life." Judy Johnson philsophized, "We would get tired from the riding, we would fuss like a bunch of chickens, but when you put the suit on it was different. We just knew that was your job, and you'd just do it. We used to have a lot of fun, and then there were some sad days too, but there was always sun shining someplace."

The Heat of the Harlem Moon

4

Entry into the life of the Negro leagues in the North was exhilarating. When Moberly, Missouri's Jimmy Crutchfield walked down Harlem's 125th Street for the first time he experienced "a feeling of freedom I had never felt before." For Mountain Jesse Hubbard, who came to New York a hulk of a country boy, it was the "sporting class of people" who dazzled him, and who then became the model to emulate.

The big-city black communities, particularly Harlem and Chicago, opened their arms to the Negro leaguers with an effusive enthusiasm. "The new players that don the uniforms of the Giants will be given a welcome that will go on as long as they are connected with baseball," crowed the *Defender* in 1920. "Chicago is known to lead in all things."

Why the wholehearted embrace for baseball on the part of the newly urbanized black masses? Buck O'Neil of the Monarchs, himself a rural Southerner who was part of the great migration to the urban North, noted that players of his generation and background "didn't know how to eat, they didn't know how to dress, and most of all they didn't know how to act. But they knew baseball and they could fit in going to a ball game." This was no small matter to the almost two hundred thousand blacks added to Chicago's Negro population between 1910 and 1930, or the millions who migrated north between the World Wars. In cities where blacks were largely first-generation immigrants from the South, the teams evolved into a vital component of community building, and a city without a Negro league team was almost by definition a second-rate black community. Washington, D.C., for example, felt keenly the stigma of being a teamless city, and strenuously sought to bring a ballclub to the nation's capital. It was a bitter blow when Washington lost the Elite Giants to Baltimore in the mid-thirties, and only the arrangement negotiated between Cum Posey and Clark Griffith to share the Homestead Grays in 1939 salvaged a measure of Washington's pride.

For the black community, Negro league games quickly became a rallying point for a host of mundane and not so mundane purposes. "The prize-sepia beauties of the greater Cincinnati district will vie in the second annual bathing beauty contest," Cincinnati Tiger baseball fans were informed in 1937. It was an event sure to increase attendance. Mary Jo Wheeler, crowned Miss Monarch in 1940, was selected from twenty Kansas City beauties. A merchant's sponsorship was required to enter the Miss Monarch Contest; Miss Wheeler's five-dollar entry fee was paid by Gold Crown Liquors.

Invariably Alabama Day, Tennessee Day, and Virginia Day punctuated the Negro league schedule, for Southerners maintained a divided loyalty in the North. When the Memphis Red Sox, Atlanta Black Crackers, and Jacksonville Red Caps joined the league in the late thirties, regional promotions became even more prevalent.

However, probably the most remarkable special day in Negro baseball history was Newark owner Effa Manley's "Stop Lynching" campaign in Ruppert Stadium. As New Jersey Treasurer of the NAACP, Effa was a born organizer and promoter. "I was always good with money," she modestly admitted. Decorating her usherettes with sashes that read "Stop Lynching," she sent them gladhanding through the crowd, fund raising for the number-one civil-rights issue of the day. "We didn't make all that much," she reported, "but I was glad to do it." On another occasion she invited the entire 372nd Regiment, the nation's top black military unit, to an Eagle game, all twenty-five hundred of them. During the war she organized black entertainers, including her friends Florence Mills and Eubie Blake, who used the Newark bus to reach Fort Dix and put on special productions for the "colored troops."

The black community used baseball in a traditional American way. Marching bands, drum majorettes, and parades featuring black dignitaries were staples of the league—particularly in connection with the big Sunday games or special events like the East-West Classic. Opening day of course required a prominent figure, and by the thirties astute white politicians realized that appearing at the league's opener was a proven vote-getter. The women too found an arena to parade in. "They had eyes on all the ballplayers," Lahoma Paige acknowledged, speaking of herself, too. "Each girl would dress up in fashion so that when the boys looked up out of the dugout into the grandstand they would catch the guy's eyes."

Baseball was a unifying element for black communities in transition, communities in the process of development. Clint Thomas, Hilldale and Black Yankee outfielder, kept a poem, published in 1923 in Philadelphia, as a treasured part of his scrapbook. That poem accurately depicted the warm and heartfelt adoption of the ballplayers by their new communities. The poem also captured the joyous flavor and spontaneity of the early black press, qualities which to some degree overshadowed their literary weaknesses:

We are all deep dyed
With that old civic pride
 When a product is stamped as home grown!
We'll swear by a stack
We've the best apple-jack,
 And our soil, it's the world's richest loam.

But listen here, bo
And tis no tale of woe,
 We've a weakness for imported skates;
For here in Kendrick's domain,
We got guys grabbing fame.
 A Legend I now will relate.

A full-gazebo,
Was Phil Cockrell, you
 Ere he peeped up at Bill Penn,
Now then at August, Ga.
Is where Phil first saw th' day
 But Quaker fans say "he's now one of them."

Allen is another from that Cotton State,
Where Sherman's pilgrimage made rebels
 abate,

> *While Mackey, George Johnson and Louis*
> *Santop,*
> *Have all wandered here from Sam Houston's*
> *plot*
> *For Texas produced these three knights of swat.*
> *That fair Philadelphia's been proud to adopt.*

> *Along with a many thousand more,*
> *Maryland's far famed Eastern Shore,*
> *Turned out "Judy" of Johnson fame;*
> *Clint Thomas, Joe Lewis and Mervyn th' red,*
> *And all of the others are foreign bred,*
> *But they're ours, Philadelphians acclaim.*

> *Sure, he may come from Walla Walla,*
> *Or hail from Possum Hollow,*
> *And to him League Island is unknown;*
> *But we'll rear up just th' same,*
> *And reverberate his name,*
> *If he's plugging fo th' town we call our own.*

In the urban areas, the Negro leaguers became celebrities whose exploits were heralded throughout black America. Of course, the most championed of all was the astounding Satchel Paige. Paige combined an awesome fastball with an accuracy that made him almost unbeatable even though the batter might know that a fastball was coming. (A story, probably apocryphal, has Paige writing in large letters on the bottom of his long left shoe "FAST-BALL.")

Paige was saved for the last innings in the 1941 East-West game. The crowd naturally agitated for their superstar, while the opposing East squad fearfully watched, for they knew "Paige didn't like little games, he liked the big games, the best games." The first batter facing Paige in the seventh inning was Lennie Pearson, an excellent hitter. Monte Irvin was on deck. Paige, to the delight of the crowd, overpowered Pearson, striking him out on three pitches! As Pearson headed to the dugout Irvin looked up and asked, "What's he throwing today?" "I don't know," muttered Pearson, "I didn't see it." Players reported that Satchel threw a small ball—many calling it a "pea ball"—as though it got smaller as it approached the plate.

The greatest single episode of Paige's lengthy career occurred in Forbes Field on July 21, 1942, when Paige had his penultimate showdown with Josh Gibson. That hot July day Paige knew he really had his stuff and he baffled and teased the Grays through six innings. With a 4-0 lead, he was a picture of nonchalance, as he put the first two men out in the seventh. Then lead-off man Jerry Benjamin tripled.

Satchel motioned for first baseman John "Buck" O'Neil, the Monarchs' captain, to approach the mound. "Hey, Nancy," yelled Paige, using the nickname he gave O'Neil, "I'm gonna put Howard Esterling on base; I'm gonna put Buck Leonard on base; I'm gonna pitch to Josh!"

"Oh, Satchel, you got to be crazy," moaned O'Neil, who was accustomed to Satchel's antics.

Behind the scene was this story.* When both Satchel and Josh had been rising young stars with the Pittsburgh Crawfords years before, Paige had told Josh, "Some day we're gonna meet up. You're the greatest hitter in Negro baseball, and I'm the greatest pitcher, and we're gonna see who's best."

So on that day in 1942, Paige walked Howard Es-

*Originally reported in *The Sporting News*, July 18, 1981.

terling so that Buck Leonard entered the batter's box and Gibson reached the on-deck circle. "Hey, Josh, you remember that time when I told you about this," roared Paige as he began deliberately to walk Leonard. "Now is the time."

"Okay, Satchel, okay," cackled Gibson in his high-pitched voice. In repartee, Gibson was not ready to challenge the voluble Paige.

"I'm gonna put Buck on. I'm gonna put him on, and pitch to you. I want this to happen," Satchel told Josh.

Now the fans began to realize just what was happening. They stood and cheered. And then, as Leonard hustled to first, loading the bases, they turned oddly silent.

"Now I'm gonna throw you a fastball, but I'm not gonna trick you. I'll tell you what, I'm gonna give you a good fastball," said Paige as Gibson stepped in.

Boom! It was a knee-high fastball. Josh didn't swing. Strike one.

"Now, I'm gonna throw you another fastball, but I'm not gonna try and trick you. Only it's gonna be a little faster than that other one," teased Satchel.

Boom! Again, Josh didn't swing the bat. Strike two.

"Now Josh, that's two strikes," laughed Paige. "Now I'm not gonna try to trick you. I'm not gonna throw any smoke around your yoke. I'm gonna throw a pea on your knee, only it's gonna be faster than that last one."

Boom! It was a fastball, knee high on the outside corner, and Josh didn't swing. Strike three.

As Paige walked off the mound even the Grays' fans cheered. "I told you, I was the greatest in the world," said Satchel Paige, who at that moment was his most magnificent essential self. At a result of such magic moments, Paige became part of the nation's sporting lore. "The Lord always had his arm 'round Satchel," swore his teammate Jimmie Crutchfield.

Once Paige became truly famous, first among blacks in the early thirties and then among whites in the middle and late thirties, a player could make his reputation simply by getting a hit off Satchel. "They didn't even want to let a person foul-tip his ball," said his wife Lahoma. "If they tipped his ball they'd say, Satchel hasn't got it today." But the reality was that Paige was a half step ahead of most Negro leaguers in ability and a full step ahead in showmanship. "We had quite a few who hit that ball," Satchel Paige complimented his fellow Negro leaguers. "I know you had to do some pitching to get by them." For Lahoma, Paige's third wife, it often was too great a strain. "I would leave the ball park and just go sit in the car because I didn't want to see him lose," she said. "I would build up a terrible feeling inside. I didn't want him to make any mistakes because of the pressure of the fans."

But almost invariably Satchel Paige rose to the occasion, and so he won special devotion from black fans. While playing for the Pittsburgh Crawfords he loaded the bases with Philadelphia Stars. Third baseman Judy Johnson called for the ball, and while rubbing it up, informed Paige that "the fellows were kinda hoping you'd get in this spot." "They did, did they?" questioned Paige. "Yeah they did," answered Johnson. "They said you were such a pop off." Paige fulminated a couple of minutes and then struck out the side on nine pitches. Quickly he walked toward the Stars dugout and boasted, "Now go back to Philadelphia and tell that!" Like Jack Johnson before him and Muhammad Ali afterwards, Paige added that intangible dimension of personality which enhanced his standing in the black community. Proud, capable, and direct, Paige more than any other Negro leaguer brought excitement to black baseball.

However, the public at large never understood the inner Satchel Paige. He was a loner, and not particularly beloved by teammates and friends. The better Negro leaguers resented the attention and ten to fifteen percent of the gate that he commanded. Yet he also bubbled with a humor and flair for life that captivated all who knew him. "He could laugh, and dance, and sing," said Newt Allen. "He was a man who just loved life itself." As the drawing power of black baseball, he was above the rules. He traveled to ball games alone or with a handpicked companion. More often than not he would arrive late, and the park would already be buzzing with "where's Satchel?" Sometimes several innings passed before the mercurial Paige reached the game. Yet as Jimmie Crutchfield wistfully observed, "When Satchel got to that ball park it was like the sun just came out." (Not to disappoint a rural crowd, on one occasion the Monarchs passed Booker McDaniel off as Satchel Paige, and the fans never knew the difference.)

When Satchel Paige died, a United States Senator gave the eulogy and the family pastor told the world, "Don't be sad, at least not for Satchel, because Satchel Paige has pitched a complete inning."

Once established, city life for the Negro leaguer became exciting, even adventurous. The players swiftly moved from the watchful eyes of relatives and managers and took lodging in rooming houses and the prominent black hotels that functioned almost like community centers. Until they married—which most eventually did—the players found permanent apartments an unnecessary expense. They were men half the time on the road and abroad a good part of the year.

The black grand hotels such as the Theresa and Woodside in Harlem, the Vincennes and Grand in Chicago, the Gotham in Detroit, the Dunbar in Los Angeles, the Grand on Market Street in Newark, the Street Hotel at 18th and Paseo in Kansas City, the Hotel Nacional in Havana, and even the Rush Hotel on 14th Street in Birmingham—all were only slightly seedier versions of the best hotels of their day. It was here that the players played, and ate, and had many a misadventure. In 1935 the Grand Hotel in Chicago was the headquarters for the East-West game. Shortstop Paul Jake Stevens, weighing about 115 pounds, roomed with third baseman Boojum Wilson who was at least 220 and one of the toughest men in the league. Stevens got drunk after the game, insanely challenged Wilson, and even took a couple of swipes at him. Wilson, with one hand, simply held Stevens by the throat out a fourth floor window until he cooled off.

In the urban centers the ballplayers had every temptation. "The gin bottle killed many a ballplayer," Elmer Knox reported. And Negro leaguers spoke with awe of the Memphis catcher whom they'd dry out just in time to get to the ball park "where he'd play a hell of a game." Then, too, being young, mostly single, with money in their pockets and the status of star athletes, the players found women all too accessible. When Leon Day was asked if the fellows had "had a girl in every town," he laughed, and replied "They still do." But the reality was that to be a top-flight ballplayer, a

man had to limit his excesses; most of the truly prof-
ligate passed out of the league rather quickly.

The ballplayers became an ingredient, and a major
one, of the black entertainment world. In an era when
black successes were few, they were among the most
applauded of their race. Those closest to the ballplayers in lifestyle were the musicians, and strong
friendships developed between the two groups of
young, male, black achievers. Louis Armstrong, Eubie
Blake, Fats Waller, Count Basie, Lionel Hampton, and
Cab Calloway were their associates and the bandmen
their friends. "Fats Waller used to stay at the ballpark," recalled Jesse Hubbard, pointing out that the
Lafayette Theater was not too far from the oldest Negro league park in New York, Dyckman's Oval. Lionel
Hampton was such a Monarch fan that one year the
Monarchs made him an honorary coach and let him
handle the third baseline. The Mills Brothers were so
enamoured of the "Minstrel of the Mound," Satchel
Paige, they had him "jumping" and playing catch in
the alley behind the Woodside Hotel.

The black entertainer most intimately associated
with black baseball was Bill Robinson. Robinson, "Mr.
Bojangles," usually interrupted his Harlem revue to
travel to Chicago for the East-West Classic, where his
attendance was front-page news. His involvement with
black baseball was deep, for Robinson was quite an
athlete in his own right. Having trained himself to
run backwards with great speed, Robinson once defeated world-class sprinter Ralph Metcalfe running
backwards seventy-five yards to Metcalfe's one
hundred yards straight. If Robinson was playing the
Kansas City Orpheum or another major "race thea-

ter," he would often put on his exhibition in conjunction with a nearby Negro league game. He was idolized by most of the black players.

Robinson developed lasting friendships with most of the key Negro league personalities, and indeed, virtually his dying act was to summon Jackie Robinson and Roy Campanella to his death bed. Wheezing in his oxygen tent, Bill Robinson held their hands and offered a prayer for their success in the major leagues.

In the white mind the Harlem Renaissance did not mean the poetry of Langston Hughes or the writings of Claude McKay; it meant the Cotton Club or other Harlem joints where intrepid whites first tasted the delights of Harlem's sensual night life. Ironically, many of the revues and dives were owned by white gangsters and the average Harlemite never went within. But the ballplayers did. As Dick Seay told his friends, "I've been to the Cotton Club, Connie's Inn, Small's Paradise, been to all those places. Not with the gangsters. The musicians always had a table and they'd invite us to come up there with them." Lured by Harlem's city lights, and its black celebrity life, virtually all of the Negro league stars, in one way or another, called it home.

However, not only the musicians provided Negro leaguers entrée to the outwardly glamorous and sometimes dangerous life of the racketeers. After 1930, with Rube Foster gone, the numbers racketeers became, for want of a legitimate stewardship, the most important leadership of the black league.

The "policy racket" or "policy wheel," as the numbers racket was frequently called, had a strong foothold in poor neighborhoods, white and black, throughout the East. And as the Depression squeezed the economy, the small bet/big payoff of the numbers became more and more attractive.

The black community had its own numbers men, and every black ghetto from Chicago to the Eastern Seaboard had a local "numbers king," and sometimes several. In Harlem, Jersey City, Philadelphia, Pittsburgh, and, indeed, in all the large centers of black population, the black numbers operation became very sophisticated indeed.

There was no stigma attached to being a numbers boss. As Richard Wright argued, "They would have been steel tycoons, Wall Street brokers, auto moguls had they been white." The numbers racketeers in the black community were black entrepreneurs and community leaders at the same time. They were men with money and they were expected to support the community. For many, this obligation meant backing the black baseball team.

Although underworld figures Tom Wilson of Nashville, Alex Pompez of Harlem and Dick Kent of St. Louis were all involved with baseball prior to Gus Greenlee's creation of the Pittsburgh Crawfords, it was Greenlee, with his leadership ability and his willingness to spend money for the Crawfords, who brought the gangsters center stage.

Greenlee's stature in Pittsburgh was based upon his absolute control of the North Side numbers game, a position he won when he became the only numbers banker to pay off after a particularly "large hit" during the late '20s. (More than one black racketeer owed his standing to an ability to pay off in a pinch and thereby earn a reputation for "honesty." There were literally hundreds of people—astrologers, palm readers, cabbies, horse players—providing tips on the numbers, and a numbers banker could easily be wiped out by an unfortunate coincidence or a rigged set of winning numbers.)

After Greenlee made the decision in the early thirties to build a black baseball powerhouse, he knew that the Negro league had to be reorganized. The death of Foster in 1930 and the extremely difficult times required a significant infusion of capital. As Greenlee could plainly see, there was only one readily available source of black capital in the Northern cities: the gangsters. Greenlee mobilized the society-conscious racketeers, aware that baseball was a route to legitimacy in the eyes of the common people.

Greenlee, at the outset of his restructuring of the Negro leagues, understood that "baseball wasn't paying." He knew that the Depression meant that Negro league baseball would probably remain unprofitable for the near future. He himself claimed to have lost fifty thousand dollars in baseball in 1933. Nonetheless, he "hoped to surround himself with men of financial strength who would be willing to count any losses as an investment."

But an investment in what? Good will certainly, for the numbers men basked in the reflected glory of the beloved baseball team. As the Grays' Cum Posey wrote, "Regardless of opinions concerning the owners of the clubs it is helping the Negro Race morally and financially." When Alex Pompez's troubles with the law became headline news in the late 1930s, the *Courier* editorialized, "Any person who has the honor of knowing Pompez personally is well aware that he is in no way a hardened criminal and does not look at life through the eyes of a criminal." The black community evaluation, expressed by the *Courier*, was that "Pompez has been many more times a benefactor in the life of Harlem than he has been a nuisance."

In general, the Negro leaguers had affection for their gangster bosses. "My memories of Gus Greenlee are very pleasant ones," said Ted Page. "I think Gus had one of the finest operations in baseball. There are no limits as to how far Gus would go with a buck in order to make sure his players were comfortable." Greenlee advertised extensively in the black newspapers, set up placards by his restaurant, and even sent sound trucks through the Negro neighborhoods.

In the winter of 1932, to keep Ted Page around, Greenlee hired his outfielder as a numbers lookout. Page sat in a chair from eleven o'clock in the morning to three in the afternoon six days a week, while Greenlee and his confederates counted the day's money. Page's salary was fifteen dollars a week—a black man did not disparage a fifteen-dollar-a-week job in the winter of 1932—and his only assignment was to ring a buzzer should the police or anybody suspicious appear.

Greenlee was flashy in every way. He bought new cars—preferably Lincolns—every year, and he lavished money on his sports promotions. Though it was rumored that he supplemented his income by robbing liquor trucks in the hills of western Pennsylvania, nobody in Pittsburgh had a mean word for Greenlee while he was on top.

The only gangster-owners who were universally condemned by the Negro leaguers were Ed Semler, the Black Yankee owner, and Robert Cole, who had Cole's American Giants in Chicago after Foster's death. Semler was a cheap owner who tried to get by on the drawing power of over-the-hill stars. The charge against Cole was more serious. In 1932, realizing that the team was going bankrupt, Cole, to extract his money from the operation, approached Willie Wells, the universally respected manager, and offered to put his salary in a special account if Wells would encourage the rest of the team to keep playing without their salaries in hopes of a better day. (Wells refused and left the team.)

Some Negro league baseball owners also may have used baseball to hide or launder money gained from the rackets. With baseball they could conceal their illicit activities and avoid the dreaded income tax. Evidence for this hypothesis is Effa Manley's assertion that Abe, her husband, Jersey City's numbers banker, "always paid his taxes," as if this was unusually honest behavior for the times. She boasted, perhaps too much, of the legality of his tax return. It seems probable, given the massive ignorance of white authorities about Negro baseball, that the numbers income was shielded as baseball profits. And of course, both baseball admissions and gambling receipts were almost always cash.

Under Greenlee's leadership, Negro National League meetings were conclaves of the most powerful black gangsters in the nation. Ed "Soldier Boy" Semler had the Black Yankees; Tom Wilson, the Baltimore Elite Giants; Abe Manley, the Newark Eagles; Alex Pompez, the New York Cubans; and Ed Bolden, the Philadelphia Stars (Bolden's white partner and confidant was Eddie Gottlieb, the second most prominent sports figure in Philadelphia after Connie Mack, and future owner of Philadelphia's Warriors). Even the Homestead Grays' were forced to obtain a gang-

ster supporter, Rufus Jackson, under relentless pressure from Greenlee's operation. Jackson was not quite
in the same category with Greenlee and the other
owners, though he too "wore diamonds and big rings."
Jackson had the "Night Roll" in Homestead, a well-
publicized crap shoot that paid off on winning numbers the next morning. He also "ran piccolos up and
down the Monongahela"; that is, he had a piece of
the early jukebox action, just then becoming lucrative.

Thus the entire 1937 Negro National League was
run by the numbers boys. And numbers girl. For no
figure cast a larger shadow in Negro baseball in its
late period than the amazing Effa Manley, the wife of
Abe Manley.

Effa was born in turn-of-the-century Philadelphia
—an illegitimate white offspring in a family with
mulatto children, a black stepfather and a white im-
migrant mother. "My mother was German, but she
married a Negro and had four children before I came
along," Effa reported. After Effa's birth, her mother
married another black man and had two children with
him. "She was one of those women way ahead of her
time, she believed in integration." Effa claimed that
her mother's first husband sued her father for alienation of affection, "the first case in America history
of a black man suing a white man for that." "I'm really
white," she acknowledged. "I was this little, blond,
hazel-eyed white girl always with these Negro children."

While still a young woman she left Philadelphia for
New York where she worked as a white, accepted white
wages, and then took the "A" train back to an apart-
ment in Harlem. Many of her Harlem friends and

baseball associates had no knowledge of her background; and in those days one didn't ask. (One of her players of long standing described Effa as "a very light-skinned black woman.")

Effa met Abe at the 1932 World Series and they married shortly thereafter. She was young, smart, beautiful, and she loved baseball. He was twenty years her senior, a racketeer and a baseball fanatic, too. And when Abe acted on his lifelong dream and built a Negro National League franchise in Newark, Effa was there with him. "Cap," as Abe was affectionately nicknamed, was a true baseball lover and gradually became a sharp judge of baseball talent. But in everything but scouting, the power passed into Effa's hands. "Her husband was supposed to run the team," recalled Pat Patterson, "but she ran it."

She handled the business matters. She handled the public relations. And she handled the personal relations too. Once, when she wanted some girlfriends to see how handsome her favorite pitcher Terris McDuffie was, she ordered her manager to pitch him — out of the regular rotation. The Newark managers of integrity — in particular, Willie Wells and Biz Mackey — had difficulty working for her.

But this remarkable woman was more than a dilettante. As the treasurer of the New Jersey NAACP, she was a strong voice for integration, and she was a charter member of the Citizens League for Fair Play — the group which desegregated Harlem department-store employment in the thirties. "Don't buy where you can't work" was the slogan which broke Blumberg's Department Store in 1934, and Effa was the first one on that picket line.

Abe always took Effa to the business meeting of the

Negro National League, for her hardheaded manner and fiery skill in debate made her a terror throughout the league. At one East-West game she put down a threatened players' strike by assuring the players on the strike committee that "no Newark Eagle was gonna strike, period." Later Effa would become the most outspoken of all in her condemnation of the major-league raids upon the Negro leagues.

Indeed, only the great Satchel Paige had more charisma than Effa. Effa and Abe did everything possible to obtain Paige for the Newark Eagles. In 1937 when Gus Greenlee was having difficulties with Paige, Greenlee sold him to the Eagles for $5,000; but the quixotic Paige, unreliable as always, went to Latin America instead. Effa claimed that Paige, before he left the country, wrote her a letter indicating that he would become an Eagle if Effa would become his sideline girlfriend. "I didn't know what to say," she laughed over forty years later, "so I just threw it away."

Probably the most well-liked, well-respected of all the owners was Alessandro Pompez, the proprietor of Dyckman's Oval, Harlem's baseball and amusement park. Pompez (pronounced "Pompei"), was born of Cuban parents in Key West, where he became a baseball manager and sports promoter. His talents and trustworthiness were apparent as early as 1924, when he was selected as one of the negotiators of the agreement that created the first Negro World Series.

Capitalizing on his baseball contacts and reputation, Pompez entered the numbers business in the twenties and became an important cog in the Dutch Schultz mob and a prime figure in the Harlem rackets.

By the thirties he was a major Harlem celebrity and one of the wealthiest men in Harlem. Pompez's charm and talent swiftly led him to a top position in the black-controlled rackets of New York, and rumors had it that his yearly trips to Havana involved more than baseball scouting. Due to Harlem's preeminent position in black life, Pompez was among the most illustrious black-community gangsters in the nation by the mid-thirties.

Certainly New York Attorney General Thomas Dewey considered Pompez an estimable opponent when he chose Pompez as the main target of a massive crackdown on the Harlem rackets in 1937. Preparing a race for the governorship, Dewey saw the obvious propaganda benefits to be derived from "busting" the apparently vulnerable Cuban racketeer. After sixteen months of preparation, Dewey had "perfected his plan [to nab Pompez] to the last degree," according to the *New York Times*. Yet, on the project day of arrest, much to Dewey's chagrin, Pompez "disappeared without a trace."

Well not exactly. Juan Mirabel, Cuban Star pitcher and Pompez's assistant, was with Pompez that day as he returned to his Harlem office off Lenox Avenue. As they entered the elevator both immediately sensed that something was wrong, for the operator kept nodding his head and raising his eyebrows. Pompez needed no additional warning. He stopped the elevator several floors below his destination, climbed out a fire escape, and disappeared among the Harlem multitudes. However, the $34,000 in cash awaiting him was grabbed by Dewey's men.

Protected by an underground railroad of Negro

baseball men, Pompez easily eluded the Federal drag-
net and escaped to Mexico, crossing the border near
Tucson after what seemed an interminable bus ride.
Only when Pompez resumed his flamboyant lifestyle
in Mexico did the Mexican authorities arrest him,
prodded by Dewey's near-frantic attempt to prove his
prosecutorial abilities. Reportedly, when the Mexican
federales did seize him, it was as he was stepping into
a bulletproof sedan with "Chicago" license plates.

Through the bars of a Mexican jail Pompez yelled
to the New York reporters, "I got lots of friends in
New York." And he apparently had lots of friends in
Mexico, too, for to Dewey's amazement, the New York
attorney general's request for extradition was declined.

Harlem seethed with unconfirmed rumors that
Pompez was about to shift his operation to Mexico,
while Pompez seethed with cultural schizophrenia:
was he an American? A Cuban? Latin American? At
this critical junction in his life, after much soulsearch-
ing, Pompez decided to turn state's evidence and return to New York. As his friend Leon Day put it less
kindly, "He became the only guy who ever snitched
on the mob and lived to tell about it."

After he turned state's evidence, all that was left for
Pompez was baseball. He continued to run the Cuban
Stars, and, turning his enormous energies and talents
to the team, built the Stars and later the Cuban Giants
into pennant contenders and a Negro league pennant
winner. Using the Polo Grounds as his home field for
the forties, he became an intimate of Horace Stoneham, the New York Giants' owner, and was ultimately
responsible for the entry of most of the black Latin
Americans into organized baseball during the 1950s.

Pompez had the pleasure of signing his close friend Perucho Cepeda's son Orlando to a Giant contract, and, had his strong recommendation that the Giants sign Hank Aaron been acted upon a trifle less slowly and halfheartedly, Aaron would also have become a Giant.

In 1948 Pompez even made the Cuban Giants a New York Giant farm team, the only time a Negro league team was formally associated with the major leagues. In the 1970s, when the movement began to recognize Negro league players, Pompez served on the committee that sent a few Negro leaguers belatedly into the Hall of Fame.

It is a profound irony that this former gangster was one of the most loved and respected baseball men in America at a time when baseball officialdom went to great lengths to avoid even the hint of impropriety. Although, for example, Mays could be barred from close association with baseball because he picked up a paycheck from a casino, Eddie Gottlieb and Alex Pompez, who associated with racketeers their whole lives, served on official baseball committees.

But the fact that Greenlee, Pompez, Effa Manley, and the rest were racketeers had its cost too. When baseball finally integrated in 1946, the numbers men still dominated the Negro league ownership in the East. They had established business dealings with the major-league moguls, though neither side was particularly eager to emphasize the extent of its relationship with the other. When, to the Negro league owners' considerable anger, Branch Rickey fended off questions about the Negro league with the charge that "they were in the zone of a racket," the owners of Negro baseball took it for what it was: an implied threat to destroy them if they became too open in their condemnation of the major leagues.

Negro league teams were placed in a difficult situation: white dollars were critical to all the teams' finances, yet they feared too close a scrutiny, for their business practices were not aboveboard. Gambling was ubiquitous in Negro league parks, and it also flourished at some of the better Eastern semi-pro stadiums and in the semi-pro leagues of the upper Midwest that were such an important part of the black baseball world.

"They would come to you," acknowledged pitcher Andy Porter, speaking of the gamblers. "I was in the bullpen once and a guy offered money to let them win." "No kind of way," was Porter's response. A truly tragicomic gambling baseball incident occurred during the mid-thirties in the most famous semi-pro park of all—Dexter Park, home of the Bushwicks of Brooklyn, a white team.

During a game with the Crawfords, the Bushwicks had the bases loaded with two out in the bottom of the ninth. Then Josh Gibson, not known for his fielding, dropped a pop fly. Theolic Smith, the Crawfords' knuckleball pitcher, tells the rest of the story, recalling that "the big wheels and the gangsters too would bet heavily on the black teams that came in. When Josh dropped that pop-up, the fans threatened us, and they said there was a bomb placed in our bus, and we had two or three squad cars escort us back to New York City. We was afraid," he said.

Ironically, this incident acquired so much significance that Judge Landis, the commissioner of the major leagues, called the Crawfords to account. He met personally with the Crawfords to determine, in his paternalistic way, whether Josh had thrown the game. Judge Landis always kept a wary eye on the Negro leagues.

This incident also illustrates another significant aspect of Negro league baseball in the urban North: there was a rich black/white baseball interaction that took place outside the major leagues. The Bushwicks were the best of many white semi-pro teams operating throughout the nation. The Bushwicks employed former and future major leaguers and had consistently good success against the pros. But the best money for Bushwick came in games against the Negro league teams, particularly in the Bushwicks' Dexter Park. Owned by Nat C. Strong and later by Dizzy Dean, the Bushwicks were a critical part of Eastern baseball. Raucous, exuberant, gambling, integrated crowds of over ten thousand were not extraordinary—a head count not lost on Branch Rickey when he moved from St. Louis to Brooklyn in the 1940s.

Many players with the Bushwicks and other topflight semi-pros had major-league ability. They chose not to play professional ball because the pay was comparatively small in the thirties and forties, and because travel was difficult. The Bushwicks, or the Farmers of New Jersey, Studebakers of South Bend, and Chryslers of Detroit were all powerful teams by any standard, and urban barnstorming was profitable for both the white independents and Negro league teams. Finally, these contests also gave sizable white populations a look at the better black ballplayers.

As the Negro leaguers rose above the black masses, their very prominence thrust them into association with the black elite. To be invited up to Sugar Hill, Harlem's prime residential area, to dine with the

Manleys was a symbolic journey from cotton field to mansion.

The relationship between the ballplayers and the black bourgeoisie was complex. The elite, mimicking white class distinctions, wanted to keep its distance from the black masses. And yet, the black bourgeoisie needed the black masses, for who else was there to witness their role playing? The black elite also needed to win legitimacy from the community they sought to lead. What less incendiary, more popular cause than baseball integration?

The black elite vigorously used their propaganda arm, the black newspapers, to support the Negro leagues. However, in the urban North they also used baseball to act out Franklin Frazier's "world of make-believe."

"Socialites to Attend East-West Ball Game," blared the lead of a black society page in August of 1935 that listed the prominent blacks coming to Chicago for the game. "The East-West baseball game has been popularized to a fine social point," the *Defender* reported. "Social registerites take a greater interest in the game now than ever before. Rest assured that society will be represented at Comiskey."

Parading at the East-West game as "exclusives" or "registerites," they thought of themselves as "a cultured crowd." They bought the dollar-and-a-half box seats so the sixty-cent, general-admission fan might look upon them. At an East-West game or other big sporting event, they escaped from their positon of inferiority and inconsequence in American society.

The players in turn shared an ambivalence toward the elite. "We knew them, but we weren't part of them," Hilton Smith ruefully asserted. "They'd come to our games, and we'd talk to them, but we didn't get too close," added Elite Giant pitcher Andrew Porter. Most of the Negro leaguers had no aspirations to enter the black elite anyway. The Negro leaguers in the North merely participated in the most variable and exciting life possible for black Americans in the period. As performers they engaged in a creative experience, and as urbanites with money, they tasted the possibilities of the North. Finally, as legitimate celebrities, they transcended their roots and mixed with people of all classes and races.

On the Road 5

The black ink of black baseball was earned not in the so-called sepia metropolis, where the great mass of migrators congregated and worshipped baseball, but in the countryside, where the players entertained a white public starved for baseball. All the Negro league teams supplemented their city income by scheduling exhibitions "on the road" before, during, and after the league season. Indeed, the majority of games played by Negro league teams were not the bitterly contested league games but instead exhibitions held wherever a profitable afternoon beckoned. It was pure economics: white people had more money.

Booking agents arranged these (usually interracial) baseball attractions. In return for ten to forty percent of the gate, the booking agents did everything from selling tickets to driving the busses. The Negro league owners did not particularly like working with the booking agents. But in the periodic baseball wars with Nat C. Strong, Ed Gottlieb, or Eddie Loesch, the Negro league owners learned that accommodation was more profitable than conflict. The booking agents controlled the independent baseball parks that the Negro league needed to round out its schedule, and since money, not race, was the bottom line, a compromise was inevitable.

In time the booking agents, and sometimes the teams themselves, created a baseball circuit which was followed year in and year out. The Kansas City Monarchs, for example, had Kansas City as their home base but developed a traveling routine including St. Joseph, Des Moines, Wichita, and Tulsa as regular stops on the itinerary. It was on May 5, 1929, that Bob Feller's father—as a special treat—took his son to Des Moines to watch the Des Moines Demons meet the Kansas City Monarchs, an event which introduced him to Negro baseball. Several times a season, the itinerary expanded dramatically, and then Winnipeg, Denver, and New Orleans would be treated to the Monarchs, too.

Lowest on the scale of those who played against the Negro league teams were local teams in small towns who played the touring black professionals as celebrity entertainment. Every small American town had a ball park and the potential to raise a credible nine on short notice. The arrival of the black professional team created a carnival atmosphere, and, in fact, on occasion the Negro league team brought a carnival with them. "Then we got *all* their money," said old-timer Arthur Hardy. These games were characterized by good fellowship rather than good baseball. The locals were no match for the Negro league professionals. The Negro leaguers treated the low-quality games lightly. "We got it easy tonight...you play my position and I'll play yours," recalled Dick Seay. "They had no chance."

In these games the Negro leaguers consciously held down the score because they wanted to return the following year. After quickly obtaining a comfortable lead, the task was merely to maintain the entertainment interest. Sometimes clowning kept the games amusing: a batter might hit one-handed or on his knees, or a runner might circle the bases in the wrong direction. Increasing the entertainment value of baseball on the road were comedy attractions such as Jesse Owens's challenge to "cars, motorcycles, racehorses, and guys from the college," in the hundred-yard dash. If the game was the expected rout, the players might adjourn the game in the seventh inning for some "prize running."

The presence of an attraction like Jesse Owens made all the difference at the gate during the Depression era. Accompanying the Toledo Crawfords in 1939, Owens drew better than the team itself. His exhibition running invariably brought out the best local talent to test him. In small towns he sometimes ran hurdles while the opponent ran straight, to enhance the contest. Then too, he would occasionally give his local adversary ten yards, which the latter inevitably learned was an insufficient handicap in racing against a 9.6 sprinter. Of even more appeal was Owens's challenge to race horses, though then Owens took the ten-yard advantage. One day in Texas, a match was made against a race horse whose owner refused to spot Owens ten yards in front of a large, paying crowd. "I'm not gonna let my pony spot you ten yards," the redneck ruffian said. "Don't run," urged the Crawfords, as Owens assessed the crowd. Jesse jogged a couple times around the stadium and then reported, "Naw, I'm gonna run him." "And you know what?" said Connie Johnson, "he beat that horse too. He flew that night, and came back to us and said, you know that's one of the greatest races I ever run."

Only if racism crept into the encounter did the Negro leaguers "run twenty, twenty-five runs on 'em, so they'd leave the park whispering." But that was rare indeed, because the arrival of a Negro league team was a festive occasion. In the small towns of the rural Midwest, just the sight of a band of Negroes was an attraction, and the typical rural American was not naive enough to expect local boys to be the equal of the best black athletes.

Often, to present a more substantial game, the Negro league teams joined together to put on their own exhibition. These games did not count in the league standings, but since money was split unevenly, usually sixty-forty, there was every incentive to play hard. In the South, this was the main barnstorming style, either because white opponents were not available or because, in many Southern states, laws prevented interracial sports contests.

While in the South, barnstorming Negro teams also played the Southern city teams such as the New Orleans Black Pelicans, the Atlanta Black Crackers, or the Jacksonville Red Caps. Most all-black Southern barnstorming games took place as a part of spring training, but in some years Northern Negro league teams made in-season Southern forays that received great publicity, as did the Chicago American Giant tour of Alabama in August of 1923.

An even better draw than a Negro league team in the small towns of the Midwest and North was a high-quality white opponent, not necessarily a major-league team. Between the wars, baseball salaries were

low and talented players frequently passed up professional careers for more lucrative positions. Some of
the natural ballplayers used baseball as an avocation,
playing for excellent oil-company or automobile-
manufacturing teams. The Studebakers of South Bend
were a noteworthy example. Occasionally a college
player played with a semi-pro team to supplement his
income. The New York Black Yankees were featured
every year at the great guest hotels in the Poconos
and Catskills. Usually such games meant easy money,
but more than once the Black Yankees ran into college
teams or a bewhiskered lad like Lou Gehrig making
money on the side. Once Hal Schumacher of the Chicago Cubs was the "collegiate" ringer, and the Black
Yankees were particularly impressed with the talent
Niagara and St. Lawrence were able to obtain "under
the table."

John Welau, later a white outfielder for the Washington Senators, started out playing illegally on semi-
pro teams. By his senior year in high school, he was
earning one hundred dollars a week as a tramp ballplayer, playing anyone, anywhere, as long as he would
make money. One night he faced Satchel Paige in
South Boundbrook, New Jersey, as part of a team
comprised mostly of New York-area major leaguers
(Urbanski, Medwick, Greenberg, Moore). "We had this
truck pumping up the lights on three twenty-four-foot
ladders," he recalled, and then, thinking of Paige, Welau added, "lucky we had a full moon, let's put it that
way." Welau was the seventh hitter. "I was the first
one to even tick him," Welau remembered. "I faced
him as if I was gonna bunt." After the ball rolled foul
Paige walked off the mound and shook Welau's hand.
"Son, you're gonna be a major leaguer," he said.

During the 1920s the Kansas City Monarchs played against strong city teams in the upper Midwest. These teams took any good ballplayer they could find, including major leaguers ejected as a result of the Black Sox scandal of 1919. Buck Weaver was at Sauk City, Wisconsin, and Swede Risberg was in Minnesota. Chet Brewer said, "We played against all those big leaguers and drew real fine crowds." By playing against them, Brewer also learned how to evaluate the quality of Negro league play: "At that time I knew, if given a chance, we could play in the major leagues, 'cause all those fellows were top major leaguers," he recalled.

But, of course, the opponent most desired by the Negro league was a team of major-league players. Sometimes, in the days before Landis became commissioner, an intact major-league team was induced to play a top Negro team. And in Latin America, where the commissioner had less clout, major-league teams met Negro leaguers on their winter barnstorming tours. In 1936 in Puerto Rico, the Cincinnati Reds were thumped two straight by a Negro league all-star group, after which the Reds decided to play the Negro leaguers no more. But usually black-vs.-white encounters were promoted as "all-star exhibitions" to diffuse the inherent meaning of the contest. This sleight of hand had little effect on the black population, which always considered the games a fair measure of comparative ability. For the whites, however, calling the games "exhibitions" and playing as all-stars enabled them to dismiss defeat as meaningless.

Nonetheless, almost every important white pitcher in the first half of the twentieth century lost a game to a Negro team. The victimized included Rube Wadell, Walter Johnson, Lefty Grove, Grover Cleveland

Alexander, Dizzy Dean, Bob Lemon, and Bob Feller. The all-star contests were tremendously successful. The black population wanted to see how its heroes measured up, and whites were attracted by the much-heralded names of major leaguers and also out of curiosity about the blacks. The better black players quickly developed fine reputations among the major leaguers, and colorful, well-traveled Negro leaguers such as Satchel Paige or Josh Gibson earned the admiration of white fans and players alike. Birdie Tebbetts said bluntly, "We were in awe of Satchel Paige."

Major-league-vs.-Negro-league games were held every year. There is probably not a single white superstar of the period who did not participate in them. In the 1920s Babe Ruth competed with enthusiasm against the Negro league teams—one reason that less capable, more prejudiced players referred to him derisively as "Nigger lips" and falsely questioned his patrimony. (The black players themselves idolized Ruth.) In the 1930s Dizzy Dean confronted the Negro league players virtually every season. The Satchel Paige/Dizzy Dean pitching duels of the mid-thirties were the most publicized pitching confrontations of the decade; they served to spread the reputation of the Negro league, and particularly of "that old colored boy—Satchel Paige," as Dizzy Dean described him. In the 1940s, Bob Feller replaced Dizzy Dean as Satchel Paige's prime antagonist. In 1946 Bob Feller rented two Flying Tiger aircraft retired from the China theater for a dollar a mile and, with the assistance of the Kansas City Monarch ownership, toured the nation. Satchel Paige and the black all-stars had their separate and, this time, equal plane. They played all across the nation that year, working their way west to California.

While Bob Feller and Satchel Paige were the names used for promotion, the format minimized their actual role. Paige and Feller pitched only the first few innings and then turned the game over to the likes of Bob Lemon for the major leaguers and Hilton Smith for the Negro leaguers.

Scrutiny of the 1946 Bob Feller-Satchel Paige tour provides an indication of how important and lucrative barnstorming had become by the time Robinson entered the majors in 1947. The all-stars played thirty-two games in twenty-six days and drew over four hundred thousand fans. Stan Musial missed several of the first games because of the World Series that year, but Feller still paid him his $10,000 share for participating. A World Series share at the same time was less than $4,000. Later that fall, Musial gave a talk at the Dapper Dan Dinner in Pittsburgh, where he castigated the league for not returning more money to the players. He pointedly observed that he could earn more barnstorming against the black stars than he could by winning a pennant for his team. This was a revelation that "scared the heck out of the league," according to Feller.

The Satchel Paige-Bob Feller confrontations were so successful that at one game, Bob Lemon's mother was not able to get a seat. Feller, a born promoter, hired Jackie Price and Max Patkin to entertain on the side. Price caught flies in a jeep and performed other tricks. Feller paid Larry MacPhail twenty-five percent of the gate to arrange the booking and gave him an additional ten percent for distribution to local sportswriters for publicity. The sportswriters, as poorly paid as the ballplayers, were glad to accept the money. But their publicity was effective. Satchel Paige and the accomplishments of the better Negro leaguers became even more well known as a result of their journalism.

Anytime the Negro leaguers played major leaguers the adrenaline flowed and the Negro leaguers played their best. But no amount of glamorization disguised the hardships on the road. Weeks of suitcase or bedroll living were the norm. Throughout their careers players often slept in dugouts, buses, and on the side of the road. "I can remember a town in Arkansas. When you turned on the light you'd see the bed bugs start to go for cover," said one player. "Many a time we put up in homes or hotels where you'd have to sleep with the lights on, because if you didn't those little gremlins would come out and you wouldn't get any sleep anyhow." Sometimes there would be two or three players assigned one bed.

The ballplayers endured. The riding was rough, no matter how nice the bus (and many a bus was not nice at all). Hilldale played a doubleheader in Chicago on a Sunday, packing the bus prior to game time. After the game they ate dinner and rode directly to Philadelphia, where they played a doubleheader as soon as they got off the bus. And that wasn't all that unusual. Satchel Paige's longest jump was from Nashville to Los Angeles, straight through, and then from automobile to ball park.

The amazing thing was how stoically the players accepted it all. "They took pride in what they were doing, just living loose," said Lahoma Paige. "No place to sleep, you got to go four hundred miles to the next town. Okay. Then you get some bologna and crackers. You sing bass? Okay man." Someone would pull a battered guitar or ukulele from his bedroll, "hit two or three strings, then somebody would pretend to blow a horn and down the highway they'd go."

"Most all our baseball teams had singing groups," said Buck Leonard, one of the league's better singers. "It would kill our worries and our tiredness to sing as we went from one town to another at night." Teasing the bus driver was also a favorite pastime, noted Leonard. "I used to tell the bus driver, don't pay any attention to the fellows, they were just doing something to kill the time."

Eventually the days and the towns flowed together and the players wore down. The Homestead Grays were one of the hardest-traveling teams. For Willie Wells the pace was too much. "Traveling all the years I traveled, over those hills, you just got tired of it, at least I did," he said. "We played a ball game in Pittsburgh on a Friday. You know where we played the next day? Toronto, Canada, you know where we played the next day? Detroit, Michigan." For three days Wells did not sleep in a bed. He had not gotten to sleep before three o'clock in the morning. Finally, things came to a head. They knocked on Wells's door. "Let's go," said Cum Posey. "Go where," answered Wells. "We got a game tonight," Posey called. "Not me," Wells said. "We gonna give you some more money, Wells," Posey offered. "I don't want no more money. I want my health and I want to live," insisted Wells. He left the Grays shortly thereafter. As one Kansas City Monarch summed it up: "We'd eat and ride and play. That was the size of it. It wasn't easy street."

The travel problem became particularly acute after the Kansas City Monarchs pioneered electric lights for baseball in 1929. Wilkinson experimented with generators that powered a portable lighting system mounted on several trucks. Chet Brewer participated in that first night game, held in Enid, Oklahoma. "Boy, they'd kick that thing over and the floor lights would light up that park like day. And people would come from miles around to see that baseball could be played at night! In Enid, Oklahoma, you never saw so many people." In fact, the lights were feeble, at least by today's standards, and only just good enough for play.

Once night baseball took hold, conditions worsened for the players. The combination of a Depression and portable lights encouraged the strapped owners to squeeze in as many games as possible. The Monarch bus became the home of the generator and the Monarchs themselves took to cars. As Judy Johnson later recalled, "We'd play three games at a time, a doubleheader and a night game, and you'd get back to the hotel and you were tired as a yard dog."

Compounding the difficulties of a life of hectic baseball travel was the ubiquitous presence of segregation and bigotry. The Negro leaguers obviously knew what was expected of them in the Deep South, where everything social was segregated. But as for the rest of their territory, only in northern New England and parts of Canada was everything integrated. Jesse Hubbard, whose barnstorming took place in the twenties said, "in Jersey, Pennsylvania, Delaware, Maryland, shoot, I'd just as soon be down in Georgia."

The worst racial incident was probably one that involved the Philadelphia Stars. After playing in Laurel, Mississippi, they were returning through the Delta. Stopped for gas in Cleveland, Mississippi, they heard a commotion and, upon inquiring, were told by the station attendant that "they took a little colored boy off his bicycle and put an airhose up his rectum and blew him to pieces." Jack Marshall reported that the Stars just shook their heads "and went on."

Petty segregation was everything in the South; lodging was always as a black hotel, black rooming house, or family homes. Only in Birmingham, where the owner of the Rush Hotel also owned the Black Barons for a time, or in Miami, where there were several excellent black hotels, were accommodations even adequate. (Because the ballplayers stayed in so many homes, over so many years, they built up a national skein of acquaintances. Roy Campanella, when he first traveled with the Dodgers, was not allowed to stay in hotels with his team. Instead, he stayed with black families. Meanwhile, the Dodgers made a small fortune off Southern blacks eager to sit in segregated bleachers and glimpse Robinson and Campanella.)

There were no black restaurants on the road where the players could sit and eat, and so the ballplayers usually bought sandwiches to go, or cold cuts and soda pop. "The best we could do was get one of those Bell fruit jars and put some sardines and pork and beans in it," remarked one old ballplayer. "We had to travel in a hardship way."

Sometimes even the Negro leaguer's money was not good enough. Once en route from Birmingham to Montgomery, the Newark Eagles stopped at a road cafe. They approached the cafe owner, who immediately started shaking her head. "Why are you saying 'no'?" asked Monte Irvin, "when you don't even know what we want." "Whatever it is, we don't have any," she responded. "Won't you sell us some soft drinks, some Pepsi-Cola or Coca-Cola?" he asked again. "No," she told him bluntly. Finally one of the Eagles said, "It's awfully hot, could we use your well out back?" She thought about it and acquiesced. The team had a good drink and thanked her, but when they got back to the bus and looked back, she was breaking the drinking gourd in pieces. "How could she hate us so?" lamented Monte Irvin. "She didn't even know us."

For the Northerners this petty segregation was most discouraging; moreover, they were shocked to see the ease with which their Southern teammates fell into the etiquette of segregation. "I about fell out the first time I went South," reported Dick Seay, who was raised in upper New York State. The ballplayers, who always had a little free time in strange cities, patronized the barbershops, laundries, and movie theaters of segregated America. "In Memphis you'd have to go around the alley, up the fire escape, way up to the top, and sit where the projector was, and they called it the Buzzard Roost," sarcastically complained Chet Brewer. "You knew what was expected of you," said Baton Rouge native Pepper Bassett. "You didn't like it, but you couldn't change it."

Vic Harris's wife Dorothy traveled with her husband, the manager of the Homestead Grays, for many years. One year during the thirties the Grays, hoping to avoid some of the difficulties they experienced in the Deep South, went to spring training in Oklahoma. "They thought the Homestead Grays was a white team," remembered Mrs. Harris, "so they booked us into a very nice hotel. See Posey was traveling secretary, and he was fair-skinned," she noted. "So he went in and got the rooms and everything and they started to unload the bus and when the players got off, they said, 'Oh, no, you can't stay here, this is a white hotel.'"

Some Negro leaguers could "pass" easily in white society. (Bill Battle, who played with the Chicago American Giants and then pioneered in Negro tennis, played in white tennis tournaments without provoking so much as a murmur.) Homestead Gray pitcher Wilmur Fields was lighter than almost all the Cubans playing in America. Once while traveling through Mississippi in the forties, Josh Gibson told Fields to get the team some sandwiches. They parked the bus out of sight and Fields entered a cafe and ordered. He had no difficulty, until another player, in a potentially dangerous lark, came in. After a speechless moment, the startled cafe owner shouted, "Are you with him?" pointing at the dark-skinned teammate. "Get the hell outta here." Wilmur Fields, who was raised black in Manassas, Virginia, had never given passing a thought.

The Kansas City Monarchs' solution to prejudice in lodging was to camp out. The sight of several old Dodge cars loaded with tents, cots, blankets, cooking utensils, and the team of wandering black ballplayers was a sight indeed. They shared the road with a tragic group of travelers, the refugees from the Dust Bowl. "It wasn't a pretty sight," recalled Newt Allen. "Everything was burnt up. Hot weather in the Dakotas had people packing up and moving west. Every day you'd see people with stuff on the top of their cars, trucks. In 1937 during the drought, everything was so hot we played seven-inning ball games. Golf balls were melting." On more than one occasion, the Monarchs shared a meal with the Depression pilgrims.

After 1936 the Monarchs had a "sleeper trailer," an

accommodation that was considered very modern. However, the Monarchs were not that far from their roots that they were prevented from carrying shotguns and hunting rabbits and pheasant along the way. They found greatly amusing Satchel Paige's notorious inaccuracy with a shotgun. "He couldn't hit a thing," laughed Newt Allen. "Newt Joseph was the best shot. And if we hit a pheasant [driving along], we'd take him."

Despite fatigue, heat, discomfort, and an occasional spring snow, barnstorming remained a wonderful memory of many old-timers. Satchel Paige, who traveled more than anyone else, said it rather eloquently when he noted, "I stopped [barnstorming] twice, but I had the misery with me. You stay out a month and you get that itch on you. You can't stay home. I got myself weaned to it." (Later Satchel blamed "all those dusty roads" for the emphysema which shortened his breath and then his life.)

Although the Negro leaguer adjusted to the hardships of travel, he was never able to reconcile the hardships of segregation. In general, a Negro leaguer was not about to fight a battle he could not win, but there were limits to patience, tolerance, and passivity. Negro league players were not passive in the face of injustice. Satchel Paige, for example, when he became the drawing power of Negro baseball, sometimes refused to play in towns where he was denied lodging or food. J. L. Wilkinson made special eating arrangements for his players, aware that the indignities of petty segregation could be more painful than racial epithets muttered by bigots.

Stories of irreverence toward segregation became

staples of Negro league lore. Satchel Paige, who loved fast cars and had a tongue as sharp as his fastball, was legendary for getting "one up" on the white man. Double Duty Radcliffe relates that once Paige got a speeding ticket while zooming through a small Kansas town in his new Lincoln. A policeman escorted him to the local judge, who fined him forty dollars and asked if he had anything to say for himself. According to Radcliffe, "Paige pulled eighty dollars from his wallet and said, 'Here you go judge, 'cause I'm coming back tomorrow.'"

Eugene Benson was rudely awakened once as he traveled by train through Arkansas on his way to Mexico. Told by a belligerent passenger to get to the Jim Crow car, Philadelphia-raised Benson responded with a right cross that would have done justice to his idol, Joe Louis.

Quincy Trouppe was managing the Cleveland Buckeyes when they too ran into racial problems in Arkansas. Some white men came over and looked at the Cleveland Buckeye bus. "Might have known you coons is from the North," said one of them. "I guess we gonna have to show these shines..." said his red-faced companion. "That was as far as they got," said Trouppe. "My two players lit into them and planted knuckle sandwiches all over their heads. When it was all over two Southern white men were laying stretched out cold in the hard, sun-baked ground of Arkansas." Quickly Trouppe instructed the team, "Okay, you guys, let's saddle up and get out of here." And they did. North by northwest, they headed for the Missouri line.

Racial encounters on the field were less frequent, although once in West Texas, Pat Patterson took one slur too many from a drunken bench jockey on the third-base line. Patterson was over the railing in an instant, but a moment later his teammates, terrified that they might have to fight a ball park of Texans, pulled him back, to a chorus of boos. Wilkinson fined the usually soft-spoken Patterson fifty dollars for violating the one irrevocable rule of barnstorming baseball: the fans, since they are paying, can say anything they want.

A similar incident took place on a northern ballfield when Judy Johnson was a rookie with Hilldale. Playing a white team in the coal region near Mackinaw City, Hilldale encountered a home umpire who happened to double as the local sheriff. "The ball'd be over your head and if there were two strikes, you'd be out," recalled Johnson. At that time, Hilldale's catcher was Louis Santop. He was a "wonderful catcher. [He was] called the Black Babe Ruth, that was before Josh," Johnson went on. "And Santop went out to the pitcher and said, 'Throw a hard one, and I'll let it go by and hit him.'" Sure enough, the ball hit the umpire—in the groin. "He couldn't breathe and was choking; it broke up the game," remembered Johnson. "We had to get in the car with our baseball clothes and they chased us six miles down the road. I was really scared."

Once in San Diego, during a black barnstorming game, when the Negro league pitcher was pulled from the mound, the band struck up "Bye Bye Blackbird."

Incidents like these were rare—surprisingly rare. Buck Leonard said, "I never remember any ballplayer calling us 'niggers.' They might have called us that, but we didn't hear them." Newt Allen added, "Ballplayers were pretty much good fellows. Very seldom did you run into a real snotty one." Among major-league players who met Negro leaguers in off-season games, racial animosity was rarer yet; though Bobo Newsome, one of the best pitchers in the American League, did mutter, after a tough defeat in California, "I'm not going back to the major leagues 'til I beat these niggers." To which Cool Papa Bell, a soft talker, replied, "We're gonna keep you out here 'bout two more years." When Frank Demaree of the Chicago Cubs was foolish enough to slur a Satchel Paige team, Paige let his pitching do the talking. He deliberately walked batters until the bases were loaded. Then he called in his outfield and ordered all his infielders to sit down. Then, he struck out Demaree on three pitches. And for Ty Cobb and his manifest prejudice, black players felt a contempt that was passed down from one Negro league generation to the next.

Much more typical of race relations were instances when a white ballplayer stood up for his black opponent, or, after integration, for his black teammate. Chet Brewer, in the late forties, was the first black to play on a team in Michigan City. The team stopped in Fort Wayne, Indiana, at a beer parlor and restaurant. "They didn't give me a beer and weren't going to get me any food," recalled Brewer. "The waitress said, 'Sorry we can't serve you.'" Brewer's teammate Bill Fuchs was furious. "Why the hell can't you serve him?" screamed Fuchs. "He's just a ballplayer like the rest of us." And then Fuchs turned over the table and it took six players to calm him down.

The overall picture, then, is of race relations in some flux, of blacks encroaching on the limits of segregation, and of greatly varying white attitudes. Black ballplayers understood segregation; they were prepared to cope. Yet they did not spend their lives fretting because they could not eat or sleep in restaurants and first-class hotels; every black man at that time had to live with segregation as best he could. Though hampered, their lives were not soured by segregation.

Barnstorming baseball had tremendous impact on the developing push for major-league baseball integration. Especially influential were the Midwestern (actually Plains States) baseball tournaments, which became regional events of significance in the 1930s.

During the era of the Negro leagues, Midwestern baseball tournaments provided the best, most competitive matches available west of a Chicago-St. Louis line. Western baseball fans simply did not get to see major-league baseball during the season. Consequently, strong minor leagues evolved and semi-professional teams flourished west of the Mississippi. To cap the baseball season, to intensify regional rivalries, to assist the region's promoters, and, finally, just as a logical outgrowth of their baseball development, prize tournaments evolved into major events.

The most established of the tournaments was the Denver Post Tournament, sponsored each August by the newspaper. Having begun as a city semi-pro tournament in 1915, by the early thirties the event attracted teams from all over the nation competing for the $7500 first prize. Entry to the double-elimination tournament was by invitation. Although Denver had a strong black team, until 1934 no black club was ever invited. Then a wave of excitement swept through black baseball. The Kansas City Monarchs, through the efforts of Ollie Marcelle, a great Negro league third baseman, received an invitation. (Marcelle's Negro league career ended shortly after a celebrated Havana dice-game brawl in which Frank Warefield bit off Marcelle's nose.) The invitation extended to the Monarchs was "the most significant announcement of a decade insofar as Negro baseball was concerned" according to the jubilant *Pittsburgh Courier*. The *Courier* argued that, for the first time on the ballfield, a Negro league team was demonstrating its ability in a truly measurable situation. It would be impossible to dismiss success at the Denver Post Tournament in the same way that white opinion dismissed exhibition victories.

The Monarchs placed second in the 1934 tournament. Ironically, the winning team, the House of David, had recruited Satchel Paige, and in the climactic game, Paige defeated Chet Brewer of the Monarchs, 2-1. The House of David baseball team had begun as an amusement for a Midwestern religious cult, but by the thirties had become a major touring attraction. The House of David picked up "ringers," disguised them with the mandatory beards that typified cult members, and barnstormed the land. The Negro league teams—especially the Monarchs—became their most fabled opponent. To heighten their appeal, they at one time also employed Babe Didrickson Zaharias as a pitcher. "She threw overhand and as hard as a man," recalled Pepper Bassett.

Nearly every year after 1934 a Negro league team, usually the Monarchs, won the Denver Post Tournament, and black teams of every sort participated. In 1935 Buck O'Neil was barnstorming with the Miami

Giants, anticipating a lucrative payday for a "June-
teenth" game in Wichita Falls, Texas. June 19th, the
day news of the Emancipation Proclamation had
reached Texas, was a traditional black holiday in the
state. Unfortunately for the Giants, an unusually severe storm had caused the river in Austin, Texas, to
rise, and the Wichita Falls team could not get back
for the game. "So we were in the town, no money,
nothing. We were stranded," reminisced O'Neil. Then
the Giants heard of the Denver Post Tournament. "We
hoboed from Wichita Falls to Denver," continued
O'Neil. "Got there in the morning, got to the station,
washed up, got in the soup line, and played in the
Denver Post Tournament."

The second major Midwestern baseball tournament
was the National Baseball Congress Tournament held
in Wichita, Kansas, beginning in 1935. The sponsors
of this tournament, in an effort to one-up the Denver
Post, offered a $10,000 first prize. The tournament was
run by Ray Dumont, president of the National Baseball Congress and a close friend of Monarch owner
J. L. Wilkinson. Dumont was perhaps the most prominent individual in all Midwestern baseball. Under
Dumont's auspices, Negro league teams and independents with black players were invited every year. In
the initial year Bismarck, North Dakota, won the tournament. Their team featured Satchel Paige, Double
Duty Radcliffe, Hilton Smith, Chet Brewer, and Quincy
Trouppe, all first-line Negro league players.

Buck O'Neil's Miami Giants also participated in
that first Wichita tournament. "We still didn't have
any transportation," said O'Neil, recalling the plight
of his team in Denver after the Denver Post Tournament. "However, we met a fellow with a Graham-

Paige, a beautiful car; he put nine of us in his car and took us to Wichita." After Bismarck won, O'Neil became homesick for Sarasota. "I called Mama. Tell Papa I want to come home. They sent me a ticket, no money. I had 75¢, and the first time I had any food was in Chattanooga, Tennessee. When I got home I tell you I ate so much my mother cried. I slept two days. I said, 'Mama, I'll never leave again.'" And then with a twinkle in his eyes and a laugh in his throat, O'Neil added that in 1936 he began "throwing that ball" and was ready to go again.

With victories in the Denver Post Tournament and the Wichita Tournament, the Negro league's reputation for having the best baseball outside the majors was firmly established. Major-league scouts, of course, attended the tournament games, and, of course, reported back to their employers. At one Wichita tournament game, Ray Dumont reported that a major-league scout valued Negro leaguer Quincy Trouppe at "$100,000 if he were white." While the Midwestern tournaments did not result in the opening of the major-league door, playing in such contests was a milestone for the Negro leagues. It was the first time that Negro leaguers were accepted as true equals in baseball. They were were not exotic outsiders in these tournaments but a valued part of the Midwestern baseball world.

With the assistance of events like the prize tournaments, integrated baseball was taking hold in the Midwest in the 1930s. This phenomenon was most obvious in the Dakotas, where Bismarck emerged as a great team after they began recruiting Negro leaguers for their predominantly white club. Under the leadership of Mayor Winston Churchill, Bismarck set out on a round of baseball boosterism. Suddenly, North Dakota businessmen were haunting Negro league hangouts with offers of hard cash for a summer's work in the Dakota League. In 1934 Quincy Trouppe left the Chicago American Giants for an extra thirty-five dollars a month, raising his salary to one hundred seventy-five dollars a month. When Satchel Paige went to Bismarck in 1935, it took four hundred dollars a month, a car, and the right to hire himself out to other teams. With Satchel Paige as part of the team, Bismarck easily dominated Dakota baseball. Other teams were forced to compete for Negro league players and, by the end of 1935, the heart of many Dakota city teams was made up of three or four Negro league players, including a couple of pitchers. Dakota ball was a wild affair with lots of betting and bragging.

Quickly the Negro leaguers became sure of their abilities against the best white semi-pros. Then in 1937, the Trujillo All-Stars won the Denver Post Tournament. The Trujillo All-Stars were in fact an all-Negro league aggregation, back from a sojourn in the Dominican Republic. The team featured Satchel Paige, Josh Gibson, Cool Papa Bell, George Scales, and other Negro leaguers. A fascinating incident illustrates the ambiguity with which the Negro league regulars viewed Satchel Paige. With Leroy Madlock on the mound the Trujillo All-Stars swept into the semi-final game of the double-elimination tournament. Then, with an eye on the gate, the tournament promoters pressured them to let Paige join the team and pitch what could be the decisive game. (Paige wanted the $1,000 bonus promised the winning pitcher of the final game.) The Trujillo All-Stars felt Madlock deserved his chance at the thousand dollars. "So we didn't perform," reported an infielder on the team. They lost 2-0. "The ball was hit to you and you just didn't get to it." Then Madlock came on and the Trujillo All-Stars won the climactic game 17-3.

As the Denver Post Tournament, the Wichita tournament, and Bismarck's success served to demonstrate, the Negro leaguers really had no competition on the road, except for the major leaguers whom they played every October. Thus as entertainers the Negro leaguers were confronted by a profound problem: how to keep interest in a baseball game in which they were embarrassingly superior to the opposition. The solution, given race relations, was almost inevitable: defuse the agonistic elements in the game by comedy and exhibitionism. All the black teams incorporated some comic elements into the game as insurance against a racial confrontation. Teams were ordered not to win by too much, and ebullient pre-game entertainments were frequent.

While all the Negro league teams employed a bit of showmanship in the countryside, only one team was an exception to the unwritten rule by which Negro league teams insisted on the primacy of their professional baseball. Unfortunately for the historical assessment of Negro baseball, that one exceptional team, which actually had a rather shortlived existence in the Negro league, overwhelmed every other popular image of the league. The "Clowns," as they styled themselves, conformed closely to the racial stereotypes of the period and, in the mythmaking about black baseball, they possessed an irresistible lure. The Clowns' fame depended upon a well-practiced comedy act incorporated into a serious effort to play first-rate baseball. At the height of their notoriety in the late thirties and forties, the Clowns packed major-league ball parks such as Yankee Stadium and Comiskey Park where they offered their zany antics against Negro league teams or the House of David. Sometimes they drew over forty thousand people.

The Clowns' act depended upon a long tradition of comedy deeply imbedded in black American folk culture. Two nonplaying comics worked the crowd. Spec Bebop, a dwarf from Florida, and Philadelphia's King Tut were a comedy pair that in the heyday of the Clowns were almost as well-known as Amos and Andy. Bebop would exasperate Tut to the breaking point, and then Tut would take off after Bebop, only to just miss capturing him. Tut's character was the pompous overdrawn hick in fancy clothes; his uniform sometimes consisted of tuxedo and top hat. He would play dice against himself, lose his coat, and then, stripped down to polka-dotted underwear, win it all back. Bebop would enter the stands, sit on women's laps, and have his picture taken. Between innings Bebop practiced hitting. Running to first with those short little legs was sure to get him a laugh. Tut's and Bebop's banter was hilarious. Here was a minstrel show on a ballfield: here was William Toll's "aristocratic nigger," and "dandy darkie." Bebop illustrated the "exaggerated physical deformities common to all minstrel blacks."

The Clown first baseman also had a critical comic role, filled brilliantly after 1942 by Goose Tatum. Goose Tatum was a great baseball player—but above all he was a showman, a comedian, and a natural.

Tatum's forte was his sense of timing, and crowds loved his ability to touch the bag casually just an instant before the runner reached safely. He talked to the crowd, the opposing bench, and to his own pitcher. Sometimes the Tatum costume included a huge first-baseman's mitt three or four feet long that Tatum wore on his foot. With it he handled grounders, and he was famous for backhanding a ball. Sometimes he even wore a dress.

Other Clown members had lesser comic roles, though catcher Pepper Bassett developed a following as the "Rocking Chair Catcher." Bassett began playing with the New Orleans Crescent Stars in the thirties, when they were not drawing very well. "I had to figure out a way to put some people in the park," recalled Bassett. He went to the owner and suggested that he try catching in a rocking chair. "It's all right with me," said the owner. "The chair was a rocking chair with the back out so I could throw the bases. I had a good strong arm then," said Bassett. Around New Orleans and then Austin, Texas, Bassett became a major attraction. An old white Texan who saw him made Bassett's popularity clear. "I didn't care if I was the only white man in the stands, I was gonna see that nigger in the rocking chair," he exclaimed.

Bassett, however, was sufficiently outstanding to enter the Negro league with the Philadelphia Stars as a regular catcher. Later he moved over to the Pittsburgh Crawfords. With these teams he almost never used the rocking chair. After he went to the Cincinnati (later Indianapolis) Clowns, as part of the show, he caught a few innings in the chair. "Never at the first of the game, in the middle. I didn't do it every day now. Only in the big cities, like Minneapolis [and] Winnipeg. It was easy catching in the chair. And they went for it."

For the infielders, glory came during the pepperball and shadowball routine. "You'd throw the ball around the field and take infield practice [at a faster and faster tempo]. Then, you'd throw the ball away and go through the same motion without the ball." (The Harlem Globetrotters borrowed this act, set it to the music *Sweet Georgia Brown*, and even hired Goose Tatum, who was almost as deft on the court as on the diamond.) "A couple of times we'd go in and they'd pay us extra money just to do it over again," recalled Dave Barnhill. "That's how good it was."

The high point of the Clowns' show was their midgame vaudeville skits. Between the fifth and seventh inning, baseball took a back seat to the distilled essence of a hundred years of black comedy. The "Fishing Act" was probably the most well-known of these show-stoppers. Bebop, Tut, and sometimes Goose Tatum pretended that they were fishing and rowing on a river that ran through the pitcher's mound. One of them looked up, and immediately a bird "shit in his eye." Then Tut caught a big one, but after a struggle, with victory almost in his grasp, he managed to fall out of the boat (by then the fans could almost see it). Tut tried to swim to safety, flailing the dirt around the mound. Little Bebop dragged the unconscious Tut ashore, but nothing revived him until Bebop removed his shoe and passed it daintily before Tut's nose.

There was always room for improvisation, and certain bits were used only in special situations.

Of course, to be effective, the Clowns had to win. "If we got a lot of runs on a team the guys would go to third instead of going to first," explained Buster Haywood, a Clown manager. "That's when we had a lot of runs now. You couldn't go into a town and get run to death, noooh."

But the Clowns, who officially joined the Negro league in 1943, were only an overt manifestation of a tendency which had existed in black baseball almost from its inception. James Weldon Johnson wrote of the nineteenth-century Cuban Giants in his classic *Black Manhattan*, that they "brought something entirely new to the professional diamond; they originated and introduced baseball comedy. The coaches kept up a constant banter that was spontaneous and amusing. They often staged a comic pantomime for the benefit of the spectators...[and] generally after a good play the whole team would for a moment cut the monkey shines that would make the grandstand and bleachers roar." According to Sol White, the only authority on nineteenth-century black baseball, "Every man on a team would do a funny stunt during the game in the eighties and nineties."

However, the comedy teams were antithetical to the purposes of Negro baseball; consequently when the league was founded, they were shunted aside. In fact, in New York City in the twenties, comedy teams could not get dates. "You don't see no major leaguers clowning," insisted Nat C. Strong, who controlled the New York booking. "Be like major leaguers," admonished Strong.

Thus comedy-centered Negro baseball was forced back to a baseball minstrel circuit of very small towns and not much profit. The Tennessee Rats kept the tradition alive by barnstorming the Midwest each summer in run-down cars. The team played comedy baseball during the day and put on a show in the evening. Much of the competitiveness of the baseball experience was stripped from the games. Instead, caricatured blacks played baseball with great agility and guile, thereby reinforcing racial stereotypes.

In the East, in the early thirties, the Zulu Cannibals superseded the Tennessee Rats. Charley Henry, a black man based in Louisville, owned and promoted the Zulus; he put them in grass skirts and painted their faces. They would "do war dances like Indians, hollering and crying—oh boy was that something to see," said one Zulu. Henry would leave Louisville with just a catcher and by the time he reached Miami, he would have a full ball club. All along the way he had hired black ballplayers and taught them the routines.

That same winter, in the early 1930s, Johnny Pierce was creating the Miami Clowns. Following the example of Henry's Zulus, a group of black ballplayers who hung out around a little baseball park on 17th Street and 2nd Avenue in Miami decided to "get up a traveling ballclub." The Miami Clowns also painted their faces and sometimes wore clown costumes over their uniforms. Piled into two old Cadillacs with running boards, the Clowns and all their baseball paraphernalia set out on the road.

In 1935, events beyond America reinvigorated the comedic tradition in black baseball. The 1935 Ethiopian-Italian conflict spawned an interest by black Americans in all things African. Ironically, the core Zulu and Clown acts strengthened common misconceptions about Africa shared by whites and blacks alike. As "invaders, their grass skirts, long hair, and war painted faces and bodies, causing spasms of laughter," the Pittsburgh *Courier's* Wendell Smith noted, the Zulus were obviously drawn from the Tarzan movies of the day. They often played barefooted and employed a drum section. With names like "Anghol," "Takloore," "Bissagos," "Impo," "Selassie," "King Tut," and even "Tarzan," the Clowns and Zulus were more entertainment acts than baseball teams; nevertheless Goose Tatum, Dave Barnhill, Buck O'Neil, and other team members went on to distinguished careers in more organized ball.

When the Clowns went on the road in 1935, Johnny Pierce came to rely on Syd Pollack for bookings. A prominent agent in the upper Midwest, Pollack had already experimented with a team called the Canadian Clowns, a white team, which had played the Canadian Pacific Line in 1933. After Pollack booked Henry's team, he was surprised to discover the revenue potential of a black comedy-team.

With his ability to control the booking, Pollack offered Pierce a small sum, and in effect took the Clowns from him. Johnny Pierce returned to Miami and grew embittered as time passed and the Clowns' fame grew.

Although the Zulus continued as an important independent team until the forties, the Clowns gradually came to dominate the black comedy-market because Pollack had contracts with the right booking agents throughout the land. The Clowns, based first in Cincinnati and then Indianapolis, cast a wider and wider net. (In the late thirties they played the Zulus in Louisville in what must have been the funniest game in history.)

After 1935 the Clowns also were a force in Negro league baseball. They commanded good dates and attracted better-and-better-paying crowds. The Negro league teams with their blatantly capitalistic values solicited the Clowns. They were well aware that though they might refuse to play the Clowns, the Clowns would play white teams such as the House of David. (In fact, the Clowns preferred to play the House of David because the black-vs.-white confrontation meshed more successfully with the racial imagery projected in the Clowns' act.) Then too, the Negro league feared the Clowns' success because its better players owed allegiance only to their paychecks.

As the Clowns became an ever greater attraction, the issue of their propriety loomed larger. Although they were very successful with black crowds, they were even more successful with whites. This fact disturbed the black press, which began to attack them vigorously. Wrote one paper, "The team has been capitalizing on slap-stick comedy and the kind of nonsense which many white people like to believe is typical and characteristic of all Negroes." And the players themselves drew a sharp distinction between the comedians who paced the Clowns and the ballplayers themselves. Andrew Porter observed that "they had special guys for that, people who called themselves clowns. You ask one of the ballplayers to go out and do something like that, he'd have a fit."

The Negro league teams realized they stood to gain by incorporating the Clowns into the league, and they were invited in 1943 to enter formally. But a scheduling relationship with the Negro leagues had existed long before. The Clowns benefited by securing steady-playing dates; moreover, they still maintained the potential to barnstorm the majority of their games. The Negro leagues gained at the box office and as a result of increased publicity among whites. Finally, the arrangement prevented the Clowns from raiding Negro league teams—an important consideration.

At the time the Clowns entered the league they were called "Ethiopian Clowns," a reference to the minstrel tradition. The Negro league, however, insisted that the name be changed, because, as Effa Manley put it, "We didn't want anything Bessie"—a common pejorative allusion to a house servant. The Negro newspapers also rejected the "repulsive moniker," and they were no less happy about the team itself. "Negroes must realize the danger in insisting that ballplayers paint their faces and go through minstrel show revues before each ball game," editorialized Wendell Smith. "Every Negro in public life stands for something more than the role he is portraying. Every Negro in the theatrical and sports world is somewhat of an ambassador for the Negro race—whether he likes it or not."

The Clowns entered the league but proved a mediocre team by Negro league standards. The Clowns franchise was shifted between Cincinnati and Indianapolis and only achieved real success in 1950, when the Negro league was in steep decline. In 1952 the Clowns obtained a promising rookie named Henry Aaron. (The shy youngster's nickname was "Pork Chops" because he at first ate only pork chops and French fries on the road.)

Because of the persistent power of the Clown imagery, perpetuated in the sportsworld by the successful Harlem Globetrotters, the Clowns' style of baseball came in the public mind to stand for the entire Negro league style. The movie *Bingo Long and the Traveling All-Stars and Motor Kings*, a major popular culture treatment of black baseball, concerned the same small story. In fact, Bingo Long was not really a Negro league story at all but rather a representation of the Tennessee Rats, the Zulu Cannibal Giants, and Miami Clowns, and a plethora of other obscure teams that more properly belong in the history of black entertainment than in the mainstream of Negro league baseball history.

Buck Leonard, almost unanimously regarded as the greatest first baseman of Negro baseball, a Hall of Fame member, and one of black baseball's most respected figures, summed up the consensus Negro league opinion of *Bingo Long* when he said, "I was disgusted when I saw the film, because I know that wasn't the way we played baseball." Leonard added, "We didn't go in a town and put on our uniform and parade all around the town before we played. They showed where we got on a truck and rode all through the town cutting the monkey. We didn't do that." Buck Leonard was so incensed that he called the film's producer. He was told by the producer that using this approach was the only way he could "sell" that picture. Buck Leonard shook his head and concluded, "It's portraying something that never happened."

The tragedy of the film version of Bingo Long (over which author Bill Brashler had almost no control), was that it trivialized the so-very-important black baseball experience of life on the road. Life on the road tempered the exuberance of urban black baseball; it deepened the black baseball experience. Negro leaguers gained a perspective on white culture afforded few members of their race. They faced hardship and discrimination, but that was not the whole story. They also were cheered by all-white crowds and admired by white ballplayers less proficient than themselves. In their daily encounters with white players they were usually accorded meaningful respect for their talents. While they never forgot or forgave the brutal and petty harassments of a society which discriminated on the basis of color, they also experienced the accolades of a culture which celebrated competence and achievement.

The Latin Connection

6

The spread of baseball to the Caribbean was a nineteenth-century phenomenon which occurred almost by osmosis. By the 1880s, a scant decade after the founding of the National League, baseball was already an enormous success in Cuba. Wenceslao Galvez y Delmonte wrote of the "baseball that had rooted itself so strongly in this land as proven by the hundreds of clubs in almost all parts of the Island." With characteristic passion, he insisted that the "baseball fields of Cuba will persist longer than the cockfight and the bullring," and indeed, Havana and Almendares, the premier Havana-area teams, had as intense a nineteenth-century rivalry as the Dodgers and Yankees did in the 1950s.

As Cuban baseball developed, the Cubans hired American players to supplement their teams and to act as teachers. American catchers especially commanded a premium as the finer points of baseball technique were transported to Cuban shores. But well before the twentieth century, Cuban baseball players were as proficient as those in the United States, and if anything, the Cuban emotional attachment to the game was greater still. In fact, Cubans denigrated the American approach to the game. "At various times Yankee baseball players came to Cuba," noted Galvez y Delmonte, "always for speculation, since they do not understand baseball in any other way."

However, as Cuban baseball thrived, Cubans too profited from baseball, creating, by the twentieth century, Cuban leagues and highly successful commercial teams. By 1900, major-league-team visits to Cuba were in no way extraordinary, and the first all-black baseball team had already sailed across the Florida Keys for a game.

At a slightly later period, Cuban teams started to tour the United States. But the Cuban teams which came to the States were invariably integrated teams, well stocked with black Cubans. Consequently, the Cubans played in a black context in America, despite the presence of white players on their teams. With the descriptive name "Cuban Stars" usually stenciled on their uniforms, they were a collection of better Cuban players in search of American dollars.

Two very light-skinned men, Rafael Almeida and Armando Marsans, played on the early-twentieth-century Cuban Stars. Clearly, these men passed as white for, after seeing them play, the Cincinnati Reds signed them to major-league contracts in 1911, the first Cubans in big-league ball.

Black baseball watched this development with enthusiasm, anticipating the selection of Almeida and Marsans as the wedge for baseball integration. "Now that the first shock is over it would not be surprising to see a Cuban a few shades darker than Almeida and Marsans breaking into the professional ranks," editorialized Booker T. Washington's *New York Age* in 1911. "With the admission of Cubans of a darker hue in the two big leagues it would then be easy for colored players who are citizens of this country to get into fast company." The *Age* commented further that "the Negro in this country has more varied hues than even the Cubans," and suggested that "until the public gets accustomed to seeing native Negroes on big league [teams] the colored players could keep their mouths shut and pass for Cubans"—not the last time that this ploy would be encouraged.

But not only complete teams went to Cuba. In the teens the Cuban league grew stronger, and the better American players discovered that they could make reasonable salaries by joining Cuban teams as individuals, negotiating their own contracts. The Cubans, to protect their own players' livelihood, limited the "imports," as they called them, to only a few players per team. Thus Tris Speaker, Rogers Hornsby, and other established major leaguers ventured down in quest of winter paydays. They were there joined by black stars such as John Henry Lloyd and Ollie Marcelle. (As foreign attractions, the Americans, white or black, generally received greater pay than their Cuban counterparts for the same performance level, a disparity that resulted in some bitterness.)

As far as baseball itself went, race mattered little in Cuba; black Americans competed with major leaguers on an equal basis for positions on Cuban teams. The result was that selection by a Cuban team became the single best criterion to evaluate baseball ability. As Quincy Trouppe put it, "you didn't get to go to Cuba unless you were a well-seasoned ballplayer."

Based upon his Cuban experiences during the teens, Rube Foster knew that a Cuban team was a desirable addition to the first Negro National League. He realized that the Cubans possessed a wealth of talent and worked cheaply. Also, he understood the inherent drawing power of the word Cuban among black Americans eager to learn more about their exotic brothers. Displaying amazing stamina, the first Cuban Negro league teams played without a home field, consigned to a whole season on the road. For some of the greater Cuban players, the Cuban Stars was a stop on their way to more established Negro league teams. Cristobel Torrienti of the Chicago American Giants and Jose Mendez of the Kansas City Monarchs both became celebrities in the black communities of their adopted cities, but only after a painful stint with the early Cuban Stars.

When the Eastern Colored League was established in 1923, it too wanted a Cuban entry; young Alessandro Pompez was chosen to manage the Eastern Cuban Stars. "Those babies could play out of this world" was Jesse Hubbard's first impression of them; Cy Young's comments after the Cuban Stars beat him and a major-league all-star group near Miami in April of 1923 are not recorded.

The extensive, sustained interaction between Cuban and Negro league baseball was of enormous significance to the Negro leagues. First, it enabled the best Negro leaguers to become full-time professionals. Negro leaguers earned winter income in the Caribbean, at first chiefly in Cuba and later in Puerto Rico, Venezuela, Mexico, Panama, and the Dominican Republic. Of equal importance was that in Latin countries, the Negro players competed as equals against whites. Since the great white players, the Ty Cobbs and Babe Ruths, participated in the Cuban Leagues, a Negro leaguer knew after a few Cuban seasons whether or not he was a player of major-league caliber.

However, the inherent injustice of their predicament weighed on the black Cubans and Negro leaguers alike. Luis Tiant, Sr., the ace lefty of the Cuban Stars in the thirties and forties, despaired over the harsh life he had chosen, and discouraged his son and namesake from following in his footsteps.

When that son, Luis Tiant, Jr., became a famous major-league pitcher in the era of integration, he was startled to discover that many old-time baseball men believed his father, the Negro leaguer, had been a better pitcher than he was. "It made me proud that people say my father was a better pitcher than me," Tiant said, though he vividly remembers the months his father was gone and the presents sent from America. "He supported eleven of us," Tiant, Jr., recalled, "and once he was gone two whole years." The "fatherless" oldest son honed his baseball talents while awaiting his father's return. Tiant's father's experiences were not all pleasant. He drilled into his son the memories of horrendous, grueling bus trips, and unaccustomed segregation. "He didn't want me to be a ballplayer," remembers Luis Tiant, Jr. "He said the life was too hard."

Luis "Lefty" Tiant entered Negro league lore for one incident which still brings a smile to the Negro leaguers who witnessed it. Tiant had the niftiest move to first in the league. With an assortment of off-speed pitches and the herky-jerky motion that his son inherited, Tiant was a tough hombre to face anytime. In the twilight games of Negro league competition, he was almost invincible. One day, as dusk settled on a game between the Baltimore Elite Giants and the Cuban Stars, Tiant was facing Goose Curry at bat, with a man on first. After wasting a pitch, Tiant bobbed through his motion, hesitated, and then, deftly, attempted to pick off the runner. In the diminished sunlight Curry thought he saw the ball coming, and he swung. The ump drew a deep breath and yelled "strike." Curry wheeled toward the umpire, and pointing to first, disputed the call. But the umpire, taking command in his most imperial manner, hollered, "If you were stupid enough to swing it's still a strike."

Lefty Tiant and all the Cubans were regarded as fierce competitors. In a game against the Philadelphia Stars, Tiant gave up hits to outfielder Ted Page in his first two trips to the plate. On the third at-bat the ball came directly at Page's head, landing with a loud plunk. The helmetless Page lay still for a moment; when he came to, Tiant was leaning over him and chuckling, "You not hit thata one too well."

Americans were procured for the Cuban League by Cubans, both white and black, who played summers in the United States and then returned to their homeland for the winter league. Thus the Cubans became a traditional and important conduit of baseball information between white and black American players. The white Cincinnati pitcher, Adolph "Red" Luque, managed for both Almendares and Marianao in the Cuban League, where he used Negro league players as regulars. While in the States he scouted Negro league games and maintained his Negro league friendships during the season.

Luque was probably the most important Cuban baseball man during the Negro league heyday. With his fiery temper, he was a dominating figure as a player, a manager, and later, an owner. Once, while managing Almendares, his pitcher, Negro leaguer Terris McDuffie, refused to go into a game after only two days' rest. Luque motioned McDuffie through the dressing room and into his office. Reaching into a desk drawer he pulled out a revolver and sharply asked McDuffie again if he was ready to pitch. "Gimme the ball," gulped McDuffie, and he went out and pitched a two-hitter.

Many Negro leaguers believed that the only mechanism for a black to enter organized baseball was "to pass" into the major leagues as a foreigner, probably a Cuban. At the turn of the century John McGraw of the New York Giants actually tried to pass a Negro ballplayer named Charley Grant off as an Indian, "Chief Tokohoma," but without success. In later years blacks emphasized the wide variety of exotic nationalities accepted in organized baseball. With Indians such as "Chief" Albert Bender, "Chief" John Meyers, "Chief" Ben Tincup, Jim Thorpe, and Chief Yellowhorse playing in the major leagues, and Cubans such as Adolph Luque, Mike Gonzales, and Tommy de la Cruz accepted, and even Japanese and Chinese playing minor-league baseball, the black press vehemently protested that something was "missing in the color scheme of the national pastime, and that color is black."

In the 1920s, power hitter Cristobel Torrienti of the American Giants supposedly missed his opportunity to join a major-league team because of "kinky" hair.

Quincy Trouppe related that one Sunday in the late twenties, "a baseball scout came down from the stands and asked him if he was interested in playing in the big leagues." The scout suggested that Trouppe go to a Latin country and learn Spanish, explaining that if he could speak the language, he would have a good chance to play organized ball. Art Rust, Jr., the sports editor of the *Amsterdam News*, was even more explicit. "I have always been convinced that Jackie Robinson was not the first black man in the modern major leagues," he wrote. "The Washington Senators in the mid-thirties and forties were loaded with Latin players of darker hue, who because they spoke Spanish got by with it." John Welau, an outfielder with the Senators in the forties, said that most of the Senators considered Robert Estalella black. Even more frequent testimony points to Mike Gonzales as one of the "black" Senators. Rust specifically mentions Gonzales, calling him "a light-skinned black man." Corroborating Rust's assertion is Willie Wells's that while he, Wells, was playing for the Almendares team under Gonzales, he was told by Cubans, "Willie, his momma black." (In Cuba, Almendares seemed to recruit black players more vigorously than did their arch-rival, Havana.)

Additional evidence comes from none other than Branch Rickey himself. When integration finally came to organized baseball, Clark Griffith of the Senators objected, arguing that integration would destroy the Negro leagues and his lucrative business arrangement with the Homestead Grays. However, in an aside to Red Smith, Branch Rickey snickered that Griffith had already hired blacks. In Red Smith's classic phraseology, "Ricky responded that hiring Negroes was nothing new to Clark Giffith. This seems to imply that there was a Senegambian somewhere in the Cuban batpile where Senatorial timber is seasoned."

The origins of every prominent Cuban in the major leagues were suspect because of the uniquely American view that every man with any black blood was a Negro. Adolph Luque, Tommy De La Cruz, Mike Gonzales, Robert Estalella, and Armando Marsans were all called black by Negro leaguers at one time or another.

For the Negro leaguers, Cuba served as an escape valve from repressive racism. In Cuba the players led more "normal" lives: they played a single game each day and their travel was negligible. Then too, they were experiencing de facto integration. During the winter months the status hierarchy of American baseball was forgotten. Ray Dandridge (Taluah), Willie Wells (El Diablito), and John Henry Lloyd (Cunchado) were every bit as much Cuban heroes as Ty Cobb and Babe Ruth. When a rookie Dodger pitcher named Tommy Lasorda arrived in Cuba, it was to Dandridge or Willard Brown that he looked up to, at least to the same degree as he did to his Dodger teammates. "Willard Brown was one of the greatest hitters I ever saw," Lasorda insisted even after a decade at the Dodger helm.

While the player had a more professional existence in Cuba, the game itself was characterized by a passion and exuberance not found in the major leagues. Gambling in the stands was a given, and sometimes after a great play or hit, a ballplayer pulled hundreds of dollars from the screening; these were the gifts of appreciative fans. Piper Davis won a crucial game

Ciudad Trujillo team with their manager, 1937. *(Courtesy Craig Davidson)*

Season's Greetings from the 1946 Newark Eagles. *(Courtesy Effa Manley)*

Poster from a wartime Negro World Series game, early 1940s. *(Courtesy Craig Davidson)*

Team photo sent by the Brooklyn Eagles (also known as the Newark Eagles) to their "gal," owner Mrs. Effa Manley, 1940s. *(Courtesy Dick Seay)*

Effa Manley, Newark Eagles' owner from 1934 to 1948. *(Courtesy Craig Davidson)*

Group of Negro leaguers on the docks in Cuba with wives and girlfriends, late 1930s. *(Courtesy Buck Leonard)*

Newark Eagles' Max Manning, Dodgers' Carl Erskine and Frank Meagher, and an unidentified Cuban player (rear) of the integrated Cienfuegos team, 1949. *(Author's collection)*

Buck Leonard batting in Durango, late 1940s. *(Courtesy Buck Leonard)*

Poster advertising the Mexican League All-Stars vs. Negro League All-Stars game in Los Angeles, 1938. *(Courtesy Craig Davidson)*

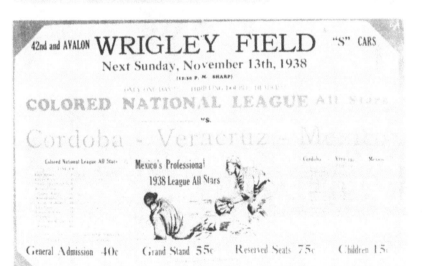

42nd and AVALON **WRIGLEY FIELD** "S" CARS

Next Sunday, November 13th, 1938

(12:30 P. M. SHARP)

ONLY ONE DAY! HIRPLING HORSE BUICK

COLORED NATIONAL LEAGUE All Stars

"S.

Cordoba - Veracruz - Mexico

Colored National League All Stars

Mexico's Professional 1938 League All Stars

Cordoba   Veracruz   Mexico

General Admission 40c   Grand Stand 55c   Reserved Seats 75c   Children 15c

Negro BASEBALL

Pictorial ★ Year Book   25¢

1944 Records ★ World's Series Review
East-West Classic ★ All-America Team

Wartime Negro baseball magazine edited by Art Carter, 1944. *(Courtesy Art Carter)*

Lena Horne throws out the first ball in a 1945 exhibition game in Los Angeles between Chet Brewer's Black All-Stars and a white All-Star team. The blacks won, 4-3. *(Courtesy Chet Brewer)*

Satchel's All-Stars and their Flying Tiger, 1946. On the ground, from left: Hilton Smith (Kansas City Monarchs), Howard Easterling (Homestead Greys), Barney Brown (Philadelphia Stars), Sam Jethroe (Cleveland Buckeyes), Gentry Jessup (Chicago American Giants), Hank Thompson (Monarchs), Max Manning (Newark Eagles), Othello Renfroe (Monarchs), Refus Lewis (Eagles), Gene Benson (Stars), Buck O'Neil (Monarchs), Frank Duncan (Monarchs), Artie Wilson (Birmingham Black Barons), Quincy Trouppe (Buckeyes). On steps: Dizzy Dismukes, the All-Stars' business manager. In doorway: Satchel Paige (right) and his valet. *(Courtesy Phil Dixon)*

AMERICAN ALL STARS

BARNSTORMING CHAMPIONS IN CARACAS, VENE-

After Jackie Robinson signed with the Dodgers, he went to Venezuela with a black barnstorming team in 1945. Roy Campanella is standing at far left, Quincy Trouppe is standing fourth from left, Buck Leonard is standing at far right, and Robinson is kneeling at front left. *(Courtesy Phil Dixon)*

Barnstorming poster, early 1940s. *(Courtesy National Baseball Hall of Fame Library, Cooperstown, NY)*

BASE BALL

ALL STAR GAME OHIO STATE LEAGUE HALLORAN PARK

LIMA-OHIO

COLORED ALL STARS The Best Colored Players in the State By Wayne Xenia and other Leading Clubs

— VS —

WHITE ALL STARS The Pick of Best Players from Northwestern Ohio SEMI-PRO Teams

Children 15¢ — Adults 40¢
ANY PLACE IN THE PARK

THE BIG GAME OF THE SEASON

TUES. NITE 8:30 P.M. UNDER LIGHTS **AUG. 22**

Pat Patterson at the plate, 1939. *(Courtesy Pat Patterson)*

Kansas City Monarchs team photo, 1945. Hilton Smith is at top left, Satchel Paige is standing fourth from left, Jackie Robinson is kneeling at far right. *(Courtesy Hilton Smith)*

The Clowns, ca. 1948. *(Courtesy Phil Dixon)*

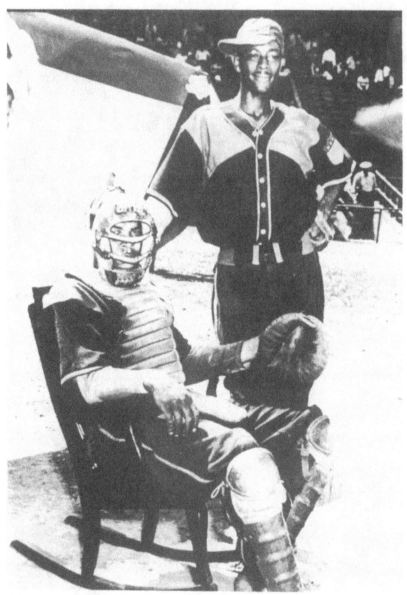

Pepper Bassett, the "rocking chair catcher," with an unidentified player. *(Courtesy Bassett family)*

Hall of Fame induction picture, 1973, the year Monte Irvin (top, third from left) of the Newark Eagles entered the Hall of Fame. Satchel Paige (top, second from right) and Buck Leonard (top, fourth from right) preceded Irvin. *(Courtesy Monte Irvin)*

Photo taken at home plate during the fiftieth anniversary celebration of the All-Star game, Comiskey Park, Chicago, 1983. Invited Negro league veterans of the East-West Classic were Buck Leonard, Judy Johnson, Willie Wells, and Cool Papa Bell. *(Courtesy Craig Davidson)*

Negro league reunion, 1981. Effa Manley (center) is flanked by Hall-of-Famers Ray Dandridge (at left) and Buck Leonard. Note guest Bob Feller (top, second from left). *(Courtesy Craig Davidson)*

Satchel Paige on the set of the made-for-TV movie *Don't Look Back,* 1980s. *(Courtesy Mark Petty)*

Author interviewing Satchel Paige, 1980. *(Courtesy Mark Petty)*

At a 1980 Negro league reunion were, from left: Webster McDonald, Buck Leonard, Chet Brewer, Clint Thomas, Monte Irvin, Buck O'Neil, unidentified man, Judy Johnson, Joe Black, Ted Page, Gene Benson, and, kneeling for the catch, Ray Dandridge. *(Courtesy Craig Davidson)*

1982 Negro league reunion, the best attended of all Negro league reunions. Five Hall-of-Famers are pictured—bottom row: Judy Johnson, second from left; Buck Leonard, sixth from left; Cool Papa Bell, sixth from right; Ray Dandridge, fifth from right; top row: Monte Irvin, fifth from right. (*Courtesy National Baseball Hall of Fame Library, Cooperstown, NY*)

with a smashing homer out of Tropical Stadium in Havana. When the batboy returned with the loot, it totaled over two hundred dollars at the current exchange rate. (The best Cuban fans were the sailmakers and the men on the docks.)

In Cuba old conflicts might be resolved away from the eyes of Negro league authorities. Ray Dandridge had a score to settle with Roy Campanella dating back to an "unnecessary" spiking. "I had him out from here to the door, and boom, he cut me." Dandridge took a long breath. "I told him, all right, I'm gonna get you one of these days or bust." Retribution came in Havana, Cuba. Campanella was catching. Dandridge was camped on second when a teammate hit a sharp single to left. "It came to me all of a sudden," he said, " 'cause I know they can throw me out." As Dandridge rounded third like a miniature locomotive, he was hollering at Campanella, "I got you now!" With a smile of satisfaction Dandridge added, "I guess you know I came in safe; he was practically up in the stands." (And then, with the slate even once again, they resumed their friendship.)

With excitement like that, no wonder Cuban winter-league baseball was the most popular Cuban sport, and making it into the Cuban league the dream of every young Cuban boy. Fidel Castro had that dream. As a boy he loved to attend Cuban winter-league games; he followed the famed Negro leaguers to the park, and on one occasion, was allowed to play catch with the ballplayers before a game. (Castro evolved into a pretty fair pitcher. When he assumed power, he reportedly gave formal assurances that the Cuban entry in the International League—the Havana Sugar

Kings—would not be expropriated, but the Eisen-
hower Administration pressured baseball to pull the
team from Cuba anyway.)

Cuba also provided the opportunity to sow wild
oats away from unsympathetic parents and wives. One
Negro leaguer bet another that he could "screw every
whore in Havana during a winter league season." He
made it through the season, fell in love, and married
a Cuban woman. In Cuba, without stealth, the Negro
leaguers who wanted to could meet white women,
sleep with them, be jilted, and jilt them back. In Cuba
their dollars were as good as the next man's. They
attended the best clubs, ate the best food, and stayed
in the finer hotels. Negro leaguers fortunate enough
to be selected to play in the Caribbean were given the
opportunity to become more fully human in the lush
tropical environment.

Cuban ball was an education for the white major
leaguers too. "Where'd you come from?" was a frequent major-league refrain, as the big leaguers discovered talented black players already entrenched.
The major leaguer, like the Negro leaguer, had to adjust to the Latin rhythms blaring from the loudspeak-
ers at Tropical Stadium, and to the spicy food, which
most American players, white and black, seemed to
abhor. A few had to adjust to Cuban race relations
also. Willie Wells and Johnny Dunlap of the Boston
Braves became friends after becoming teammates on
Almendares. One day, while at the race track, Dunlap
spied Early Wynn, who was pitching for Havana that
year. "Earl, come on over and have a beer," invited
Dunlap. Wynn took one look at Dunlap's dark-com-
plexioned companion and said, "I don't drink with
niggers." "What'd you say?" quizzed Dunlap. "You

heard what I said, I don't drink with niggers," responded Early Wynn. Dunlap swiftly got up and broke Early Wynn's jaw. Wynn pitched no more in the winter league that year.

In its heyday, from the 1930s to the 1950s, the Cuban League was usually a four-team winter league. Havana and Almendares were based in Havana, while Marinao, Cienfuegos, and its precursor Santa Clara represented more outlying regions. At one time Santa Clara had a tremendously strong team, so strong that Rudolpho Fernandez, one of the most prominent of Cuban pitchers, believed the Santa Clara team of the late thirties was Cuban baseball's greatest team. (Negro league superstars Oscar Charleston, Frank Duncan, and Ollie Marcelle played on that team.)

Once Cuba wholeheartedly adopted baseball as the Cuban national game, the rest of the Caribbean, with the exception of the West Indies, quickly fell in line and embraced baseball. However, even Jamaica had its baseball devotees, with Chester Brooks becoming the single most outstanding West Indian Negro leaguer.

As might be expected, Puerto Rico followed most closely the Cuban baseball model. During the thirties a strong Puerto Rican winter league sprang up, aided by a 1934 tour of Puerto Rico by an elite group of Negro leaguers. That team, coordinated by the Brooklyn Eagles, was led by Josh Gibson, Rap Dixon, and Dick Seay. The emotionalism of the Latin fan shocked even the Negro leaguers. "They were fanatics," laughed Dick Seay. "They'd throw oranges or lemons at us depending on whether they liked us or disliked us." Shortly after the 1934 tour, a five-team league developed: San Juan, Aquadilla, Caguas, Ponce, and Santurce. The rise of Puerto Rican baseball was welcomed, for it meant additional winter jobs.

The Puerto Rican promoters, especially Pete Zorilla of San Juan, understood the box-office appeal of the Negro league stars. The most famous Negro leaguer in Puerto Rico was Willard Brown, the "Babe Ruth of Puerto Rico." A home-run hitter of extraordinary power and natural ability, Brown was a fixture at the LaFrance Hotel in San Juan, where most of the Negro leaguers stayed. Dick Seay, the second baseman of San Juan and later Santurce, loved Puerto Rico so much that he settled there when his playing days were over. The attractions were the lack of discrimination and the warm weather. Almost all the Negro leaguers who spent any time at all in the Caribbean or Mexico developed a facility with the Spanish language.

An indication of the value that the Puerto Rican fan placed on baseball is Pete Zorilla's willingness to pay $1,000 and all expenses to Satchel Paige for a single barnstorming appearance in the 1940s. Dick Seay had been instructed to find Paige and buy his services. Seay found Paige in Kansas City, who told him that his price was $1,000. Seay informed Zorilla, and the money was wired back the next day. That was how Negro baseball and Satchel Paige worked.

By the end of the thirties, most of the Spanish-speaking Caribbean had a flourishing baseball tradition. Panama and Venezuela, encouraged by the Panama Canal authorities and American oil companies, quickly emulated the Cuban model. Negro league shortstop Bill Yancey went down in the thirties to help Panama field a team for the 1936 Olympic games. (A baseball exhibition was scheduled for Berlin as part of the games!) Yancey helped create two national teams dubbed Atlantic Side and Pacific Side, and was so successful in implanting the game that over a dozen Panamanians ultimately became Negro leaguers.

Later the Panamanian league developed into a four-team organization sponsored by the more important Panamanian industries: Chesterfield, Spur Cola, Cerveceria, and Carta Viejo—cigarettes, soft drinks, beer, and a rum company.

Chet Brewer, the Negro league standout, developed a true love for Panama and became a winter-regular there for a number of years. One day while he was pitching—his leg cocked high at the top of his wind-up—he heard the rat-a-tat-tat of machine-gun fire. "You talk about getting prone right now," he exclaimed. "It was those college students raising Cain." That, too, was part of the Caribbean baseball.

For the Americans and the Cubans, who had the strongest baseball tradition, the most difficult Caribbean country, until the forties, was Venezuela. The money was acceptable, but the forlorn note of Venezuelan isolation from the baseball world was captured in a postcard from the Cuban star Pelayo Chacon to his friend Clint Thomas. "I hope you be well," he wrote in pidgin English, "I be well. Thomas, I have been here 14 month, and I am weary. Regards to all boys. Your friend Chacon." It was sent from La Guaira, Venezuela, dated June 3, 1933. Venezuela simply could not produce the level of ball provided by the Negro leaguers. When Negro league all-star groups went to Caracas, they dominated the Venezuelan teams. In 1945, a team which included Jackie Robinson, Roy Campanella, Quincy Trouppe, Buck Leonard, and about seven more Negro league all-stars so embarrassed the Venezuelans they asked the Negro leaguers to lose or at least to lighten up some. The Negro leaguers refused the offer, though they did subdivide themselves and played additional exhibitions. The best Venezuelan player at the time was probably the Magallanes shortstop Luis Aparacio, Sr., whose son made it all the way to the major leagues.

In the Dominican Republic, under the leadership of the American Sugar Company, baseball also was played within a league structure. Santiago, San Pedro de Macoris, and Ciudad Trujillo comprised the Dominican league. (Rafael Trujillo had changed the name of the capital from Santo Domingo.) In 1937, facing one of the toughest fights in his political career, Trujillo decided to enhance his reputation by winning the Dominican pennant. His method was to import the best Negro leaguers, which in 1937 meant the Pittsburgh Crawfords and above all Satchel Paige. Catching up with Paige in New Orleans, Trujillo's men offered a large sum of money to Paige, a man with a notorious love of cold cash. The rather crude but effective Dominican technique involved spreading large amounts of greenbacks on a bed and encouraging the recruit to take his specified amount as an advance.

Paige left the United States, causing an enormous outcry in the Negro newspapers. Gus Greenlee threatened to sue and tried to have the U.S. State Department retrieve his ballplayer. When Frederico Nina, the "baseball mogul of Santo Domingo," arrived in Pittsburgh seeking additional players, the entire black community was furious. Manager Oscar Charleston, a man of imposing physique, caught up with Nina in a local hotel as Nina was arranging for pitcher Spoon Carter's Dominican trip. The terms were $775 for eight weeks, round-trip tickets for Carter and his wife, and all expenses; this salary was much higher than what the Negro league was paying for a journeyman like Carter. Charleston grabbed Nina by the throat and yelled, "I came here to whip you, but since you're so little, I won't do it. Why don't you go into the white leagues?" Nina and a man from the Dominican consulate were then marched to the local alderman's office, where they were promptly arrested for conspiracy. However, since the best players were already in the Dominican Republic, the cause of the Crawfords was hopeless, and the team dropped from the Negro league shortly thereafter.

These maneuvers were, however, only the beginning of the Dominican story. The other Dominican clubs began to recruit Negro league players as well, and soon all the Dominican teams had many Negro league players competing in the tight national pennant race.

The Negro league players, loyal only to their wallets, watched amused as the Dominican factions used baseball as the arena for their power struggles. One day Chet Brewer, who was playing for Santiago, went hunting for Satchel Paige, who was playing for Trujillo City, to invite him to have a beer with him. Unfortunately, Brewer couldn't find Paige. Then as Brewer recalled, "A little kid (they know all the business), he said, 'En la carcel,' that's 'jail' in Spanish. Trujillo had put them in [protective custody] before they were gonna play us. So they wouldn't 'rouse around. He was gonna have it."

The real power behind the Dominican league and Trujillo in 1937 was the American Sugar Company.

Since victory in the pennant race had political ramifications, manipulations to insure a Ciudad Trujillo victory were almost inevitable. On one occasion, the Commissioner of the Dominican League forfeited some games to Trujillo City blaming unruly fans in San Pedro de Macoris for their cancellation. But in fact a very minor outbreak of anti-Trujillo agitation was the real cause of the forfeitures. "He just took it," complained a player from San Pedro de Macoris.

Another time, when Trujillo's team lost a series to Santiago, his players returned to their hotel to discover a squad of angry militiamen. "El Presidente doesn't lose," shouted the militiamen, firing their rifles in the air. "You know you are playing for El Presidente," they shouted, and more shots rang out. Cool Papa Bell and the other Ciudad Trujillo Negro leaguers were terrified, and they swept their next series against Santiago.

After Trujillo's team won the championship, the dictator threw a huge going-away party, a "fiesta latino," for his American players. This party has entered Negro league lore, primarily because of the lavish arrangements and the presence of machine-gun-carrying troops. The dinner items were named in the players' honor.

When the Dominican season ended, the Negro leaguers from all the teams boarded a Pan Am Clipper and island-hopped back to the States, where, for a short period, they barnstormed together as the Trujillo All-Stars.

By the 1940s the Caribbean had an established baseball sportsworld that was essentially independent of the United States and the major leagues. Panama, Venezuela, Cuba, Puerto Rico, the Dominican

Republic, and Mexico all had established leagues that limited the number of Americans allowed on each team. In fact, Puerto Rico, Cuba, Panama, and Venezuela played a Caribbean World Series in which the champion of each league met to determine the Caribbean champion. The winners were feted throughout the Caribbean, and it did not particularly matter that a few Negro league Americans were prominent on most Caribbean championship teams.

Chet Brewer, for example, was the winning Panamanian pitcher the only year that Panama ever won the Caribbean Series. He was joined on the Panamanian pitching staff by Pat Scantlebury, another Negro league player. They went to Puerto Rico the year Panama won. "We were the poorest country of all of them," remembered Brewer. "The other players laughed at us when they had the pre-game ceremony and lined the players up from home to first, first to second, second to third, and third to home. They looked resplendent in their fine uniforms. We looked like boys in knickers. But we had some real ballplayers," he added. When they returned home to Panama victorious, parades and parties broke out all over Panama City. "We were some kind of heroes," acknowledged Brewer.

Winning a Caribbean Series or an important international baseball game had political repercussions throughout the Caribbean. In fact, in 1941 Venezuela and the Dominican Republic broke diplomatic relations in a controversy over a baseball game.

Mexico, too, started down the path of the Cuban model with winter-league baseball and the recruitment of Americans to supplement their teams. As early as the twenties, black ballplayers were employed in

Mexico, and Texas Negro teams—the San Antonio Giants, the Austin Black Senators, and the Galveston Crabs—made quick trips to Mexico for ballgames. Sometimes they played their way to Mexico City and back, stopping in Monterrey, Puebla, and other towns along the way. On more than one occasion, they headed straight to Mexico City, played a series, and headed home. "The first time I went to Mexico," said Willie Wells, "I had a trunkful of pesos when I reached the border. When I changed it you could put it in one pocket."

The Mexican teams came North too. For the stronger Mexican teams, playing in the United States, particularly Texas, was a lucrative opportunity. In the thirties and forties, independent Mexican teams journeyed throughout the Southwest, just like their Negro league counterparts.

However, in the 1940s Mexican baseball ambitions grew larger, and the Mexican summer league made a systematic attempt to upgrade itself by raiding big-league ballclubs. Multimillionaire Jorge Pasquel attempted to strengthen Mexican baseball with a scheme that involved stocking Mexican teams with a nucleus of Negro leaguers and then adding to this a smattering of white major leaguers. Pasquel, an important financial backer of Mexican President Aleman, hoped to fan the flames of nationalism by proving that the Mexican League was the equal of the major leagues, and by analogy, that Mexico and the United States were in the same league, too.

Pasquel's idea was to entice Americans to play in Mexico's summer league of permanent Mexican teams. Although there had been Mexican leagues prior to the

1940s, the participation of Americans promised a significant strengthening of the six-team league composed of Mexico City, Vera Cruz, Puebla, Torreon, Tampico, and Monterrey. As a summer, not winter operation, a strong Mexican League threatened the hegemony of the United States majors. While the major leagues had always viewed Latin American baseball as a useful adjunct to their own baseball empire (and not incidentally a place to make barnstorming dollars and sell baseball equipment), they were bitterly hostile to the Mexican plans. The uneasiness of major-league baseball toward Mexico was compounded by the healthy respect the majors had developed for Pasquel's operation. Major league owners knew that Pasquel had strong baseball contacts, both white and black, and, as the largest liquor importer in Mexico, he had the money to back his ambitions.

Pasquel spared no effort. He immediately went after the most famous Negro leaguers: Josh Gibson, Buck Leonard, Vic Harris, Willie Wells, and Ray Dandridge. (Satchel Paige had a sore arm in 1939–1940, when the first wave of Negro league players went into the Mexican league, though he had played in Mexico with a Nuevo Laredo team even earlier.) There was nothing subtle in Pasquel's approach. He offered the prospective players fabulous salaries. "The first player they got after on my team was Dandridge," reported Effa Manley of Newark. "He came to me with this thousand dollars in his hand, and said Mr. Pasquel had just given him this to play with his team, and if I'd give it to him he wouldn't go." Effa, who knew that if she "ever got in a bidding war they'd win," advised Dandridge to head for Mexico. Soon he was joined by

Wells, Gibson, Bankhead, Campanella, Hughes, Irvin, Trouppe, Leonard, Harris and Theolic Smith.

The Mexican experience was an important one in the life histories of all the Negro leaguers. In Mexico they lived in fashionable neighborhoods and made excellent money. They kept regular hours and were encouraged to bring their families. Pasquel even hired tutors for some of the children. "It was fun," recalled Dolores Dandridge Ramirez, Ray Dandridge's daughter. "We'd tell our friends, 'We're going to Mexico for six months,' and they'd say, 'Where's Mexico?'" Some of the players partook of the cultural opportunities available in Mexico City, either by wandering the pyramids or by visiting the remarkable Museum of Anthropology, located in an area where many of them lived. Most learned Spanish; some even became fluent. Bill Wright of the Baltimore Elite Giants found such freedom that he never came back. Willie Wells summed up his attitude toward Mexico when he said, "We are heroes here...[while] in the United States everything I did was regulated by color. Well, here in Mexico I am a man." When Pat Patterson married while in Mexico, his manager Carmona declared a team holiday and threw "a lovely party," according to Gladys Patterson. "I'd never seen a roast pig before," she confessed.

Although Wells, Gibson, Harris, and the rest had their moments of loneliness that could be dissipated only by the cases and cases of beer Pasquel provided, there were joyous moments, too. Pasquel, who owned the Mexico City stadium as well as several of the Mexican teams, attended most of the games. His modus operandi was to reward players on the spot for achievement. With the bases loaded and two outs,

Monte Irvin, playing for Mexico City, was called from the plate for a word with Pasquel. "If you win this game I'll give you $200," Pasquel told Irvin. As he took the first strike, Irvin leaned back and told Monterrey's catcher, Roy Campanella, what Pasquel had said. "Give me a fastball and I'll give you half," Irvin told his friend. Campy agreed and quickly signalled for a curve, which is exactly what Irvin had expected. Over the fence it went. As Pasquel greeted Irvin with the money in his hand, he smiled at Campanella and thanked him profusely.

Once, while playing for Vera Cruz, a Pasquel team, Josh Gibson went four for four: a triple, double, and two singles. Pasquel entered the locker room with an expression of horror. "What's amatter Jipson," he asked, mispronouncing Gibson's name as he always did. Gibson held up four fingers. "Four for four," he chuckled, "four for four." "No home run?" quizzed Pasquel. "I got Wells and Dandridge for doubles and singles. I got you for home runs."

With a nucleus of Negro leaguers in Mexico, the recruiting became even easier. In the informal business style which characterized the Negro leagues, a phone call, a letter, or even word of mouth was all it took to send a ballplayer packing for another part of the world. Ray Dandridge became such a trusted confidant of Jorge Pasquel that he was sent to the United States specifically to exercise his judgment as a recruiter and bring back ballplayers. "I didn't beat around the bush," said Dandridge. "I said, 'I'm going to tell you exactly what the man gave me and I'm not going to try and [argue] you down.'" When Dandridge decided to hire his Newark Eagle teammate Leon Day, he simply told Day, "The Mexican Consulate is over there, your visa's waiting for you." Dandridge would come to Newark for a day or two and then he'd leave with a fine ballplayer in tow.

Pasquel's influence was pervasive. For example, in 1943 Quincy Trouppe and Theolic Smith sought a draft exemption to play baseball in Mexico. After their draft boards turned them down flat, Quincy Trouppe wrote Pasquel in Mexico City and returned to his job in a Los Angeles defense factory. Soon he was contacted at home by the Mexican consul. "The representative from Mexico told me that they had loaned the United States 80,000 workers to fill the manpower shortage caused by the war and [that] all they wanted in return was two ballplayers by the name of Quincy Trouppe and Theolic Smith," recalled Trouppe.

A measure of Pasquel's power was displayed after Ray Dandridge left for the States after a salary squabble with him. Dandridge soon received a shock. While he was in a train compartment near Monterrey, the Mexican army stopped the train and came looking for him! The explanation was simple enough: Pasquel had changed his mind and was prepared to raise Dandridge's salary. Dandridge developed a deep affection for Pasquel, and when Bill Veeck offered Dandridge a contract with the Cleveland Indians in 1947, Dandridge felt enough loyalty to remain in Mexico. When they finally parted, Pasquel bought Dandridge a home in Newark.

Although Pasquel vigorously recruited the best Negro leaguers as well as the best Cuban players, he knew that to accomplish his objectives he needed major-league names as well. His money was sufficient to tempt Mickey Owens, Max Lanier, and Sal Maglie, whose collective jump into the Mexican League sent shivers through the U.S. baseball establishment. When they learned that Pasquel was negotiating with Ted Williams, the situation turned ominous for the big leagues, and they clamped down hard on the so-called "outlaw" players—by banning them from the league. The Negro league had no such power. The Mexican salaries were higher than Negro league salaries, and the Negro leaguers had little sense of loyalty to their Negro league owners. Instead, it was a general fatigue from too much time spent in a foreign culture on one hand and the general improvement in Negro baseball finances during the war on the other which brought the Negro league stars back to the States.

The story of the impact of Latin American baseball on the Negro leagues is the missing link in black baseball history. Not only was Latin America an enormously exciting place for the Negro leaguers to play baseball; more important, it was in Latin America that the critical groundwork for baseball integration occurred. In Latin America virtually every important defense of segregation was destroyed.

It was argued that blacks played an inferior brand of baseball. But in Latin America the Negro league style of play dominated the Latin American leagues. When the Yankees met Vargas in Caracas in March of 1947, Ray Dandridge, Bill Cash, Hilton Smith, and Lennie Pearson of the Negro league outperformed Rizzuto, Berra, and King Kong Keller.

As a result, when the Latin American leagues sought players they were more likely to choose a Negro league star than a major-league star, and in Latin America the best Negro leaguers had reputations greater than in their own countries.

It was argued that blacks and whites would not be

able to get along as teammates on a major-league team. But in Latin America, Negro leaguers and major leaguers were teammates and sometimes developed friendships. White players as well as black players seemed to welcome the integrated setting. A Whitey Ford or Max Lanier in Mexico found companionship with Buck Leonard and Ray Dandridge. In Latin America, for reasons of language and custom alone, the Negro leaguers and major leaguers were thrust together.

It was argued that there was no way properly to evaluate the Negro league players. However, in Latin America the managers of Latin teams evaluated white and black players on performance and performance alone. The white players did indeed know about the best Negro leaguers. When Ted Williams was inducted into the Hall of Fame in 1966 he declared, "I hope that some day Satchel Paige and Josh Gibson will be voted into the Hall of Fame as symbols of the great Negro players who are not here only because they weren't given the chance."

It was argued that blacks were not up to major-league responsibilities. How, for example, would a black catcher handle a group of white pitchers? But in Latin America, black players exercised authority over white players routinely.

When integration finally arrived, Jackie Robinson was viewed as a special kind of black man. He was supposedly more intelligent, more moral, and more disciplined than other black ballplayers, and therefore more deserving of inclusion in the major leagues.

Perhaps the choice of Robinson was a wise strategy at the time. Robinson's UCLA connections and his articulate, sensitive demeanor won for the Dodgers and the so-called noble experiment the battle of public opinion. However, this choice was a great disservice to the other Negro league players. In Latin America, they had already proved their talents and demonstrated that most of the outstanding Negro leaguers were perfectly capable of playing major-league ball without incident, animosity, or undue emotional trauma.

Dusk and Dawn 7

The story of baseball integration has usually been told as though the Negro leagues hardly existed. This was the view promulgated by the two principals of integration, Jackie Robinson and Branch Rickey. Rickey, in public, had a strongly negative opinion of Negro baseball. "They are not leagues and have no right to expect organized baseball to respect them," he declared shortly after the Robinson signing. Rickey, a sometimes bombastic moralist, objected to the presence of gamblers in the Negro league front offices. "They [the leagues] have the semblance of a racket," he said.

Robinson, too, was highly critical of the Negro leagues. As a player he threatened to quit the Monarchs on several occasions in 1945, and once, only the intervention of Hilton Smith prevented his return to Los Angeles. Shortly after his rookie season as a Dodger, Robinson wrote a highly controversial assessment of Negro league baseball in *Ebony* called "What's Wrong with Negro Baseball," in which he castigated the Negro leagues, particularly for their arduous pace. In his official biography, *I Never Had It Made*, published shortly before his death, he gave a scant three pages to the Negro leagues. Robinson summarized his experience with these words: "For me, it turned out to be a pretty miserable way to make a buck."

While Jackie Robinson did not understand his debt to black baseball, Branch Rickey certainly did. Rickey had watched Negro baseball obtain a tenuous toehold in St. Louis in the early twenties, when the St. Louis Stars were one of Negro baseball's premier teams. Rickey's Cardinals benefited from the Negro league exhibitions in Sportsman's Park, the site of frequent Negro-league-vs.-major-league all-star spectacles. Famed for his close monitoring of players, Rickey knew that his better players barnstormed with mixed results against Negro league all-star aggregations, and that some of his players were teammates of Negro leaguers in the Caribbean. He was positively livid over Dizzy Dean's excesses on the road when Dean injured his arm. As a general manager Rickey heard and analyzed the recurrent rumors that integration was at hand. Rickey also was privy to the backstage discussions about Negro baseball that invariably punctuated league meetings.

Yet when sixty-five-year-old Branch Rickey signed twenty-five-year-old Jackie Robinson, the Negro leagues were hardly mentioned. The popular perception was that Branch Rickey's benevolence and Jackie Robinson's courage had joined to shatter the color barrier. Baseball integration was *not* perceived as an inevitable consequence of the history of Negro baseball and changing race relations in the United States, a view that would have emphasized the social rather than individual dimension of baseball's integration. Instead, the drama of two fascinating men, Rickey and Robinson—the stern but loving white father and the combative young black son—obscured, at least in the white world, the forces and people who had made integration possible.

That the distorted version of history persisted so long is strong testimony to Rickey's powerful image making, Robinson's alienation from the roots of the black baseball experience, and the negligible influence of black culture on white opinion makers.

The Negro leagues were founded with the aim, ultimately, of integrating the game. "We have to be ready when the day comes," Rube Foster told Elwood Knox, one of the league's founders in 1920. And the entire history of the Negro leagues unfolded as a perverse minuet in which the black leagues mimicked the whites in the expectation that, if they were professional enough, white baseball would invite them into the major leagues. The Negro leagues referred to themselves proudly as the "Negro major leagues" and tried to create a baseball climate conducive to assimilation.

In black circles there was constant agitation for baseball integration. "Colored ballplayers in the big leagues are inevitable," wrote a Negro newspaperman in 1930, but then added, "What loop club owner will have the courage and the wisdom to see the handwriting on the wall?" Syd Pollack, a major booking agent for black baseball and, in the 1940s, a team owner, flatly challenged the major leagues with his claim that "such teams as the Cuban Stars, Homestead Grays, Pittsburgh Crawfords, Chicago American Giants could today defeat either the Washington Senators or the New York Giants in a series of seven games." During World War II the rhetoric only intensified. "Does Hitler bar Negro ballplayers?" scrawled on Los Angeles's Wrigley Field wall was a reminder of the disparity between wartime rhetoric and wartime reality. The minor leagues weren't ignored in this campaign either. "Couldn't a traveling team of Negroes and Mexicans be included in the Coast League?" asked Neil McDonald in the *Los Angeles Record*.

By the 1930s black baseball had developed important white sportswriter allies. Westbrook Pegler in 1935 spoke out against the "silly unwritten law that bars dark Babe Ruths and Deans from the fame and money they deserve." Heywood Broun in New York and Shirley Povich in the nation's capital added their voices to the demand for baseball integration. And by the late thirties, there was sufficient interest in Negro baseball in the North to spur many prominent white sports columnists to devote at least one article a year to the injustices done black baseball players. "Spring is in the air. The crack of bat against ball in organized baseball's Southern training camps is almost audible away up here," began a piece in the *Newark Star Eagle* of March 26, 1938. "But it isn't...the famous names of the majors and minors that we're starting to write about, but...Men Nobody Knows—nobody that is but thousands of baseball fans from here to Chicago and along the Atlantic seaboard. We refer to the stars of the Negro National League." Slightly later Dan Parker of the *New York Daily News* editorialized that "there is no good reason why in a country that calls itself a Democracy, intolerance should exist on the sportsfield, that most democratic of all meeting places."

White baseball men, speaking from personal experience, rose to applaud Negro league players. Leo
Durocher, called "Lippy" by the Negro leaguers whom
he barnstormed against, said in an extremely important statement that he "would hire colored players if
they were not barred by the owners. I've seen a million
good ones." Durocher's association with Negro baseball dated from 1932, when an all-star team that he
had assembled was beaten 2-1 by Dave Malarcher's
Chicago American Giants in Cincinnati. Much later
Durocher raved about a bevy of good black ballplayers including shortstop Silvio Garcia, whom he discovered in Cuba. "Where the hell have you been
hiding?" Durocher exclaimed upon seeing Garcia. "If
we could just do a little something about that skin
color." Durocher reported to his major league-friends
with astonishment, "I've seen a shortstop in Cuba
blacker than my shoes, and Marty Marion can't carry
his glove!"

Not unexpectedly, the very best white players, the
Ruths, Greenbergs, DiMaggios, Deans, and Musials,
were especially generous in their praise of the Negro
leaguers. Babe Ruth himself noted that "the colorful-
ness of Negroes and their sparkling brilliancy on the
field would have a tendency to increase attendance
at games," though the phrasing suggests that the
statement was penned by his agent, Christy Walsh.

Compounding the pressure for baseball integration
was the increasing publicity given black-vs.-white encounters. Even prior to the Negro league, black baseball players won a kind of tainted immortality by
defeating white major-league teams. The most pun-
gent of these victories was Smokey Joe Williams's
1–0 win over the Phillies. Following an unsuccessful

World Series bid, the Phillies met the Lincoln Giants in October of 1915. Ahead one to nothing in the ninth, Williams loaded the bases. He then struck out Niehoff, Bancroft, and Paskert on nine straight pitches. Williams—clearly the ace of his era, the Negro league player who, more than any other, should not have been kept from the Hall of Fame—achieved many of his wins over intact major-league teams.

Until 1923 some of the white clubs played Negro league teams, made a little money, and more important, placated their underpaid players. Such contests had only one risk, namely, that the Negro leaguers might embarrass the big boys.

Embarrass them they did with disturbing frequency, particularly Connie Mack's Philadelphia Athletics, who maintained a lively rivalry with the Hilldale Club. "Nip Winters meted out a 6-1 trimming to the boys under the big tent," read a clipping in Clint Thomas's scrapbook. "The win made it two straight for the Darby Daiseys who combed the delivery of Lefty Grove, the high priced hurler of Connie Mack's tribe, for ten safe blows, including a quartet of doubles and a lusty home run from the bat of Oscar Charleston." The Hilldale vs. Athletics games were eagerly anticipated by Philadelphia fans and players alike. "I had a lot of fun and made a lot of friends with them players," said Judy Johnson. "I knew they were strapped for money, and I was too."

Commissioner Landis, who took office in 1920, knew it was impossible to prevent the major leaguers from barnstorming with black teams, because barnstorming dollars often were a sizable part of a ballplayer's income. Yet he was determined to diminish the meaning of Negro league victories, for he realized that they struck directly at the unwritten law excluding blacks from the big leagues.

Landis first clearly revealed his feelings on the race question in baseball when he ordered that all future barnstorming games involving major leaguers be billed as "all-star contests" and forbade the wearing of the major-league uniform during such games. All the Negro leagues were incensed, though there was nothing they could do except snipe at Landis derisively—something they continued to do for twenty-four years.

On several occasions when even the "all-star" designation proved embarrassing to the major leaguers, Landis cancelled barnstorming tours by executive order. In the twenties, the Chicago American Giants under Rube Foster regularly played a major-league-caliber team put together by Harry Heilmann. After Heilmann called Rube Foster to tell him that Landis had cancelled their games, Foster went directly to the commissioner and complained. "The very idea, Judge, that you can cancel this game," he began. "This is a chance that we have every year to play against your fellows, make a little extra money. Why do you do this?" Supposedly Landis responded, "Mr. Foster, when you beat our teams it gives us a black eye."

Still, Landis was only partially successful in this policy, and the black-vs.-white barnstorming games continued even after the Landis edict, and did exert pressure on the big leagues. The Negro leaguers in these encounters proved that their best players were easily of major-league caliber. In 1934, as part of Satchel Paige's All-Stars, Willie Wells, a shortstop, pitched against a major-league all-star team—the only pitching appearance of his career. When the game was called, due to darkness, it was tied 4-4.

One year Chet Brewer's Kansas City Royals defeated the Hollywood All-Stars six games in a row; the seventh game ended in a tie, called on account of darkness. The Hollywood All-Stars were really the Hollywood Stars, the Pacific Coast League champions, but with a single player added to comply with the Commissioner's policy. Although some in white baseball consistently categorized Negro league baseball as "triple-A at best," results of such games against triple-A-quality white teams like the Hollywood Stars overwhelmingly favored the Negro leagues. In general, the Negro league made mincemeat of triple-A teams.

In time, political support mobilized for baseball integration. The Commmunist Party took up the rallying cry of baseball integration, promoting the cause at meetings and in their newspapers. In 1942 *Daily Worker* sports editor Nat Lowe tried to arrange tryouts for several Negro league players. He induced Roy Campanella to leave the Elite Giants for a nonexistent tryout and he sent Dave Barnhill a telegram which read, "Have just arranged with William Benswanger, President of the Pittsburgh Pirates team, [for] try-out soon, won't you please get in touch with me. We can make full arrangements." The black players and the black press were unimpressed by the Communist campaigns. The only truly effective step the Communists took in promoting baseball integration was their decision to picket opening day at Yankee Stadium in 1945. They received a lot of publicity, particularly in New York, where Rickey watched with fascination. The Communist cadres went so far as to try to get Negro leaguers onto the picket lines with them. Barging into the dressing rooms of Yankee Stadium one Sunday when the Grays were in town, they confronted the Homestead Grays. "Don't you fellows think you can play in the major leagues?" they asked the semi-naked ballplayers. "Yeah, we think so," was the Grays' curt answer. "Wouldn't you fellows like to play in the major leagues?" they continued. "Yeah, we'd like to play in the major leagues," a few responded. "Why don't you protest?" the Communists finally asked. "You fellows demonstrate and protest. We're gonna play," was Buck Leonard's return. As the young Communists were leaving, one called, "Well, you're part of the movement." A Negro leaguer yelled back, "No, we're part of the game." The exchange illustrated how strongly the Negro leaguers felt bound to the game and the structure that had never returned the affection. Bob Feller, commenting on this ironic and unequal situation, said to the Negro leaguers, "You've given a whole lot to baseball but baseball hasn't given much to you."

Yet, the Communists were not alone. Much more substantial white political power, especially in New York City, began to agitate for integration. Mayor Fiorello LaGuardia headed an Anti-Discrimination Committee specifically working for baseball integration, and a bill to forbid racial discrimination in hiring was moving through the New York legislature at the time Rickey signed Robinson. LaGuardia, meeting regularly with Larry MacPhail of the Yankees, publicly hinted that integration of baseball was imminent in 1945, and the mayor tried to coerce an integration pledge from Rickey, Stoneham, and MacPhail. The unions, powerful in New York City, were also beginning to stir on the issue. "As early as the year 1944," Effa Manley recalled, "we in organized Negro baseball could see quite plainly the proverbial handwriting on the wall. The gathering storm of inevitable baseball integration was approaching rapidly, ever more relentlessly."

Larry MacPhail, then of the Dodgers, certainly was aware of the increasing influence of the Negro leagues. In 1942 he intimated that he would let the Dodgers play the Kansas City Monarchs after the season ended. Several years later, after Chandler assumed the commissionership, MacPhail wrote Chandler a secret memo in which he said, "We can't stick our heads in the sand like an ostrich and ignore the problem. If we do we will have colored players in the Minor Leagues in 1945 and in the Majors thereafter."

The Negro league owners welcomed this development. As early as 1942, J. L. Wilkinson said, "I think it would be a fine thing for the game, even though we would lose some of our stars." And he recommended Satchel Paige and Josh Gibson for that historic task. The same year Gibson's owner Cum Posey declared, "If it ever comes about we wouldn't stand in the way of any of our players." After integration Posey tried unsuccessfully to give Luke Easter to the Pirates—for nothing!

However, when the Negro league owners contemplated integration, they thought almost exclusively in terms of putting an entire Negro team into the majors. After all, this was how "integration" of the California winter league had been effected, and this was how the black-vs.-white barnstorming games were played.

In the early twenties, Rube Foster's Chicago American Giants had been the team with the best shot at integration. Foster cultivated white baseball men like John McGraw with the idea of being asked some day to form a major-league team. In the 1930s Syd Pollack, the power behind the Cuban Stars, argued that the Depression-induced decline in ticket sales warranted "placing an entire Colored club in a city like Cincinnati in the National League and Boston in the American League. Imagine the drawing power of a formidable Colored aggregation playing in New York, Pittsburgh, Brooklyn, Chicago, Philadelphia, St. Louis, and Detroit."

In the 1940s the most eligible pretender was J. L. Wilkinson, whose lifelong ambition it was to bring a major-league franchise, with black players, to Kansas City. Wilkinson's Monarchs were the top baseball attraction in the vast region west of that St. Louis-Chicago line which defined the westernmost limits of major-league baseball.

The Monarchs drew very well, in spite of a strong minor-league team in Kansas City, and Wilkinson was certain that (it was in the days before jet airplanes) Kansas City was the single most desirable place for baseball expansion. Cramming Muehlebach Staddium for Sunday games, drawing crowds wherever they went, the Monarchs even had a minor-league team— the so-called Little Monarchs—a traveling team captained most of the time by Newt Joseph. On the minor-league team a rookie could be tried, or a veteran worked into shape. The great Satchel Paige was sent out with the Little Monarchs to strengthen his arm in 1939.

No one reacted to the Jackie Robinson signing with more bitterness than Wilkinson. He was never compensated for Robinson, and ultimately his team surrendered more players to the majors than any other: Satchel Paige, Jackie Robinson, Hank Thompson, Ernie Banks, Elston Howard, Connie Johnson, Willard Brown, and others. Wilkinson saw his Kansas City dream disintegrate.

But Kansas City was not the only latter-day candidate for the honor of integrating major-league ball. Strong rumors circulated throughout 1944 and 1945 that an all-black team would be put into the major leagues to represent New York. As Buck O'Neil recounted the story, it "was not an integrated ballclub, but a black ballclub to go into the National League. A black club picking the best black ballplayers and playing around New York."

Adding impetus to the drive for baseball integration was the ever-more-apparent success of the Negro leagues. Every year the East-West game continued to prove that blacks would spend in large numbers on baseball entertainment. "Social pride and prejudice must be overlooked where a business enterprise is at stake," claimed Dr. J. B. Martin, prior to one East-West game. Dave Malarcher argued that the success of the East-West game was the single greatest influence on baseball integration. When someone asked him when integration was going to occur he would always answer, "When the major leagues know we can bring some people to the park. OK, when did it happen?" he asked rhetorically. "When the major leagues saw those fifty thousand Negroes in the ball park. Branch Rickey had something else on his mind than a little black boy. He had those crowds."

Everywhere the Negro leagues went during the war years, crowds flocked to Negro baseball. The Negro

leagues were quick to support the war effort in whatever way they could. "We know that baseball is essential," said Wilkinson to a *Kansas City Call* reporter.
"And we're going to play for war workers, both day
and nightgames and on Sundays." Once the Washington Senators had a crowd of less than five thousand
for a game against the Red Sox, but twenty-nine thousand turned out that same night to see Satchel Paige
pitch against the Homestead Grays. Another day that
summer, the Monarchs outdrew the White Sox by ten
thousand fans in Chicago.

But of even greater significance than the gradual
strengthening of Negro baseball at the gate was a
series of dramatic public incidents that indicated that
change was at hand.

The first of these was the Jake Powell affair—the
first time that blacks flexed their muscles in front of
the baseball establishment and emerged triumphant.
On July 29, 1938, during a pre-game radio interview
before a Yankee-White Sox game in Chicago, Yankee
outfielder Jake Powell, asked what he did during the
off-season, replied that "he worked as a policeman in
Dayton, Ohio, where he kept in shape by cracking
niggers over the head." Powell was immediately cut
off and an apology extended by announcer Bob Elson.
Shortly thereafter, in response to the Chicago black
community's outrage, Powell was suspended for ten
days. However, the story did not die. Protest groups
in black organizations were formed. They demanded
that Powell be banned from baseball for life. When
Powell, after his suspension, returned to Chicago, he
required a police escort and was kept out of the line-
up. When Powell played in Washington, he was greeted
with a hail of bottles. In New York six thousand signed

a petition supporting the lifetime ban, and the *Amsterdam News* suggested a one-year boycott of Ruppert's beer.

Black opinion argued that the incident demonstrated the need for integration, and that racial feeling was higher in Chicago than at any time since the 1919 race riots. "Jake Powell is the type that causes race riots," insisted Faye Young.

White sportswriters, sympathetic to the Negro league fight for integration, used the incident to excoriate the baseball establishment. "Powell got his cue from the very men whose hired disciplinarian had benched him for an idle remark," Westbrook Pegler asserted. The *New York Post* in an editorial characterized the owners who criticized Powell as smug hypocrites. "Through their mouthpiece they express outward horror at Powell's hasty and uncouth comment," said the *Post*. "Then they calmly proceed with their own economic boycott against this minority people." Finally the pressure became so severe that Powell went to the *Defender's* offices to beg forgiveness, though his plea did include the gratuitous claim that "I have two members of your race taking care of my home while myself and wife are away and I think they are two of the finest people in the world." The black community was not placated. In fact, Powell's appearance in major-league parks invariably caused minor disturbances and resulted in the need for more police. In Washington, with its large black population, the bottle throwing caused the introduction of paper beer cups. The Yankees tried to trade Powell, with no takers; and when in 1940 Powell slipped from the majors due to injury, the Yankee management was delighted.

The incident was important; it demonstrated the growing power and cohesiveness of the black community. Even the mighty Yankees felt compelled to bow to black opinion. It also indicated the inherent instability in segregated baseball, where one intemperate remark had immediately embroiled the baseball world in controversy.

The second dramatic incident resulted in the extraction of a formal statement by the commissioner, denying the color barrier. 1942 was an extraordinary year for Negro league baseball. With full black employment and the Mexican league inroads a year off, Negro league attendance was booming. Meanwhile, white attendance was actually dropping. One of the weakest major-league franchises was the Washington Senators. Already in 1939, to help meet expenses, Clark Griffith had arranged for the Homestead Grays to use Griffith Stadium as a second home field. Then it was rumored that to boost Washington's sagging fortunes, Josh Gibson and Buck Leonard might soon join the Senators. Clark Griffith asked Josh Gibson and Buck Leonard to his office between games of a Negro league doubleheader. "You boys like to be in the major leagues?" he asked. "You like to be on the Senators?" Griffith questioned. Both Gibson and Leonard naturally said yes. "Well nobody wants to be the first to take blacks into the major leagues," Griffith sighed, "but we know you boys can play ball; you boys can play good baseball, and some of us would like to have you."

Although Griffith did not make a formal offer, this encounter heightened the rumors swirling through the black baseball world. With the *Pittsburgh Courier* leading the way, black newspapers tried to arrange tryouts with major-league teams, each Negro newspaper advancing their own favorite. Josh Gibson, Satchel Paige, Willie Wells, Leon Day, and Roy Campanella were all discussed. The *Courier* realized that Pittsburgh, with a dismal Pirate franchise, a weak-willed owner in Bill Benswanger, and a glorious black baseball tradition, was a likely candidate; the *Courier* reporters started courting Benswanger fiercely and got Benswanger to admit that it might be a good thing for the game to add the Negro stars to the various big-league teams. Shortly thereafter Leo Durocher made the historic comment that he would use blacks were it not for the owners' opposition. With the well-known, quotable Durocher on record, the proponents of integration doubled their efforts. Finally, with the issue splattered across all the major dailies, Landis was forced to act. Speaking directly of Durocher he said that "certain managers in organized baseball have been quoted as saying the reason Negroes are not playing organized baseball is [that the] commissioner would not permit them to do so." He went on, "Negroes are not barred from organized baseball by the commissioner and never have been during the twenty-one years I have served as commissioner. There is no rule in organized baseball prohibiting their participation and never has been to my knowledge." If Durocher wanted to "sign one, or twenty-five Negro players it was alright." At the same time, Ford Frick added that he "would welcome a Negro player in the National League," a comment sure to raise the eyebrow of the newest National League general manager, Branch Rickey.

Since Benswanger's comment made him the logical place to start, the *Courier*'s Wendell Smith, who later selected Robinson for Rickey, chose four players to upgrade the lowly Pirates. Willie Wells and Sam Bankhead, both shortstops, were chosen because "the Pirates have a hole at shortstop as big as the Broadway Limited"; the others were catcher Josh Gibson and pitcher Leon Day. Satchel Paige was not recommended because, in Ric Roberts's phrase, "he was more undependable than a secondhand pair of suspenders." Negro baseball men waited anxiously for the 1942 season to end in the expectation that the Pirates would give the foursome tryouts. However, these never materialized for reasons that may never be known.

At the same time Nat Lowe was tempting Barnhill and Campanella. Working on Phillie owner Jerry Nugent too, Lowe claimed to have a tryout arranged with both Philadelphia and Pittsburgh. Just the offer of a tryout was enough to cause massive interest in black-baseball circles; Campanella took his tryout so seriously that he jumped the Baltimore Elite Giants. When the tryouts fell through, he limped back to the Elites, quietly paid a fine, and served a short Negro league suspension.

Such "tryouts" weren't confined to the majors, either. In 1943 Clarence "Pants" Rowland, head of the Pacific Coast League, announced that Chet Brewer, Howard Esterling, and Nate Moreland would all get a shot at the Pacific Coast League. Two weeks later, for unknown reasons, his published offer was rescinded. The following year in the waning days of the season, Oakland Oaks owner Vince Devicenzi told his manager, Johnny Vergez, to give Chet Brewer a chance.

Devicenzi, who had grown up in an integrated Oakland neighborhood, was thinking perhaps of stimulating late-season attendance; though in any case he enjoyed the reputation of being the most liberal, fairminded white baseball man on the Coast. In response to the prodding of *Los Angeles Sentinel* reporter Hallie Harding, Devicenzi told Harding, "Why don't you find some colored guys you think can play. I'll tell my manager to put 'em in uniform next time we come to Los Angeles." Harding chose Chet Brewer, the most prominent black player on the Coast. When they entered the Oaks dressing room at Wrigley Field, prior to a game between the Oaks and the Los Angeles Angels, Johnny Vergez, the Oaks manager, was stunned, and he called Devicenzi to complain. According to Brewer, the heated dressing-room phone conversation led to the rejection of Brewer and the firing of Vergez during the off season.

Brewer—well liked, distinguished looking, well mannered—was a logical choice to integrate West Coast baseball. In fact, shortly before Jackie Robinson signed with the Dodgers, Brewer got a second chance when he was offered a position as player/coach at Bakersfield, a Cleveland farm team deep in the minor leagues. The Minor League Commissioner gave his approval for the acquisition of Brewer. However, Cleveland Indian General Manager Roger Peckinpah refused, saying, "Hell no, I'm not going to stick my neck out."

Branch Rickey got a taste of things, too. In 1944 Joe Bostic, sports editor of the Negro *People's Voice*, appeared at the Dodger spring-training camp in upstate New York. Bostic brought a cameraman and embarrassed Rickey into watching Newark Eagle pitcher Terris McDuffie and New York Cuban first baseman Showboat Thomas work out. Rickey watched sullenly, engaged Bostic in a heated exchange about appropriate ways to integrate baseball, and rejected the twosome.

Another unsuccessful effort involved Jackie Robinson himself, who tried out with the Boston Red Sox in 1945 prior to his signing with the Dodger organization. Boston liberals had become increasingly angered by the intransigence of organized baseball, and finally they decided to join with traditional opponents of Sunday baseball in Boston unless some blacks were given the opportunity to make a Boston team. The Red Sox approached the venerable Wendell Smith, who then brought Jackie Robinson, Sam Jethroe, and Marvin Williams for Red Sox tryouts on April 16, 1945. "There is no doubt about it that they are ballplayers," Coach Hugh Duffy said of their Fenway tryout. "They looked good to me." But, again, nothing materialized.

While there was no owner yet willing to stick his neck out, there was a prospective owner who already had a plan. Bill Veeck, the flamboyant huckstering son of ex-Cub owner William Veeck, Sr., wanted to get involved in major-league baseball. He arranged a financial package, bolstered with C.I.O. money, and successfully negotiated the purchase of the ailing Philadelphia Phillies franchise in 1943 from Jerry Nugent. Like the other teams, Philadelphia was suffering from a manpower shortage created by the war.

Unknown to Nugent, Veeck had already formulated a plan to bring a pennant to Philadelphia. Most of the good players had gone off to fight in the war. "The only fellows left were aged, ancient, injured or 4F," said Veeck, exaggerating only slightly.

In the latter years of the war, Cincinnati, for example, had eighteen players who were 4F—medically unfit for military service. Joe Nuxhall went from junior high straight to the majors. One-armed Pete Grey batted over .200 for the St. Louis Browns in 1945. Phil Wrigley was so terrified about the manpower situation that he organized the All-American Girls Baseball Association, and had women playing hardball in miniskirts, in case the manpower drain destroyed the leagues. "How do you think I felt when I saw a one-armed outfielder?" asked Chet Brewer. Under such circumstances, the great untapped reservoir of talent in the Negro leagues was more obvious than ever.

With only three confidants—his partner Rudy Schaefer, *Courier* sportswriter Wendell Smith, and Abe Saperstein, his friend from their slumming "black-and-tan joints" days in Chicago—Veeck prepared to stock the Phillies with experienced Negro leaguers. Saperstein was as close to black baseball as any white man except Wilkinson, and he knew exactly whom to get for Veeck. Satchel Paige, Josh Gibson, Buck Leonard, Willie Wells, and Ray Dandridge were all tapped for that team—a certain pennant winner.

Veeck decided that he had better inform the commissioner of his plan, for he feared an intemperate outburst. Veeck stopped at the commissioner's office on the way back to Chicago where he had a seemingly cordial meeting with Landis, and then headed straight for the Broadway Limited. When he arrived home the next morning he discovered that the Phillies had been sold to the National League overnight. Veeck immediately called Nugent, who responded, "What are you going to do, sue me?"

So long as Landis remained commissioner, as successor Happy Chandler later put it, "There wasn't going to be any black boys in the league." Kenesaw Mountain Landis was a flamboyant judge who became comissioner in large part because he aided the Major League in its antitrust battle with the Federal League. He was also one of the most reversed judges in District Court history. He was also circumspect enough never to be caught in a public admission of his racism.

The death of Landis, late in 1944, provided the necessary precondition for baseball integration. When the moguls of baseball reached into the Senate and plucked Albert "Happy" Chandler from that body to become their new Commissioner, it is doubtful that they thought much of the integration problem. If they did, they probably thought they were appointing just another Southerner. What they knew they were buying was political clout; what they didn't realize was that Chandler possessed political sensitivity, too.

For the summer game, the war years were difficult. The owners of baseball toyed with asking for special draft exemptions for their ballplayers, but decided that exemptions would be a political mistake. They viewed with trepidation the war's encroachment on their scheduling prerogatives, and they objected to the wartime-travel restrictions that forced spring training north and made road trips arduous. They wanted a commissioner who had pull on Capitol Hill— and baseball enthusiast Happy Chandler seemed ideal, though the owners really knew little about him.

But there was someone in Washington who understood Chandler, someone with sense enough to realize the opportunity at hand. Ric Roberts, sportswriter for the *Pittsburgh Courier* based in Washington, was an untutored genius with a pen—his prose was every bit the equal of Grantland Rice's or Damon Runyon's. His drawings, moreover, stamped him as a cartoonist of raw power.

As soon as Roberts heard the news that Chandler had been selected the new commissioner, he rushed to the Hill. Catching Chandler, already a casual acquaintance, he asked the Senator directly, "What about black boys?" Chandler was the chairman of the Military Affairs Sub-Committee. He had just returned, shaken, from the battlefields. He said to Roberts, "If they can fight and die on Okinawa, Guadalcanal, in the South Pacific, they can play baseball in America." And the crusty Senator added, "And when I give my word you can count on it."

Roberts, his prayers answered, rushed to a telephone and placed a call to Wendell Smith in Pittsburgh. "Get your streamers out," he shouted. The next day the story was front-page news in black newspapers.

Chandler was the answer to the Negro league's prayers, for according to the arcane structures of baseball organization, the commissioner had to approve each contract individually and could thus veto any arrangement not to his liking. Landis had used his power adroitly; all the owners had feared him. Then into the commissioner's office walked Chandler, a gentleman of the old school, who, when the black-baseball issue arose, said proudly, "I wasn't running for anything, and I wasn't running away from anything either."

The death of Landis and the assumption of power

by Chandler eased the task of any potential integrator. Whereas Rickey, Benswanger, Griffith, or any other potential integrator of baseball had had to convince not only the other owners but also the commissioner, now at least that final hurdle was removed—a change that would prove to be of great importance to Jackie Robinson and Branch Rickey a year later.

Why didn't Clark Griffith improve his club by signing Josh Gibson or Buck Leonard? Why didn't Bill Benswanger upgrade the lowly Pirates or Jerry Nugent compete more effectively in Philadelphia? The weaker team in multi-team cities such as New York, Chicago, Philadelphia, Boston, and St. Louis always stood to gain by signing a black.

One explanation is that no other owner had the guts to be first. The Yankees and Cardinals, for example, were winning pennants and earning profits and they had no reason to tamper with uncertain, and perhaps financially dangerous experiments. The weaker teams, which perhaps were weak due to weak leadership, were afraid to act. Clark Griffith preferred a pale Cuban to Josh Gibson.

Second, most owners wanted no part of integration and many were, to put it bluntly, racists. In 1946, when it appeared that Robinson would join the Dodgers the following season, a secret report on baseball integration was prepared for the owners. Written by Ford Frick (National League President), Sam Breadon (Cardinals), Phil Wrigley (Cubs), William Harridge (American League President), Larry MacPhail (Yankees) and Tom Yawkey (Red Sox), the report urged that Negroes be excluded from the major leagues. The vote on the resolution was 15-1, with only Rickey favoring integration. All copies of the document, save one, were then gathered and destroyed. (Commissioner Chandler made known the facts in the 1980s.) There was also an economic reason why owners didn't support integration: as the Negro leagues prospered, the major leagues benefited by renting their stadiums. In the secret document prepared for the owners, it was admitted that the Yankees made over one hundred thousand dollars a year from Negro league baseball—a figure larger than the profit realized by many teams.

Finally, there was the fear that if the dam were broken, a flood of Negro league players would overwhelm the major leagues. Judy Johnson, one of the most respected figures in baseball, recalled that his "first scouting job was with Mr. Connie Mack's Athletics, and we were very good friends. And I asked him one day why they wouldn't hire some Negroes since we [blacks] beat them [whites] all the time, and he said, 'Well, there just too many of you boys to go in at that.'"

Rickey, with his excellent intelligence, observed the ferment in organized baseball over the race question. He saw that integration would be impossible to avoid, particularly in New York, where white opposition to segregated baseball was strongest. Thus, if the Jackie Robinson signing, announced on October 23, 1945, came as a delightful surprise to most black Americans, black baseball was not surprised. What did surprise black America and black baseball men in general was the selection of Jackie Robinson to be the first black in the majors.

Robinson's career in Negro baseball had been extraordinarily brief. In the winter of 1944 Robinson had approached the bullpen in Wrigley Field where

Hilton Smith and Pepper Bassett were warming up. After introducing himself, he came to the point and asked Hilton Smith if he could get him a job. Smith called J. L. Wilkinson. Wilkinson invited Robinson to join the Monarchs at spring training in Houston. According to the oral tradition of baseball lore, it was already known that Robinson was a fine baseball player even though he had made his national reputation in football as "rabbit Robinson," the fullback of the UCLA Bruins, the man who punched holes for another great UCLA black athlete, tailback Kenny Washington.

With the Monarchs, Robinson tried out at shortstop the position he preferred. He was assigned veteran Newt Allen, who was to assess his talents. Allen piled Jackie and the rest of the Monarchs onto a bus and they headed for San Antonio to play Kelly Airfield. In the game Robinson hit well, and he proved that he was smart by handling some complicated baserunning chores and picking up the deliberately changing signs. But, Allen recalled, "he couldn't play shortstop" because occasionally he would have to range to his right and come quickly over the top, "with a lot on the ball. And Jackie didn't have that." Afterwards, Allen met with Wilkinson. Although strong in his praise, reporting that Robinson "could run, and he could hit, and most of all he could think," Allen was adamant that he should not play shortstop.

Wilkinson agreed, and Robinson was made a utility infielder, with the idea of grooming him as Newt Allen's successor at second base. However, when Negro league all-star shortstop Jesse Williams hurt his arm, Robinson was the best stand-in available and he was given the Monarch shortstop job.

He performed fairly well. Hilton Smith rated the
1945 Monarch shortstop as "an average fielder; he
could hit and he knew baseball. But we had better
ballplayers. Our third baseman Serrell was a better
ballplayer, Moody at first was a better hitter." Buck
Leonard recalled that "we had a whole lot better ballplayers than Jackie, but Jackie was chosen 'cause he
had played with white boys."

Robinson's personality was something of an enigma,
too. He never drank and he never smoked, and when
the Monarchs went carousing he would remain in the
hotels and play pinball or checkers. He did not fit in
very well, and his combative nature resulted in several nasty exchanges between Robinson and other Negro leaguers. He was not a popular player in Kansas
City, and, clearly, he was evaluating his own feelings
about the Negro league. When he heard that Kenny
Washington, his UCLA teammate—and his rival for
the role as most prominent UCLA black—was con-
sidering seeking a Monarch job too, he quietly passed
the word that there was room on the Monarchs for
only one ex-UCLA football star.

When news came that Jackie Robinson had signed
a Dodger organization contract, there was joy and
some concern among the Negro leaguers. A few felt
that Josh Gibson or Satchel Paige better deserved the
opportunity; that it should have been someone with
an established record and reputation, someone certain to succeed. (More than one Negro leaguer attrib-
uted Josh Gibson's death to his "grieving" at being
passed over.)

Many more were disturbed that Robinson, in terms
of playing skills, just wasn't the best choice. Any public expression of negativism, though, was out of the

question, especially since the Negro masses immediately enshrined Robinson. Even Jimmie Crutchfield, who spotted Robinson's ability during spring training, was somewhat disturbed by his rookie status. "How would you feel seeing a rookie selected?" he asked. Crutchfield was well aware of how long it took to season a ballplayer. Crutchfield knew that his teammate Sug Cornelius baffled Robinson easily by throwing him "all junk" instead of the outside fastball that his stance seemed to call for and that Robinson hit so well.

Despite immense difficulties that have been well documented in an extensive literature on Robinson's first Dodger years, Robinson became a great success on the field. He was a Rookie of the Year, and later a Most Valuable Player. Although on one occasion in 1946 he told his Negro league friends that he was coming back to the Negro league the following year because "he couldn't take it," he did take it, and rightly became an American hero in doing so.

As the years passed his fame grew. Yet he never gave Negro baseball credit for paving his way. Why should he have? For him, Negro baseball was "low salaries, sloppy umpiring, and questionable business connections of many of the team owners." He remembered "rooms dingy and dirty, and hotels of the cheapest kind." But his expectations of athletics were based upon his UCLA experience and then his career with the Dodger organization. For a mere season, and not a particularly noteworthy season at that, Robinson had sampled Negro baseball and found it wanting. In sum, the Negro leagues were not an important part of his life.

For Robinson, all depended upon the break that Branch Rickey gave him. Ever since he had started playing baseball in Pasadena, California, he had "wanted to play in organized baseball. I dreamed of being on a big league team," he told the world. And what of Branch Rickey? "I will always believe [Rickey] had reasons purely democratic in nature," Robinson answered.

Rickey's own characterization of his motives was more complex. "I couldn't face my God any longer knowing that his black children were held separate and distinct from his white children in a game that has given me all I own," he once said. But he also went to great lengths to argue that signing Robinson was simply good business.

Clearly, after the public announcement that Robinson was assigned to the Dodger's Montreal farm team, the man whose moral rigidity and certainty had earned him the nickname "Mahatma" acted with great courage and firmness to prevent any hint of a Dodger insurrection and to shield Robinson from racist incidents whenever possible. Rickey became a saint in the eyes of blacks, in part by skillfully appealing to widely held sentiments in the black community. Rickey insisted that Robinson needed and wanted no special privileges, but should have no inherent disadvantages either. This was, of course, what the black community wanted: simple justice. In retrospect, it is clear that without the personal strength, religious-based conviction, and wise leadership of Branch Rickey, baseball integration would have been a much more difficult and painful process.

In the course of the dramatic, closely scrutinized,

intensely emotional experience of baseball integration, the Negro leagues and a scrutiny of Rickey's
motives were bypassed. Rickey, who was "obviously
irked" whenever his prior treatment of the Negro
leagues was mentioned, seemed, at least after October
1945, to believe that "this is a movement that cannot
be stopped by anyone...the world is moving on and
they will move with it."

But what were Rickey's motives? Was there another
scenario lurking in the history of the Negro leagues?
For after all, Rickey was an unlikely integrator of the
game. Rickey was sixty-one years old when he joined
the Dodgers as general manager in late 1942. He left
St. Louis after spending nearly a lifetime building the
Cardinals into a powerhouse through his innovative
farm system. Yet his interest in Negro baseball was
minor at best. In all the rich lore of black-baseball
history, there is not one story that depicts Branch
Rickey as taking a real interest in Negro baseball in
St. Louis, whose St. Louis Stars were one of Negro
baseball's finer teams. When Rickey's ace Dizzy Dean
met Satchel Paige in confrontations of nearly mythic
proportions, Rickey said nothing. Some of the most
famous black-vs.-white barnstorming clashes occurred in segregated Sportsmen's Park, and, as Wendell Smith insisted, that policy of segregation was a
blot on Rickey's record. On September 1, 1945, Smith
wrote that according to Rickey, St. Louis could support only one team. "St. Louis cannot support two
major league clubs?" questioned Smith. "There is a
vast Negro population there, and it has not got into
the habit of supporting major-league baseball. Sportsmen's Park was the only major league park to have a
Jim Crow section," Smith observed. And "it is signif-

icant too, that this policy was rigidly enforced while
the same Mr. Rickey was bossing the St. Louis Cardinals."

Rickey's first mention of scouting black players occurred in January of 1943 when, at a closed meeting,
in urging the expansion of the Dodger scouting system, he said, "It might include scouting one or two
Negroes."

But given the history of integration efforts, by 1943
any prudent man would have begun to evaluate black
talent. Certainly Rickey, whose greatest achievements
involved scouting, would have wanted to protect himself if he suspected that the National League Pirates
or even the downtrodden Phils were preparing to take
black players.

In 1945 Rickey announced the formation of the
United States League—a black league composed of
Philadelphia, Chicago, Toledo, Detroit, and Brooklyn.
(Rickey's team, the Brooklyn Brown Dodgers, would
use Ebbets Field as their home field, of course.) To
the consternation and anger of the black owners, it
appeared that Rickey was trying to upstage the Negro
leagues without actually advancing integration. As
J. L. Wilkinson bitterly exclaimed: "We want Negroes
in the major leagues if they have to crawl to get there.
Rickey is no Abraham Lincoln or FDR and we won't
accept him as dictator of Negro baseball." Rickey
claimed that "he was going to make every attempt to
have the U.S. League become a working member of
organized baseball." Rickey's motive in this case was,
in all likelihood, to establish an organization that
would give him control of, and first crack at, the pool
of black talent, should the integration of the major
leagues occur. Had his venture succeeded, however,

it would also have meant the end of black control of black baseball.

The black owners, once their immediate anger subsided, decided that Rickey's league posed no threat; the major-league owners would not assist Rickey, out of fear that Rickey if successful would control black players at their source. The Negro league owners also thought that other white major-league owners would hesitate to jeopardize their lucrative relations with the established Negro league teams. Their reasoning "proved totally correct," according to Effa Manley. "Unable to get suitable playing sites and vital fan support on a widespread scale, the United States League did, in fact, fold after about two months."

Only after the failure of the United States League did Rickey turn his thoughts toward the formal, direct integration of baseball. But the bizarre, shortlived United States League holds the key to any reconsideration of Branch Rickey's motives in integrating baseball. Why did Rickey want to establish the United States League? Perhaps, as his biographer suggests, to cover his scouting of Negro baseball. But that was certainly an unnecessary way to scout, particularly when scouting Negro leaguers in Cuba, Puerto Rico, Venezuela, and California under the guise of scouting white players was so much easier. By the late forties, whites were not that uncommon at black ballparks, either.

Bill Veeck, who came so close to being the first to do what Rickey did, and who was the first integrator of the American League, has another explanation. "Rickey wanted money," Veeck said. "The Yankees and the Giants split [the Negro league money] and

Rickey wanted a third of it. The Yankees and Giants would not give him a third. And that is how he signed Jackie Robinson." Ever since the 1934 Brooklyn Eagles had left Brooklyn for Newark, Brooklyn had been without a black team. The New York Black Yankees used Yankee Stadium and the New York Cubans used the Polo Grounds, but only very rarely did the Dodgers receive extra money from a black exhibition game in Ebbets Field. With ten to twenty percent of the gate and attendance of between twenty and thirty thousand, Negro baseball was extraordinarily rewarding to the major leagues. That $100,000 Yankee advantage over the Dodgers must have loomed especially large.

Perhaps Rickey wanted to gain the income from black use of Ebbets Field? Did Rickey have Jackie Robinson sign a Dodger organization contract to manage that black team, selecting Robinson because he had so many of his own characteristics? They were after all both fiery competitors who hated to lose, but who controlled themselves with a rigid internal puritanism. Rickey once defined the ideal ballplayer as one who "will break both of your legs if you happen to be standing in his path to second base." They were both teetotalers, out of step with the hard-living men who made up the bulk of their professional colleagues. Once the United States League had folded, Rickey, whose legal training caused him to insist on the sanctity of contracts, may have still had a valid contract with Robinson.

At least such was Bill Veeck's belief. Bill Veeck always felt that Rickey used Robinson to solve his Ebbets Field problem. "Jackie wanted a three-year contract with the Brown Dodgers," claimed Veeck.

When the Brown Dodgers folded, "Rickey had three more years of Robinson. He then sent Robinson to Montreal."

But with a three-year contract, a one-year contract, or just a gentleman's agreement, it is possible that Rickey decided to send Robinson to the Montreal farm team to gain black fans for Brooklyn whether Robinson made the Dodgers or not. And there was considerable expert opinion suggesting that Robinson was not a major leaguer; certainly not at shortstop, and probably not at a new and difficult position such as second or first.

This supposition accords with the testimony of the Negro leaguers. In particular, it corroborates the account given by Jackie Robinson's roommate, Hilton Smith, of the first Rickey/Robinson meeting. Smith reported that Robinson said, "Branch Rickey asked me how would I like to manage the Brooklyn black ballclub."

In Rickey's own authorized biography, written in 1957 by his confidant, Arthur Mann, Robinson is quoted as saying he remembers nothing of their meeting but the goldfish bowl in Rickey's office and the fact that he felt very much like that fish. Mann quotes Rickey as saying, "You were brought here, Jackie, to play for the Brooklyn organization. Perhaps on Montreal to start with." There are two possible interpretations of this reconstructed conversation. One, the straightforward traditional interpretation, is that Rickey wanted Robinson to integrate baseball, told him so at the August 28 meeting, and then asked him to keep it quiet. The second interpretation is that he signed Robinson to a Brooklyn organization contract, while, with his "genius for indecision," he debated the fate of the Brown Dodgers and the impact of the impending political storm. When he came to the realization that the Brown Dodgers were a failure and that the political situation in New York made integration inevitable—soon—he decided to send Robinson to Montreal. By sending the young player to Montreal the crafty Rickey might be all things to all people. Through this tactic he immediately neutralized the political pressure placed on him by the LaGuardia Committee, on which New York Black Yankee owner Bill Robinson served. He also neutralized the Quinn-Ives Anti-Discrimination Committee of the New York Legislature, which was asking all major-league clubs in New York to sign an anti-discrimination statement. At the same time, considerable professional opinion thought that Robinson was not of major-leaguer caliber and that he would in fact never reach the Dodgers. Shortly after he signed, Bob Feller, who played against Robinson in California said, "I honestly can't see any chance for Robinson at all."

Rumors about Robinson's meeting with Rickey—for which Robinson asked and received the permission of the Monarchs—circulated through black baseball and the sports pages of the black newspapers. Wendell Smith, writing on September 8, 1945, said, "It does not seem logical he should call in a rookie player to discuss the future organization of Negro baseball," alluding to Rickey's first account of their discussion. Rickey at the time had said, "I am very interested in the promotion of Negro baseball. I would like to have him on a Negro team if I invest in one." Under the headline "Rickey, Robinson Hold Mystery Conference," Branch Rickey was quoted as saying, "We did not discuss the possibility of Robinson becoming

a member of the Brooklyn Dodger organization—that
problem was not touched."

This denial, if truthful, might explain why, consid-
ering that Rickey's scouting of Negro baseball was
very extensive, the critical scouting of Robinson was
not given real priority, and took place only "in late
August 1945." According to Mann, Rickey sent Clyde
Sukeforth to a Kansas City Monarch-Chicago American Giant game "to see that game and especially a
shortstop named Robinson. There is some doubt as
to whether he has a really good arm. Speak to him
before the game and ask him to throw the ball overhand from the hole in practice." (Robinson's shoulder
was hurt and he didn't even play!)

Of course, once Rickey made the decision to send
Robinson to Montreal, he had every incentive to emphasize his long-term plan for baseball integration
and to ignore the United States League escapade or
the Negro league's historic role. But why would he
gamble everything, against the known opposition of
his fellow owners, on a player with a fatal flaw at the
one position he normally played?

A second unusual event surfaced with the testimony
of Newark Eagle owner Effa Manley, wife of Jersey
City numbers baron Abe Manley, and perhaps the
dominant personality of the Negro National League
leadership. In 1945 Effa received a call from Rickey's
secretary inviting her to his personal box for an Ebbets Field game. Naturally, Effa Manley was most
curious as to the reason for this invitation. By any
standard the rigid, moralistic, elderly Rickey and the
vivacious, attractive Effa Manley, who had married
a black gangster twenty years her senior, must have
made an unusual pair. Manley was escorted to Rick-

ey's box. "Only awkward silence" ensued, according to her. "I was sure he wanted to talk about something," she reported. This non-meeting occurred just prior to Rickey's formation of the United States League. It is possible that Rickey contemplated asking Mrs. Manley to move her team from the Yankee-owned Ruppert Stadium in Newark back to Brooklyn; it is possible that Rickey sought information about the Negro leagues and their response to his United States League. It is even possible that Rickey hoped to co-opt the Manleys into the U.S. League. What seems impossible is that Rickey was bent merely on exchanging pleasantries.

The greatest irony of the entire United States League caper was Rickey's actual conception of the league. One of the teams was a revitalized Crawfords, owned by Gus Greenlee, who had been trying unsuccessfully to get back into the Negro league. In the late thirties, Greenlee's interest in Negro baseball waned as his interest in boxing promotion grew. His champion, John Henry Lewis, marched forward in the rankings and he grew tired of the turmoil of Negro league team ownership. He had watched nine of his best players skip the country within weeks during 1937. By 1945, however, Greenlee had changed his mind and now wanted back into Negro baseball. Only in 1945, the powerful owner of the Homestead Grays, Cumberland Posey, wanted no competition. So Greenlee's chance for baseball ownership rested entirely on Rickey's scheme.

But why "Mahatma" Rickey, who knew Greenlee's history and sources of income, would enter an arrangement with him, remains a matter for speculation. Would Rickey really have a business arrangement for a year with a known gangster if the United States League was merely a ruse? And was it moral to exploit those one hundred-odd ballplayers used in the United States League, including the first Brown Dodger manager, the magnificent Oscar Charleston?

Of course, once the decision to send Robinson to Montreal was made, Rickey, in the main, received (and deserved) nothing but credit. Rickey was smart enough to perceive the enormous benefit the Dodgers were beginning to reap from signing Robinson. Not only did whites remain loyal for the most part, but the Dodgers received a spontaneous, deep, and passionate embrace from all sectors of black society. Baseball integration was a success.

But baseball integration also meant a few difficult, bittersweet years for the Negro leaguers. Though they participated in the general euphoria that swept through black America as the direct result of the Robinson signing, their joy was tempered by their own hardheaded assessment of Robinson's abilities. "We had a whole lot of better ballplayers than Jackie," insisted Buck Leonard, "but we thought he could get the job done." "Jackie wasn't a good player, a finished player," declared Monte Irvin in speaking of Robinson's skill at the time he joined the Dodgers. "He only got good after he got to the major leagues." The consensus among the players expressed by Hilton Smith, was that "it all came down to this, he had played with white boys, he had played football with white boys."

At Montreal, Jackie Robinson was shifted to first base, where he had an adequate year defensively and a terrific year at the plate. Nonetheless, Rickey's public statements in 1946 were extremely circumspect, and he did not announce until spring training the following year that he was bringing Robinson to the major leagues. Negro league veteran Willie Wells saw Robinson that spring and was stunned to see him at second base. Robinson was less than enthusiastic himself. "Wells," he said, "they got me playing second base, and I don't even know how to pivot." Wells immediately offered his assistance. "I'll meet you out here after practice and I'll show you how to pivot," he volunteered.

Despite Robinson's temper and his general aloofness from the Negro leaguers, the players of the Negro league admired him greatly. They admired his courage in silently enduring those traumatic first seasons, and they admired what he had achieved prior to entering baseball.

But the Negro leaguers had ulterior motives, too. They hoped that integration would be rapid. They knew that if Robinson made it, there were, in the opinion of Monte Irvin, "ten, twenty, thirty guys who could just step right in." Before, when they had thought about baseball integration, they had assumed that an entire Negro team would do the integrating. Though a Negro team meant more black players than a single Jackie Robinson, it also meant less "social" integration. After Jackie Robinson signed and four other Negro leaguers were quickly added to the Dodger organization (Newcombe, Campanella, Roy Partlow, and John Wright), the Negro leaguers thought wholesale integration was at hand. Unlike the owners, they did not particularly care whether integration was individual or by means of a single black team as long as the better players were selected.

But the pace of integration proved tantalizingly slow. Only the Dodgers and Cleveland Indians seemed willing to take players on merit; the rest of the teams, when they made the decision to integrate, apparently instituted a quota system. Black players trickled into the major leagues. Not until 1959 did every team have at least one black player.

And at first only Bill Veeck was willing to acknowledge the source of those black players. "Rickey took Robinson, Newcombe, and Campanella from our Negro baseball and didn't even say thank you," huffed Effa Manley. "He took Newcombe from me, so I know what I'm talking about." The black owners couldn't protest. "The Negro fans would never have forgiven us for keeping a Negro out of the major leagues," added one owner. "It was a case of the strong taking advantage of the weak." In defense, the owners began to insist upon formal contracts for the players and almost all Negro leaguers of 1946 had written, legal contracts.

In 1947 Effa Manley negotiated the formal sale of Larry Doby to the Cleveland Indians, accepting Bill Veeck's first offer in a precedent-setting act. Yet even after the Doby deal, Rickey believed that he could ignore the Negro leagues. In 1948 Rickey signed future Hall-of-Fame member Monte Irvin to a Dodger contract. Effa Manley, who loved Irvin like a son, decided to fight. She hired a lawyer and told Rickey that since Irvin was under contract, he had to negotiate with her. "What did Branch Rickey do?" fumed Effa. "He wrote Monte back saying that Mrs. Manley was claiming him and he didn't want him." Effa was angry, disappointed, and determined to find Irvin a major-league team. She first called the Yankees, but they still were not ready to hire a Negro player. Then she called the Giants. "They paid me $5,000 lousy dollars for Monte Irvin. If he'd have been white they'd have given me $100,000...But I was glad to get it," she added. In the deepest irony of all, Monte Irvin took a pay cut to join the major leagues, dropping from $6500 to $5000 a year!

Some of the best black players in history were in effect paralyzed by the slow pace of integration. They could not speak out, for they, and black America in general, dared not jeopardize the process. Instead, the old-timers watched sadly as the youngsters they had trained slowly entered the major leagues.

For the Negro league owners, the situation was rather different. Some had coveted baseball integration because they hoped to own the integrating team. Others paid lip service to integration because any other publicly expressed view was anathema to the black community. Still others, such as Cum Posey of the Homestead Grays, were such old-time baseball men that integration was their personal goal as much as any player's. Finally, above and beyond parochial interest, as black Americans, integration was paramount.

Nonetheless the Negro leaguers did not want to be wiped out by integration. Abe Saperstein, who functioned as an advisor to the Negro leagues, counseled them to petition baseball to become an official minor league. This advice was not heeded, in part because some of the owners naively thought they could hold out, while others feared the publicity.

In the East this hesitation by the owners was immediately proven a mistake. The Newark Eagles, New York Cubans, and the Black Yankees lost all their appeal once Robinson strode to the plate in Ebbets Field. In 1947 Newark lost $22,000, and Effa begged her husband to sell the team. Other owners felt that if they moved to non-major-league areas they could maintain profitability. Houston and Memphis received shifted franchises. But the situation in Kansas City told the entire story. The Monarchs were the premier Negro league team of that period. They still had Satchel Paige and Hilton Smith. Yet the black fans of Kansas City deserted the Monarchs to take a five-hour train ride, under Jim Crow conditions, to see Jackie Robinson and the Dodgers play the St. Louis Cardinals. In disgust J. L. Wilkinson left baseball in 1948, and the remaining owners were placed in the position of maintaining an unrecognized farm system for the major leagues.

For the Negro leagues, then, integration was the beginning of the end. They passed from the scene without fanfare. Only the East-West game retained any vitality after 1947, and that only because black fans wanted to see the future major-league stars. By 1950 even the East-West game was dead.

Although it has been shunted aside in the historical record, the victory of baseball integration was of great importance. At the very least, it paved the way for other victories in civil rights. A generation of young blacks who grew up listening to Jackie Robinson's heroics on the radio and rooting for the Dodgers became a generation of activists on behalf of civil rights all across America.

And what became of the marvelous men of the Negro leagues? The decades that immediately followed baseball integration were not kind. Whether they returned to the towns of their birth or remained in the cities where they won their fame, history seemed to pass them by. Ray Dandridge sadly observed, "I'd go out on the street and the kids didn't know a thing about our Negro baseball."

In their thirties and forties, the Negro leaguers set about building new lives. Connie Johnson became a foreman in a Ford assembly plant; Willie Wells worked in a delicatessen; Pat Patterson administered segregated sports in Houston and then became the first black coach selected for the Texas Coaches Hall of Fame; Theolic Smith and Cool Papa Bell earned their living as security guards; Jimmie Crutchfield and Webster McDonald worked for the post office; Buck Leonard sold real estate; Monte Irvin became the Assistant to Commissioner of Baseball; Sammy T. Hughes worked for the Pillsbury Company; Ted Page did public relations for Gulf Oil Company; Hilton Smith taught school; Jack Marshall opened a bowling alley in Chicago; Chico Renfroe became sports director for WRGO radio in Atlanta; Clint Thomas became a page for the West Virginia legislature; Lennie Pearson ran a bar in Newark; and Dave Malarcher became a published poet. Eddie Dwight raised the first black astronaut—Eddie Dwight, Jr.—and Satchel Paige even ran for sheriff of Kansas City. Overwhelmingly, they remained solid, contributing citizens—exemplary men. And almost without exception, they stayed close to the game they loved, serving as coaches, scouts, trainers, and announcers. Yet the Negro leaguers themselves did want just one thing: recognition. "Many a time I said it didn't matter," Monte Irvin admitted, "but it really did. You wanted to be known for what you did best."

Fortunately, the Negro leaguers' on-the-field excellence was so indelibly stamped in the minds of those that saw them that eventual recognition was inevitable. At first, the major-league establishment tried to ignore the peppering of baseball aficionados who sniped at them with claims that Josh Gibson hit more home runs than Babe Ruth, that Satchel Paige was the greatest pitcher who ever lived, that Oscar Charleston and a host of other Negro leaguers belonged in the Hall of Fame, and that baseball would always be tainted unless justice was done to the reputation of the Negro league.

Then, as a result of efforts by Robert Peterson, John Holway, and SABR (Society for American Baseball Research), statistics were complied that irrefutably demonstrated the general quality of Negro league baseball (and also drew some distinctions between the best Negro league players and their more ordinary teammates). Supplementing the case for the Negro leaguers was the extraordinary oral testimony of former ballplayers—white and black. And of course, there was that outstanding record of integration's rookie class: Jackie Robinson, Hank Aaron, Roy Campanella, Willie Mays, Elston Howard, Monte Irvin, Joe Black, Don Newcombe, and Larry Doby.

Then too, America had changed. The success of the civil rights movement, in which baseball integration had played such a prominent and pathbreaking role, had created the necessary climate to give the Negro leagues their due.

Beginning in 1969 with Satchel Paige, a select group of Negro league players were voted into the baseball Hall of Fame. By 1982, nine former Negro league players and Rube Foster were enshrined in Cooperstown.

While there was a consensus among Negro league historians that this was not enough and that at least five to ten additional players had clearly earned inclusion—the symbolic importance of blacks being in Cooperstown was not to be denied. It meant a great deal to all the Negro leaguers.

Furthermore, as baseball extended tardy recognition to the great players of Negro baseball, so too did a new generation of Americans. Books were written, and a vague awareness of the Negro leagues and their accomplishments penetrated American society—particuarly amongst sports fans.

Best of all, the Negro leaguers rediscovered each other. With the help of the people of Ashland, Kentucky, Negro league reunions were held annually beginning in 1979. Men who had shared experiences of great power and poignancy suddenly were together again after forty years. A commitment to build a black baseball Hall of History was made, and memorabilia were collected. And in the twilight of their lives, the Negro leaguers finally knew, for sure, that they had been a part of a glorious chapter of black history.

Appendix A*

LEAGUE STANDINGS YEAR-BY-YEAR

1920—1950

1920

Negro National League

Clubs were the Chicago American Giants, Chicago Giants, Cuban Stars, Dayton Marcos, Detroit Stars, Indianapolis ABCs, Kansas City Monarchs, and St. Louis Giants.

No final standings were published but the American Giants were awarded the pennant.

1921

Negro National League

	W	L	Pct.
Chicago American Giants	41	21	.661
Kansas City Monarchs	50	31	.617

*From Robert Peterson's *Only the Ball Was White*.

St. Louis Giants	33	23	.589
Detroit Stars	30	27	.526
Indianapolis ABCs	30	29	.508
Columbus Buckeyes	24	38	.387
Cincinnati (Cuban Stars)	23	39	.371
Chicago Giants	10	32	.239

1922

Negro National League

	W	L	Pct.
Chicago American Giants	36	23	.610
Indianapolis ABCs	46	33	.582
Detroit Stars	43	32	.573
Kansas City Monarchs	44	33	.571
St. Louis Stars	23	23	.500
Pittsburgh Keystones	16	21	.432
Cuban Stars	19	30	.388
Cleveland Tate Stars	17	29	.370

1923

Negro National League

	W	L	Pct.
Kansas City Monarchs	57	33	.633
Detroit Stars	40	27	.597
Chicago American Giants	41	29	.586
Indianapolis ABCs	45	34	.570
Cuban Stars (West)	27	31	.466
St. Louis Stars	23	31	.426
*Toledo Tigers	11	15	.423
**Milwaukee Bears	14	32	.304

*Disbanded July 15.
**Dropped in late season.

Eastern Colored League

	W	L	Pct.
Hilldale	32	17	.673
Cuban Stars (East)	23	17	.575
Brooklyn Royal Giants	18	18	.500
Bacharach Giants	19	23	.452
Lincoln Giants	16	22	.421
Baltimore Black Sox	19	30	.388

1924

Negro National League

	W	L	Pct.
Kansas City Monarchs	55	22	.714
Chicago American Giants	49	24	.671
Detroit Stars	37	27	.578
St. Louis Stars	40	36	.526
Birmingham Black Barons	32	37	.464
*Memphis Red Sox	29	37	.439
Cuban Stars (West)	16	33	.327
Cleveland Browns	15	34	.306

*Succeeded Indianapolis ABCs, who started season in league.

Eastern Colored League

	W	L	Pct.
Hilldale	47	22	.681
Baltimore Black Sox	30	19	.612
Lincoln Giants	31	25	.554
Bacharach Giants	30	29	.508
Harrisburg Giants	26	28	.481
Brooklyn Royal Giants	16	25	.390
Washington Potomacs	21	37	.362
Cuban Stars (East)	15	31	.326

1925

Negro National League

First Half

	W	L	Pct.
Kansas City Monarchs	31	9	.775
St. Louis Stars	31	14	.689
Detroit Stars	26	20	.565
Chicago American Giants	26	22	.542
Cuban Stars (West)	12	13	.480
Memphis Red Sox	18	24	.429
Indianapolis ABCs	13	24	.351
Birmingham Black Barons	14	33	.298

Second Half

	W	L	Pct.
St. Louis Stars	38	12	.760
Kansas City Monarchs	31	11	.738
Chicago American Giants	28	18	.609
Detroit Stars	27	20	.574
Cuban Stars (West)	10	12	.454
Birmingham Black Barons	10	16	.384
Memphis Red Sox	12	24	.333
Indianapolis ABCs	4	33	.108

Kansas City defeated St. Louis, 4 games to 3, in a playoff for the league pennant.

Eastern Colored League

	W	L	Pct.
Hilldale	45	13	.775
Harrisburg Giants	37	18	.673
Baltimore Black Sox	31	19	.620

Bacharach Giants	26	26	.500
Brooklyn Royal Giants	13	20	.394
Cuban Stars (East)	15	26	.366
Lincoln Giants	7	39	.152

1926

Negro National League

First Half

	W	L	Pct.
Kansas City Monarchs	35	12	.745
Detroit Stars	33	17	.660
Chicago American Giants	28	16	.636
St. Louis Stars	29	18	.617
Indianapolis ABCs	28	18	.609
Cuban Stars (West)	6	27	.182
Dayton Marcos	7	32	.179
Cleveland Elites	5	32	.135

Second Half

	W	L	Pct.
Chicago American Giants	29	7	.806
Kansas City Monarchs	21	7	.750
St. Louis Stars	20	11	.645
Indianapolis ABCs	15	25	.375
Detroit Stars	13	23	.361
Cuban Stars (West)	10	20	.333

The American Giants defeated the Kansas City Monarchs, 5 games to 4, in a playoff for the pennant.

Eastern Colored League

	W	L	Pct.
Bacharach Giants	34	20	.629
Harrisburg Giants	25	17	.595
Hilldale	34	24	.586
Cuban Stars (East)	28	21	.572
Lincoln Giants	19	22	.463
Baltimore Black Sox	18	29	.383
Brooklyn Royal Giants	7	20	.260
*Newark Stars	1	10	.091

*Disbanded in midseason.

1927

Negro National League

First Half

	W	L	Pct.
Chicago American Giants	32	14	.696
Kansas City Monarchs	36	18	.667
St. Louis Stars	32	19	.627
Detroit Stars	28	18	.609
Birmingham Black Barons	23	29	.442
Memphis Red Sox	19	25	.432
Cuban Stars (West)	15	23	.395
Cleveland Hornets	10	37	.213

Second Half

No final standings were published, but the Birmingham Black Barons were declared second-half winners.

The American Giants defeated the Black Barons in 4 straight playoff games to win the pennant.

Eastern Colored League

First Half

	W	L	Pct.
Bacharach Giants	29	17	.630
Baltimore Black Sox	23	17	.575
Cuban Stars (East)	24	19	.558
Harrisburg Giants	25	20	.556
Hilldale	17	28	.378
Brooklyn Royal Giants	10	21	.323

Second Half

	W	L	Pct.
Bacharach Giants	25	18	.581
Harrisburg Giants	16	12	.572
Hilldale	19	17	.528
Cuban Stars (East)	9	13	.409
Baltimore Black Sox	12	18	.400
Brooklyn Royal Giants	5	10	.333

1928

Negro National League

No final standings were published for either the first or second half. The St. Louis Stars were awarded the first-half championship, the Chicago American Giants the second.

Other clubs in the league were the Birmingham Black Barons, Cuban Stars (West), and Detroit Stars.

Eastern Colored League

The league broke up in late spring. Clubs were the Bacharach Giants, Baltimore Black Sox, Cuban Stars (East), Lincoln Giants, and Philadelphia Tigers.

1929

Negro National League

First Half

	W	L	Pct.
Kansas City Monarchs	28	11	.718
St. Louis Stars	28	14	.667
Detroit Stars	24	16	.600
Birmingham Black Barons	20	24	.454
Chicago American Giants	22	29	.431
Memphis Red Sox	14	22	.389
Cuban Stars (West)	6	14	.300

Second Half

	W	L	Pct.
Kansas City Monarchs	34	6	.850
Chicago American Giants	26	9	.743
St. Louis Stars	28	16	.636
Cuban Stars (West)	12	12	.500
Detroit Stars	10	23	.303
Birmingham Black Barons	9	27	.250
Memphis Red Sox	5	22	.185

*American Negro League**

First Half

	W	L	Pct.
Baltimore Black Sox	24	11	.686
Lincoln Giants	22	11	.667
Homestead Grays	15	13	.536
Hilldale	15	20	.429
Bacharach Giants	11	20	.355
Cuban Stars (East)	6	16	.273

Second Half

	W	L	Pct.
Baltimore Black Sox	25	10	.714
Hilldale	24	15	.615
Lincoln Giants	18	15	.545
Homestead Grays	19	16	.543
Cuban Stars (East)	9	23	.281
Bacharach Giants	8	25	.242

*The first use of this league title.

1930

Negro National League

First Half

	W	L	Pct.
St. Louis Stars	41	15	.732
Kansas City Monarchs	31	14	.689
Memphis Red Sox	20	17	.541
Birmingham Black Barons	30	27	.526
Detroit Stars	26	26	.500
Cuban Stars (West)	17	23	.425
Chicago American Giants	24	39	.381
Nashville Elite Giants	13	35	.271

Second Half

	W	L	Pct.
Detroit Stars	24	7	.774
St. Louis Stars	22	7	.759
Chicago American Giants	19	12	.613
Kansas City Monarchs	8	12	.400
Nashville Elite Giants	7	12	.368
Cuban Stars (West)	6	12	.333
Memphis Red Sox	7	14	.333
Birmingham Black Barons	10	20	.333

The St. Louis Stars defeated the Detroit Stars in a playoff for the pennant.

1931

Negro National League

No final standings were published for either the first or second half, but the St. Louis Stars were declared winners of both. Other clubs were the Chicago American Giants, Cleveland Cubs, Detroit Stars, Indianapolis ABCs, and Louisville White Sox.

1933

Negro National League

First Half

	W	L	Pct.
Cole's American Giants (Chicago)	21	7	.750
Pittsburgh Crawfords	20	8	.714
Baltimore Black Sox	10	9	.526
Nashville Elite Giants	12	13	.480
Detroit Stars	13	20	.394
Columbus Blue Birds	11	18	.379

Second Half

The second-half schedule was not completed.

The American Giants claimed the pennant. Several months later, Gus Greenlee, league president, awarded the pennant to his club, the Pittsburgh Crawfords.

1934

Negro National League

First Half

	W	L	Pct.
Cole's American Giants (Chicago)	17	6	.739
Pittsburgh Crawfords	14	8	.636
Philadelphia Stars	12	9	.571
Newark Dodgers	6	5	.545
Nashville Elite Giants	9	11	.450
Cleveland Red Sox	2	22	.083

Second Half

	W	L	Pct.
Philadelphia Stars	11	4	.733
Nashville Elite Giants	6	3	.667
Pittsburgh Crawfords	15	9	.625
Cole's American Giants (Chicago)	11	9	.550
Cleveland Red Sox	2	3	.400
Newark Dodgers	5	9	.357
*Bacharach Giants	3	12	.200
*Baltimore Black Sox	1	6	.143

*Added for second half.

The Philadelphia Stars defeated Cole's American Giants, 4 games to 3, in a playoff for the pennant.

1935

Negro National League
First Half

	W	L	Pct.
Pittsburgh Crawfords	26	6	.785
Columbus Elite Giants	17	11	.607
Homestead Grays	14	13	.519
Brooklyn Eagles	15	15	.500
Cole's American Giants (Chicago)	14	16	.467
Philadelphia Stars	14	17	.452
New York Cubans	10	16	.385
Newark Dodgers	8	20	.286

Second Half

	W	L	Pct.
New York Cubans	20	7	.741
Pittsburgh Crawfords	13	9	.591
Philadelphia Stars	14	10	.583
Columbus Elite Giants	10	10	.500
Homestead Grays	9	10	.474
Brooklyn Eagles	13	16	.448
Cole's American Giants (Chicago)	7	13	.350
Newark Dodgers	9	21	.300

The Pittsburgh Crawfords defeated the New York Cubans, 4 games to 3, in a playoff for the pennant.

1936

Negro National League

First Half

	W	L	Pct.
Washington Elite Giants	14	10	.583
Philadelphia Stars	15	12	.556
Pittsburgh Crawfords	16	15	.516
Newark Eagles	15	18	.455
New York Cubans	9	11	.450
Homestead Grays	10	13	.435

Second Half

	W	L	Pct.
Pittsburgh Crawfords	20	9	.690
Newark Eagles	15	11	.577
New York Black Yankees	8	7	.533
New York Cubans	13	12	.520
Homestead Grays	12	14	.462
Philadelphia Stars	10	18	.357
Washington Elite Giants	7	14	.333

No playoff was held between the first- and second-half winners.

1937

Negro National League

First Half

	W	L	Pct.
Homestead Grays	21	9	.700
Newark Eagles	19	14	.576
Philadelphia Stars	12	11	.522

Washington Elite Giants	11	15	.423
Pittsburgh Crawfords	11	16	.407
New York Black Yankees	11	17	.393

Second Half

No final standings were published. The Homestead Grays were declared league champions.

Negro American League

First Half

	W	L	Pct.
Kansas City Monarchs	19	8	.704
Chicago American Giants	18	8	.692
Cincinnati Tigers	15	11	.577
Memphis Red Sox	13	13	.500
Detroit Stars	12	15	.444
Birmingham Black Barons	10	17	.370
Indianapolis Athletics	9	18	.333
St. Louis Stars	5	22	.185

Second Half

No final standings were published. However, the Kansas City Monarchs, first-half winners, defeated the Chicago American Giants in a series billed as a playoff, 4 games to 1.

1938

Negro National League

First Half

	W	L	Pct.
Homestead Grays	26	6	.813
Philadelphia Stars	20	11	.645
Newark Eagles	11	11	.500
Pittsburgh Crawfords	14	14	.500
Baltimore Elite Giants	12	14	.462
New York Black Yankees	4	17	.190
Washington Black Senators	1	20	.048

Second Half

No final standings were published, but the league office announced that the teams finished in this order: Homestead, Philadelphia, Pittsburgh, Baltimore, Newark, and New York. The Washington club folded during the second half.

Negro American League

First Half*

	W	L	Pct.
Memphis Red Sox	21	4	.840
Kansas City Monarchs	19	5	.792
Indianapolis ABCs	6	6	.500
Atlanta Black Crackers	9	10	.474
Jacksonville Red Caps	3	4	.429
Chicago American Giants	8	13	.381
Birmingham Black Barons	3	11	.214

*Last published standings.

Second Half

	W	L	Pct.
Atlanta Black Crackers	12	4	.750
Chicago American Giants	17	7	.708
Kansas City Monarchs	13	10	.565
Indianapolis ABCs	8	13	.381
Memphis Red Sox	8	15	.348
Birmingham Black Barons	5	12	.294

1939

Negro National League

	W	L	Pct.
Homestead Grays	33	14	.702
Newark Eagles	29	20	.592
Baltimore Elite Giants	25	21	.543
Philadelphia Stars	31	32	.492
New York Black Yankees	15	21	.417
New York Cubans	5	22	.185

To determine the champion, an elimination tourney was held among the top four teams. Baltimore defeated Newark in one series, and Homestead eliminated Philadelphia. Baltimore then beat Homestead, 2–0, and was declared the pennant-winner.

Negro American League

First Half

	W	L	Pct.
Kansas City Monarchs	17	7	.708
Chicago American Giants	17	11	.607
Memphis Red Sox	11	11	.500
Cleveland Bears	9	9	.500
St. Louis Stars	10	12	.455

Second Half

No final standings were published. The Toledo Craw-fords replaced the Indianapolis ABCs for the second half.

The Kansas City Monarchs were declared pennant-winners after defeating the St. Louis Stars, 3 games to 2, in a post-season series.

1940

Negro National League

	W	L	Pct.
Homestead Grays	28	13	.683
Baltimore Elite Giants	25	14	.641
Newark Eagles	25	17	.595
New York Cubans	12	19	.387
Philadelphia Stars	16	31	.340
New York Black Yankees	10	22	.313

Negro American League

First Half

	W	L	Pct.
Kansas City Monarchs	12	7	.632
Cleveland Bears	10	10	.500
Memphis Red Sox	12	12	.500
Birmingham Black Barons	9	9	.500
Chicago American Giants	9	15	.429
Indianapolis Crawfords	3	5	.375

Second Half

No final standings were published. The Kansas City Monarchs were declared pennant-winners.

1941

Negro National League

First Half

	W	L	Pct.
Homestead Grays	17	9	.654
Newark Eagles	11	6	.647
Baltimore Elite Giants	13	10	.565
New York Cubans	7	10	.412
Philadelphia Stars	10	18	.357
New York Black Yankees	7	13	.350

Second Half

	W	L	Pct.
New York Cubans	4	2	.667
Newark Eagles	8	5	.615
Baltimore Elite Giants	9	8	.529
Homestead Grays	8	8	.500
New York Black Yankees	5	5	.500
Philadelphia Stars	2	8	.200

The Homestead Grays defeated the New York Cubans, 3 games to 1, in a playoff for the pennant.

Negro American League

No final standings were published for either half of the split season. Clubs were Birmingham Black Barons, Chicago American Giants, Jacksonville Red Caps, Kansas City Monarchs, Memphis Red Sox, and New Orleans–St. Louis Stars.

1942

Negro National League

	W	L	Pct.
Homestead Grays	21	11	.656
Baltimore Elite Giants	21	12	.636
Newark Eagles	18	16	.529
Philadelphia Stars	16	18	.471
New York Cubans	8	14	.364
New York Black Yankees	7	20	.259

Negro American League

No final standings were published for either half of the split season. The Kansas City Monarchs were declared winners of both halves. Other clubs were the Birmingham Black Barons, Chicago American Giants, Cincinnati Buckeyes, and Jacksonville Red Caps. The Red Caps dropped out in early July.

1943

Negro National League

First Half

	W	L	Pct.
Homestead Grays	17	4	.810
New York Cubans	13	6	.684
*Harrisburg–St. Louis Stars	5	4	.556
Newark Eagles	9	10	.474
Philadelphia Stars	11	16	.407

*Suspended when they withdrew to go on a barnstorming tour with a team headed by Dizzy Dean.

Baltimore Elite Giants	9	15	.375
New York Black Yankees	2	11	.154

Second Half

	W	L	Pct.
Homestead Grays	9	3	.750
Newark Eagles	9	4	.692
New York Cubans	4	3	.571
Baltimore Elite Giants	5	6	.455
Philadelphia Stars	7	9	.438
New York Black Yankees	0	10	.000

Negro American League

First Half

No final standings were published. The Birmingham Black Barons were declared winners.

Second Half

	W	L	Pct.
Chicago American Giants	13	5	.722
Birmingham Black Barons	5	3	.625
Cleveland Buckeyes	8	5	.615
Kansas City Monarchs	6	7	.462
Cincinnati Clowns	3	7	.300
Memphis Red Sox	4	11	.267

The Birmingham Black Barons defeated the Chicago American Giants, 3 games to 2, in a playoff for the pennant.

1944

Negro National League

First Half

	W	L	Pct.
Homestead Grays	15	8	.652
Newark Eagles	13	9	.591
New York Cubans	12	10	.545
Baltimore Elite Giants	12	11	.522
Philadelphia Stars	7	11	.389
New York Black Yankees	2	13	.133

Second Half

	W	L	Pct.
Homestead Grays	12	4	.750
Philadelphia Stars	12	7	.632
Baltimore Elite Giants	12	9	.571
New York Cubans	4	4	.500
Newark Eagles	6	13	.316
New York Black Yankees	2	11	.154

Negro American League

First Half

	W	L	Pct.
Birmingham Black Barons	24	9	.727
Indianapolis–Cincinnati Clowns	18	13	.581
Cleveland Buckeyes	20	20	.500
Memphis Red Sox	20	23	.465
Kansas City Monarchs	12	19	.387
Chicago American Giants	10	20	.333

Second Half

	W	L	Pct.
Birmingham Black Barons	24	13	.649
Indianapolis–Cincinnati Clowns	22	18	.550
Chicago American Giants	22	19	.537
Cleveland Buckeyes	20	21	.488
Memphis Red Sox	24	28	.462
Kansas City Monarchs	11	23	.324

1945

Negro National League

First Half

	W	L	Pct.
Homestead Grays	18	7	.720
Philadelphia Stars	14	9	.609
Baltimore Elite Giants	13	9	.591
Newark Eagles	11	9	.550
New York Cubans	3	11	.214
New York Black Yankees	2	16	.111

Second Half

	W	L	Pct.
Homestead Grays	14	6	.700
Baltimore Elite Giants	12	8	.600
Newark Eagles	10	8	.556
Philadelphia Stars	7	10	.412
New York Black Yankees	5	10	.333
New York Cubans	3	9	.250

Negro American League

First Half

	W	L	Pct.
Cleveland Buckeyes	31	9	.775
Birmingham Black Barons	26	11	.703
Kansas City Monarchs	17	18	.486
Chicago American Giants	17	24	.415
Cincinnati Clowns	15	26	.366
Memphis Red Sox	13	31	.295

Second Half

	W	L	Pct.
Cleveland Buckeyes	22	7	.759
Chicago American Giants	22	11	.667
Kansas City Monarchs	15	12	.556
Cincinnati Clowns	15	13	.536
Birmingham Black Barons	13	19	.406
Memphis Red Sox	4	30	.118

1946

Negro National League

First Half

	W	L	Pct.
Newark Eagles	25	9	.735
Philadelphia Stars	17	12	.586
Homestead Grays	18	15	.545
New York Cubans	13	13	.500
Baltimore Elite Giants	14	17	.451
New York Black Yankees	3	24	.111

Second Half

	W	L	Pct.
Newark Eagles	22	7	.759
New York Cubans	15	8	.652
Baltimore Elite Giants	14	14	.500
Homestead Grays	9	13	.409
Philadelphia Stars	10	17	.370
New York Black Yankees	5	16	.238

Negro American League

First Half

	W	L	Pct.
Kansas City Monarchs	27	8	.771
Birmingham Black Barons	22	15	.595
Indianapolis Clowns	15	19	.441
Cleveland Buckeyes	14	17	.452
Memphis Red Sox	16	21	.432
Chicago American Giants	14	28	.333

Second Half

No final standings were published. The Kansas City Monarchs were declared winners.

1947

Negro National League

First Half

	W	L	Pct.
Newark Eagles	27	15	.643
New York Cubans	20	12	.625
Baltimore Elite Giants	23	20	.535

Homestead Grays	19	20	.487
Philadelphia Stars	13	16	.448
New York Black Yankees	6	25	.193

Second Half

No final standings were published. There was no playoff and the New York Cubans were awarded the pennant because they were said to have the best record for the full season.

Negro American League

No final standings were published for either the first or second half. The Cleveland Buckeyes were declared pennant-winners. Other clubs were the Birmingham Black Barons, Chicago American Giants, Indianapolis Clowns, Kansas City Monarchs, and Memphis Red Sox.

1948

Negro National League

No final standings were published for either half of the split season. The Baltimore Elite Giants won the first-half championship and the Homestead Grays the second-half. The Grays won 3 straight in a playoff for the title. Other clubs were the Newark Eagles, New York Black Yankees, New York Cubans, and Philadelphia Stars.

Negro American League

First Half

No final standings were published. The Birmingham Black Barons were declared winners.

Second Half

	W	L	Pct.
Kansas City Monarchs	19	7	.731
Birmingham Black Barons	17	7	.708
Memphis Red Sox	20	15	.571
Indianapolis Clowns	7	13	.350
Cleveland Buckeyes	10	21	.323
Chicago American Giants	7	17	.292

The Birmingham Black Barons defeated the Kansas City Monarchs, 4 games to 3, in a playoff for the pennant.

1949

Negro American League

Eastern Division

First Half

	W	L	Pct.
Baltimore Elite Giants	24	12	.667
New York Cubans	14	10	.583
Philadelphia Stars	13	20	.394
Indianapolis Clowns	14	23	.378
Louisville Buckeyes	8	29	.216

Second Half

No final standings were published. The Baltimore Elite Giants were declared winners.

Western Division

No final standings were published for either half of the split season. In the first half, the order of finish was: Kansas City Monarchs, Chicago American Giants, Birmingham

Black Barons, Houston Eagles, and Memphis Red Sox. For the second half, the Chicago American Giants, with a record of 23–15, were declared winners.

Kansas City, first-half champion, declined to meet the American Giants in a divisional-championship series because several of the Monarchs' best players had gone into organized ball during the season. The American Giants were therefore named Western Division champions. The Baltimore Elite Giants defeated the Chicago American Giants in four straight games for the league title.

1950

Negro American League

Eastern Division

First Half

	W	L	Pct.
Indianapolis Clowns	27	16	.628
Baltimore Elite Giants	10	9	.526
New York Cubans	12	13	.480
Philadelphia Stars	9	19	.321
*Cleveland Buckeyes	3	33	.083

*Disbanded at end of first half.

Second Half

	W	L	Pct.
New York Cubans	6	2	.750
Baltimore Elite Giants	14	11	.560
Indianapolis Clowns	18	21	.462
Philadelphia Stars	5	7	.417

Although finishing third, the Indianapolis Clowns were awarded the second-half championship because of a league ruling that the champion must play at least 30 games in a half.

Western Division

First Half

	W	L	Pct.
Kansas City Monarchs	30	11	.732
Birmingham Black Barons	38	14	.731
Houston Eagles	17	20	.459
Chicago American Giants	13	16	.448
Memphis Red Sox	11	19	.367

Second Half

	W	L	Pct.
Kansas City Monarchs	21	9	.700
Memphis Red Sox	18	8	.692
Birmingham Black Barons	13	10	.565
Houston Eagles	5	17	.227
Chicago American Giants	1	14	.067

No playoff was held between the divisional champions for the league title.

Appendix B*

EAST-WEST ALL-STAR GAMES

1933–1950

1933

East

	AB	R	H	E
Cool Papa Bell (Pittsburgh Crawfords), cf	5	1	0	0
Rap Dixon (Philadelphia Stars), rf	4	2	1	0
Oscar Charleston (Pittsburgh Crawfords), 1b	3	2	0	0
Bix Mackey (Philadelphia Stars), c	3	0	1	0
Josh Gibson (Pittsburgh Crawfords), c	2	0	1	1
Jud Wison (Philadelphia Stars), 3b	3	1	2	0
Judy Johnson (Pittsburgh Crawfords), 3b	1	0	1	0
Dick Lundy (Philadelphia Stars), ss	3	0	0	1
Vic Harris (Homestead Grays), lf	2	0	0	1
Fats Jenkins (N.Y. Black Yankees), lf	2	0	0	0
John H. Russell (Pittsburgh Crawfords), 2b	3	0	0	0
Sam Streeter (Pittsburgh Crawfords), p	3	0	0	0
Bertrum Hunter (Pittsburgh Crawfords), p	0	0	0	0
George Britt (Homestead Grays), p	1	1	1	0
	35	7	7	3

*From Robert Peterson's *Only the Ball Was White*.

West

	AB	R	H	E
Turkey Stearns (Chicago American Giants), cf	5	1	2	0
Willie Wells (Chicago American Giants), ss	4	2	2	0
W. Davis (Chicago American Giants), lf	3	2	2	0
Alex Radcliffe (Chicago American Giants), 3b	4	1	2	0
Mule Suttles (Chicago American Giants), 1b	4	2	2	0
Leroy Morney (Cleveland Giants), 2b	4	0	1	3
Sam Bankhead (Nashville Elite Giants), rf	4	2	1	0
Larry Brown (Chicago American Giants), c	4	0	2	0
Willie Foster (Chicago American Giants), p	4	1	1	0
	36	11	15	3

EAST	000	320	002—7	
WEST	001	303	31×—11	

2B—Stearns, Wells, Davis (2), Radcliffe. 3B—Brown. HR—Suttles. SB—Dixon, Charleston, Bankhead. SH—Dixon, Gibson, Russell. DP—Wells, Morney, and Suttles; Bankhead and Radcliffe. SO—by Foster, 4; Streeter, 4; Britt, 1. BB—off Foster, 3. Hits—off Streeter, 7 in 5⅓ innings; Hunter, 4 in ⅔; Britt, 4 in 2. HP—by Foster, 2.
Losing pitcher—Streeter.
Attendance—20,000.

1934

East

	AB	R	H	E
Cool Papa Bell (Pittsburgh Crawfords), cf	3	1	0	0
Jimmy Crutchfield (Pittsburgh Crawfords), rf	3	0	0	0
W. G. Perkins (Pittsburgh Crawfords), c	1	0	0	0
Oscar Charleston (Pittsburgh Crawfords), 1b	4	0	0	1
Jud Wilson (Philadelphia Stars), 3b	3	0	1	0
Josh Gibson (Pittsburgh Crawfords), c-lf	4	0	2	0
Vic Harris (Pittsburgh Crawfords), lf	2	0	1	0
Dick Lundy (Newark Dodgers), ss	4	0	0	0
Chester Williams (Pittsburgh Crawfords), 2b	4	0	3	0
Slim Jones (Philadelphia Stars), p	1	0	0	0
Harry Kincannon (Pittsburgh Crawfords), p	1	0	1	0
Satchel Paige (Pittsburgh Crawfords), p	2	0	0	0
	32	1	8	1

West

	AB	R	H	E
Willie Wells (Chicago American Giants), ss	3	0	1	0
Alex Radcliffe (Chicago American Giants), 3b	4	0	0	0
Turkey Stearns (Chicago American Giants), cf	4	0	0	0
Mule Suttles (Chicago American Giants), 1b	4	0	3	1
Red Parnell (Nashville Elite Giants), lf	3	0	0	0
Sam Bankhead (Nashville Elite Giants), rf	3	0	1	0
Larry Brown (Chicago American Giants), c	3	0	1	0
Sammy T. Hughes (Nashville Elite Giants), 2b	2	0	0	0
J. Patterson (Cleveland Red Sox), 2b	1	0	0	0
Theodore Trent (Chicago American Giants), p	1	0	0	0
Chet Brewer (Kansas City Monarchs), p	1	0	0	0
Willie Foster (Chicago American Giants), p	1	0	1	0
	30	0	7	1

EAST	000	000	010—1	
WEST	000	000	000—0	

RBI—Wilson. 2B—Gibson, Williams, Wells. 3B—Suttles. SB—Bell. LOB—East, 8; West, 5. SO—by Jones, 4; Trent, 3; Brewer, 1; Paige 5; Foster, 2. BB—off Brewer, 1; Jones, 1; Foster, 1.

Winning pitcher—Paige; loser—Foster.

Attendance—30,000.

1935

East

	AB	R	H	E
Paul Stevens (Philadelphia Stars), ss	6	1	2	1
George Giles (Brooklyn Eagles), 1b	5	1	0	0
Martin Dihigo (N.Y. Cubans), cf-p	5	1	1	2
Jud Wilson (Philadelphia Stars), 3b	5	1	2	0
Alejandro Oms (N.Y. Cubans), rf	4	1	2	0
Biz Mackey (Philadelphia Stars), c	5	1	0	0
Fats Jenkins (Brooklyn Eagles), lf	5	1	0	0
Dick Seay (Philadelphia Stars), 2b	3	0	1	2
Slim Jones (Philadelphia Stars), p	2	1	2	0
Leon Day (Brooklyn Eagles), p	1	0	0	0
Ed Stone (Brooklyn Eagles)	1	0	0	0

Ray Dandridge (Newark Dodgers), 2b	1	0	1	0
Luis Tiant (N.Y. Cubans), p	2	0	0	0
Paul Arnold (Newark Dodgers), cf	0	0	0	0
	45	8	11	5

West

	AB	R	H	E
Cool Papa Bell (Pittsburgh, Crawfords), cf	4	2	1	1
Sammy T. Hughes (Columbus Elite Giants), 2b	4	0	1	0
Willie Wells (Chicago American Giants), ss	3	0	0	1
Josh Gibson (Pittsburgh Crawfords), c	5	3	4	1
Mule Suttles (Chicago American Giants), lf	2	3	1	0
Oscar Charleston (Pittsburgh Crawfords), 1b	3	1	0	1
Alex Radcliffe (Chicago American Giants), 3b	5	1	2	0
Jimmy Crutchfield (Pittsburgh Crawfords), rf	2	0	0	0
Raymond Brown (Homestead Grays), p	1	0	0	0
Leroy Matlock (Pittsburgh Crawfords), p	2	0	0	0
Turkey Stearns (Chicago American Giants)	3	0	1	0
Buck Leonard (Homestead Grays), 1b	3	0	0	0
Theodore Trent (Chicago American Giants), p	0	0	0	0
Chester Williams (Pittsburgh Crawfords), ss	2	1	0	1
Bill Wright (Columbus Elite Giants)	1	0	0	0
Bob Griffith (Columbus Elite Giants), p	0	0	0	0
Felton Snow (Columbus Elite Giants)	1	0	1	0
Willie Cornelius (Chicago American Giants), p	0	0	0	0
	41	11	11	5

EAST	200	110	000	40—8
WEST	000	003	100	43—11

There were two outs in the eleventh inning when Mule Suttles hit a home run with two men on base.

2B—Gibson (2). HR—Jones, Suttles. SB—Dihigo, Giles. SH—Hughes (2), Oms. DP—Wilson unassisted. SO—by Jones, 1; Brown, 1; Day, 3; Matlock, 1; Griffith, 3; Dihigo, 1. BB—off Jones, 2; Day, 2; Trent, 2; Griffith, 2; Tiant, 2; Dihigo, 1. PB—Gibson.

Winning pitcher—Cornelius; losing pitcher, Dihigo.

Attendance—25,000.

1936

East

	AB	R	H	E
Cool Papa Bell (Pittsburgh Crawfords), cf	3	1	3	0
Bill Wright (Washington Elite Giants), cf	2	0	0	0
Sammy T. Hughes (Washington Elite Giants), 2b	5	2	1	1
Sam Bankhead (Pittsburgh Crawfords), lf	4	1	2	0
Biz Mackey (Washington Elite Giants), c	2	0	2	0
Josh Gibson (Pittsburgh Crawfords), c	3	2	2	0
Jimmy Crutchfield (Pittsburgh Crawfords), rf	2	0	0	0
Zolley Wright (Washington Elite Giants), rf	1	2	1	0
Chester Williams (Pittsburgh Crawfords), ss	4	0	0	1
Jim West (Washington Elite Giants), 1b	3	1	1	1
John Washington (Pittsburgh Crawfords), 1b	1	0	0	1
Judy Johnson (Pittsburgh Crawfords), 3b	1	0	0	1
Felton Snow (Washington Elite Giants), 3b	2	1	1	0
Leroy Matlock (Pittsburgh Crawfords), p	1	0	0	0
Bill Byrd (Washington Elite Giants), p	3	0	0	0
Satchel Paige (Pittsburgh Crawfords), p	1	0	0	0
	38	10	13	5

West

	AB	R	H	E
Eddie Dwight (Kansas City Monarchs), cf	2	0	0	0
Henry Milton (Kansas City Monarchs), cf	2	0	0	0
Newt Allen (Kansas City Monarchs), 2b, ss	5	0	0	0
Wilson Redus (Chicago American Giants), rf	2	0	0	0
Odem Dials (Chicago American Giants), rf	2	0	0	1
Alex Radcliffe (Chicago American Giants), 3b	4	1	3	0
Bullet Rogan (Kansas City Monarchs), lf	1	0	0	0
Herman Dunlap (Chicago American Giants), lf	2	1	1	0
Harry Else (Kansas City Monarchs), c	0	0	0	0
Subby Byas (Chicago American Giants), c	3	0	1	0
Willard Brown (Kansas City Monarchs), ss	1	0	0	1
Pat Patterson (Kansas City Monarchs), 2b	2	0	2	0
Popsickle Harris (Kansas City Monarchs), 1b	4	0	1	0
Willie Cornelius (Chicago American Giants), p	1	0	0	0
Floyd Kranson (Kansas City Monarchs), p	0	0	0	0
Andy Cooper (Kansas City Monarchs), p	0	0	0	0
Theodore Trent (Chicago American Giants), p	0	0	0	0
	31	2	8	2

EAST	200	130	220—10
WEST	000	001	010—2

RBI—Mackey (2), Bell, Z. Wright (2), Johnson, Gibson, Williams, Patterson. 2B—Bell, Hughes, Bankhead, Patterson. SB—Bell, Gibson, Snow. SO—by Cornelius, 2; Kranson, 1; Byrd, 4; Trent, 1. BB—off Cornelius, 1; Matlock, 1; Kranson, 1; Byrd, 1; Trent, 2. DP—Cornelius, Allen, and Harris. Hits—off Matlock, 2 in 3 innings; Cornelius, 5 in 3; Kranson, 4 in 2; Cooper, 1 in 1; Byrd, 4 in 3; Trent, 3 in 3; Paige, 2 in 3. PB—Gibson. HP—by Kranson (West).

Winning pitcher—Matlock; loser—Cornelius.

Attendance—30,000.

1937

East

	AB	R	H	E
Jerry Benjamin (Homestead Grays), rf	5	0	1	0
Willie Wells (Newark Eagles), ss	5	2	1	0
Bill Wright (Washington Elite Giants), cf	5	1	3	0
Buck Leonard (Homestead Grays), 1b	4	1	2	1
Mule Suttles (Newark Eagles), lf	3	0	1	0
Chester Williams (Pittsburgh Crawfords), 2b	3	0	0	0
Jake Dunn (Philadelphia Stars), 2b	1	0	0	0
Ray Dandridge (Newark Eagles), 3b	5	2	1	0
Pepper Bassett (Pittsburgh Crawfords), c	3	0	0	0
Barney Morris (Pittsburgh Crawfords), p	2	0	0	0
Barney Brown (N.Y. Black Yankees), p	1	0	1	0
Leon Day (Newark Eagles), p	1	1	1	0
	38	7	11	1

West

	AB	R	H	E
Newt Allen (Kansas City Monarchs), 2b-ss	4	0	0	0
Lloyd Davenport (Cincinnati Tigers), rf	4	1	1	0
Wilson Redus (Chicago American Giants), rf	0	0	0	0
Ted Strong (Indianapolis Athletics), 1b	4	1	2	2
Turkey Stearns (Detroit Stars), cf	4	0	0	0
Willard Brown (Kansas City Monarchs), lf	2	0	0	0
Alex Radcliffe (Chicago American Giants), 3b	3	0	1	0
Howard Easterling (Cincinnati Tigers), ss	2	0	0	0

Rainey Bibbs (Cincinnati Tigers), 2b	1	0	1	0
Ted Radcliffe (Cincinnati Tigers), c	3	0	0	1
Theodore Trent (Chicago American Giants), p	0	0	0	0
Hilton Smith (Kansas City Monarchs), p	0	0	0	1
Porter Moss (Cincinnati Tigers), p	2	0	0	0
Henry Milton (Kansas City Monarchs)	1	0	0	0
Subby Byas (Chicago American Giants)	1	0	0	0
Eldridge Mayweather (Kansas City Monarchs)	1	0	0	0
	32	2	5	4

EAST	010	200	130—7
WEST	000	101	000—2

2B—Allen, Wright, Bibbs, Day. HR—Leonard, Strong. SB—Dandridge, Wright, Suttles. DP—Moss, T. Radcliffe, and Strong; Wells, Dunn, and Leonard; Allen and Strong.

Winning pitcher—Morris; loser—Smith.

Attendance—20,000.

1938

East

	AB	R	H	E
Vic Harris (Homestead Grays), lf	5	1	1	0
Sammy T. Hughes (Baltimore Elite Giants), 2b	5	1	1	0
Willie Wells (Newark Eagles), ss	4	1	2	0
Buck Leonard (Homestead Grays), 1b	4	0	1	0
Rev Cannady (N.Y. Black Yankees), 3b	3	1	1	0
Sam Bankhead (Pittsburgh Crawfords), cf	4	0	2	0
Bill Wright (Baltimore Elite Giants), rf	4	0	2	0
Biz Mackey (Baltimore Elite Giants), c	4	0	0	0
Edsell Walker (Homestead Grays), p	0	0	0	0
Barney Brown (N.Y. Black Yankees), p	2	0	1	0
Johnny Taylor (Pittsburgh Crawfords), p	0	0	0	0
——— Fisher	1	0	1	0
	36	4	11	0

West

	AB	R	H	E
Henry Milton (Kansas City Monarchs), rf	3	2	1	0
Newt Allen (Kansas City Monarchs), 2b	4	0	0	1
Alex Radcliffe (Chicago American Giants), 3b	4	1	2	0

Ted Strong (Indianapolis ABCs), 1b	3	1	0	0
Quincy Trouppe (Indianapolis ABCs), lf	4	0	0	0
Neil Robinson (Memphis Red Sox), cf	4	1	3	0
Frank Duncan (Chicago American Giants), c	1	0	0	0
Larry Brown (Memphis Red Sox), c	0	0	0	0
Byron Johnson (Kansas City Monarchs), ss	4	0	1	0
Willie Cornelius (Chicago American Giants), p	0	0	0	0
Hilton Smith (Kansas City Monarchs), p	2	0	1	0
Ted Radcliffe (Memphis Red Sox), p	2	0	1	0
	31	5	9	1

EAST	300	010	000—4
WEST	104	000	00x—5

RBI—Wells, Cannady, Bankhead, A. Radcliffe (2), Robinson (3), Leonard. 2B—Harris, Cannady, Hughes. 3B—Wells. HR—Robinson. SH—Cannady. DP—Duncan and Radcliffe. LOB—East, 7; West, 8. Hits—off Cornelius, 5 in 1 inning; Walker, 4 in 3; Smith, 3 in 4; Brown, 2 in 3; Radcliffe, 3 in 4; Taylor, 3 in 2. SO—by Walker, 3; Smith, 3; Brown, 1; Taylor, 2. BB—off Smith, 1; Walker, 3; Taylor, 1. HP—by Smith. PB—Mackey.

Winning pitcher—Smith; loser—Walker.
Attendance—30,000.

1939

East

	AB	R	H	E
Bill Wright (Baltimore Elite Giants), cf	4	0	2	0
Willie Wells (Newark Eagles), ss	3	0	1	0
Josh Gibson (Homestead Grays), c	3	0	0	0
Mule Suttles (Newark Eagles), rf	4	0	0	0
Buck Leonard (Homestead Grays), 1b	3	1	0	0
Pat Patterson (Philadelphia Stars), 3b	4	1	1	0
Sammy T. Hughes (Baltimore Elite Giants), 2b	3	0	1	0
Roy Parnell (Philadelphia Stars), lf	3	0	0	0
Bill Byrd (Baltimore Elite Giants), p	1	0	0	0
Leon Day (Newark Eagles), p	1	0	0	0
Roy Partlow (Homestead Grays), p	1	0	0	0
Bill Holland (N.Y. Black Yankees), p	0	0	0	0
	30	2	5	0

West

	AB	R	H	E
Henry Milton (Kansas City Monarchs), rf	3	0	1	0
Parnell Woods (Cleveland Bears), 3b	0	0	0	0
Dan Wilson (St. Louis Stars), lf	3	1	1	0
Alex Radcliffe (Chicago American Giants), 3b-ss	5	1	1	0
Neil Robinson (Memphis Red Sox), cf	4	1	3	0
Ted Strong (Kansas City Monarchs), ss-1b	2	0	0	1
Jelly Taylor (Memphis Red Sox), 1b	1	0	0	0
Billy Horn (Chicago American Giants), 2b	2	0	1	0
Leroy Morney (Toledo Crawfords), 2b-ss	1	0	0	0
Jim Williams (Toledo Crawfords), rf	2	0	0	0
Pepper Bassett (Chicago American Giants), c	1	0	0	0
Larry Brown (Memphis Red Sox), c	2	0	0	0
Theolic Smith (St. Louis Stars), p	0	0	0	0
Hilton Smith (Kansas City Monarchs), p	1	0	0	0
Ted Radcliffe (Memphis Red Sox), p	1	1	1	0
	28	4	8	1

EAST	020	000	000—2	
WEST	000	000	13x—4	

RBI—Hughes (2), Wilson (2), Robinson, Horn. 2B—Wright, Robinson. HR—Wilson, Robinson. SB—Patterson. DP—T. Smith, Bassett, and Taylor. SO—by T. Smith, 1; T. Radcliffe, 1; H. Smith, 3; Byrd, 1; Day, 1. BB—off T. Smith, 1; T. Radcliffe, 2; Byrd, 1; Day, 2; Holland, 1. Hits— off T. Smith, 4 in 3 innings; H. Smith, 0 in 3; T. Radcliffe, 1 in 3; Byrd, 2 in 3; Day, 0 in 3; Partlow, 4 in 1⅓; Holland, 2 in ⅔.

Winning pitcher—T. Radcliffe; loser—Partlow.
Attendance—40,000.

1940

East

	AB	R	H	E
Gene Benson (Philadelphia Stars), cf	6	1	2	0
Rabbit Martinez (N.Y. Cubans), ss	3	1	1	0
Bus Clarkson (Newark Eagles), ss	2	1	0	0
Ed Stone (Newark Eagles), rf	3	0	0	0
Alejandro Crespo (N.Y. Cubans), lf	2	2	1	0

Buck Leonard (Homestead Grays), 1b	4	2	2	0
Howard Easterling (Homestead Grays), 3b	5	1	2	0
Marvin Barker (N.Y. Black Yankees), cf-rf	5	1	2	0
W. G. Perkins (Baltimore Elite Giants), c	5	0	2	0
Robert Clarke (N.Y. Black Yankees), c	0	0	0	0
Dick Seay (N.Y. Black Yankees), 2b	4	1	0	0
Henry McHenry (Philadelphia Stars), p	0	0	0	0
Poppa Ruiz (N.Y. Cubans), p	2	1	0	0
Raymond Brown (Homestead Grays), p	2	0	0	0
	43	11	12	0

West

	AB	R	H	E
Henry Milton (Kansas City Monarchs), rf	4	0	1	0
Parnell Woods (Birmingham Black Barons), 3b	4	0	1	0
Eldridge Mayweather (N.O.–St. L. Stars), 1b	3	0	1	0
Neil Robinson (Memphis Red Sox), cf	2	0	0	0
Leslie Green (N.O.–St. L. Stars), cf	2	0	1	0
Donald Reeves (Chicago American Giants), lf	4	0	0	0
James Green (Kansas City Monarchs), c	2	0	0	1
Larry Brown (Memphis Red Sox), c	1	0	1	0
Leroy Morney (Chicago American Giants), ss	2	0	0	4
Curt Henderson (Indianapolis Crawfords), ss	1	0	0	0
Tommy Sampson (Birmingham Black Barons), 2b	2	0	0	0
Marshall Riddle (N.O.–St. L. Stars), 2b	1	0	0	1
Gene Bremmer (Memphis Red Sox), p	0	0	0	0
Walt Calhoun (N.O.–St. L. Stars), p	1	0	0	0
Cliff Johnson (Indianapolis Crawfords), p	0	0	0	0
Hilton Smith (Kansas City Monarchs), p	1	0	0	0
Jelly Taylor (Memphis Red Sox)	1	0	0	0
	31	0	5	6

EAST	200	114	030—11
WEST	000	000	000—0

2B—Benson. 3B—Crespo. SB—Leonard. DP—Seay, Clarkson, and Leonard; Morney, Sampson, and Mayweather. SO—by Bremmer, 2; Calhoun, 1; Johnson, 1; Smith, 3; McHenry, 1. BB—off Bremmer, 5; Johnson, 1; Smith, 4; McHenry, 1; Ruiz, 2.

Winning pitcher—McHenry; loser—Bremmer.

Attendance—25,000.

1941

East

	AB	R	H	E
Henry Kimbro (N.Y. Black Yankees), cf	3	1	1	0
Lennie Pearson (Newark Eagles), cf	2	0	0	0
Al Coimbre (N.Y. Cubans), rf	5	2	0	1
Bill Hoskins (Baltimore Elite Giants), lf	5	1	1	0
Buck Leonard (Homestead Grays), 1b	5	1	2	0
Monte Irvin (Newark Eagles), 3b	5	0	2	0
Roy Campanella (Baltimore Elite Giants), c	5	0	1	1
Horacio Martinez (N.Y. Cubans), ss	4	1	2	1
Dick Seay (N.Y. Black Yankees), 2b	4	1	0	1
Terris McDuffie (Homestead Grays), p	0	0	0	0
Dave Barnhill (N.Y. Cubans), p	2	1	2	0
Henry McHenry (Philadelphia Stars), p	0	0	0	0
Jimmy Hill (Newark Eagles), p	0	0	0	0
Bill Byrd (Baltimore Elite Giants), p	0	0	0	0
	40	8	11	4

West

	AB	R	H	E
Dan Wilson (St. Louis Stars), lf	2	0	0	1
Jimmy Crutchfield (Chicago American Giants), lf	3	0	1	0
Newt Allen (Kansas City Monarchs), ss	2	0	0	2
Billy Horn (Chicago American Giants), ss	2	0	0	0
Neil Robinson (Memphis Red Sox), cf	2	1	1	0
Buddy Armour (St. Louis Stars), cf	2	1	1	0
Ted Strong (Kansas City Monarchs), rf	4	0	2	0
Jelly Taylor (Memphis Red Sox), 1b	2	0	1	0
Lyman Bostock (Birmingham Black Barons), 1b	2	1	1	0
Parnell Woods (Jacksonville Red Caps), 3b	4	0	0	0
Tommy Sampson (Birmingham Black Barons), 2b	0	0	0	1
Bill Ford (St. Louis Stars), 2b	3	0	0	0
Pepper Bassett (Chicago American Giants), c	1	0	0	0
Larry Brown (Memphis Red Sox), c	3	0	0	1
Hilton Smith (Kansas City Monarchs), p	1	0	0	0
Ted Radcliffe (Memphis Red Sox), p	0	0	0	0
Leo Henry (Jacksonville Red Caps), p	0	0	0	0
Dan Bankhead (Memphis Red Sox), p	0	0	0	0
Satchel Paige (Kansas City Monarchs), p	1	0	0	0

Verdel Mathis (Memphis Red Sox)	0	0	0	0
Howard Cleveland (Jacksonville Red Caps)	1	0	1	0
Henry Hudson (Chicago American Giants)	1	0	0	0
George Mitchell (St. Louis Stars)	0	0	0	0
	36	3	8	5

EAST	200	600	000—8
WEST	100	000	020—3

RBI—Kimbro, Coimbre, Hoskins, Leonard (3), Barnhill, Strong, Bostock, Woods. 2B—Strong, Irvin. 3B—Strong. HR—Leonard. SH—Leonard, Martinez, Barnhill. SB—Kimbro (2), Irvin, Martinez, Taylor. LOB—East, 10; West, 7. DP—Campanella and Martinez. SO—by Barnhill, 2; Hill, 1; Smith, 1; Radcliffe, 1; Henry, 1; Paige, 2. BB—off Radcliffe, 1; Bankhead, 1; Paige, 1. Hits—off McDuffie, 3 in 2 innings; Barnhill, 2 in 3; McHenry, 2 in 2; Hill, 0 in 1; Byrd, 1 in 1; Smith, 2 in 3; Radcliffe, 4 in ⅔; Henry, 3 in 1⅓; Bankhead, 1 in 2; Paige, 1 in 2. PB—Bassett.

Winning pitcher—McDuffie; loser—Smith.

Attendance—50,256.

1942

East

	AB	R	H	E
Dan Wilson (N.Y. Black Yankees), lf	4	3	2	0
Sam Bankhead (Homestead Grays), 2b-cf	5	1	2	0
Willie Wells (Newark Eagles), ss	5	0	1	0
Josh Gibson (Homestead Grays), c	3	0	2	0
Bill Wright (Baltimore Elite Giants), rf	5	0	2	0
Jim West (Philadelphia Stars), 1b	4	0	0	0
Pat Patterson (Philadelphia Stars), 3b	3	0	0	2
Tetelo Vargas (N.Y. Cubans), cf	3	0	1	0
Herberto Blanco (N.Y. Cubans), 2b	0	0	0	0
Jonas Gaines (Baltimore Elite Giants), p	1	0	0	0
Vic Harris (Homestead Grays)	1	0	0	0
Lennis Pearson (Newark Eagles)	1	1	1	0
Dave Barnhill (N.Y. Cubans), p	0	0	0	0
Barney Brown (Philadelphia Stars), p	0	0	0	0
Leon Day (Newark Eagles), p	1	0	0	0
	36	5	11	2

West

	AB	R	H	E
Cool Papa Bell (Chicago American Giants), cf	4	0	1	0
Parnell Woods (Cincinnati Buckeyes), 3b	3	1	1	0
Marlin Carter (Memphis Red Sox), 3b	1	0	0	0
Ted Strong (Kansas City Monarchs), rf	3	0	1	0
Willard Brown (Kansas City Monarchs), lf	4	0	1	0
James Green (Kansas City Monarchs), c	4	0	0	0
John O'Neil (Kansas City Monarchs), 1b	4	0	0	1
Tommy Sampson (Birmingham Black Barons), 2b	3	0	0	1
Art Pennington (Chicago American Giants)	1	0	0	0
T. J. Brown (Memphis Red Sox), ss	3	0	0	0
Lloyd Davenport (Birmingham Black Barons)	1	0	0	0
Hilton Smith (Kansas City Monarchs), p	1	0	0	0
Fred Bankhead (Memphis Red Sox)	0	1	0	0
Porter Moss (Memphis Red Sox), p	0	0	0	0
Eugene Bremmer (Cincinnati Buckeyes), p	0	0	0	0
Satchel Paige (Kansas City Monarchs), p	1	0	1	0
Sam Jethroe (Cincinnati Buckeyes)	1	0	0	0
	34	2	5	2

EAST	001	010	102—5
WEST	001	001	000—2

RBI—Wright (2), Bankhead (2), Gibson, Green. 2B—Wilson, Bankhead, W. Brown, Pearson. 3B—Woods. SH—Wells. SB—Patterson, Wilson (2), Wells, Vargas. LOB—East, 8; West, 6. DP—Sampson, T. Brown, and O'Neil (2). SO—by H. Smith, 2; Moss, 1; Barnhill, 4; Bremmer, 1; Paige, 2; Day, 5. BB—off Moss, 2; Barnhill, 1; Paige, 1. Hits—off Smith, 4 in 3 innings; Moss, 2 in 2; Bremmer, 0 in 1; Paige, 5 in 3; Gaines, 1 in 3; Barnhill, 2 in 3; B. Brown, 2 in ⅔; Day, 0 in 2⅓.

Winning pitcher—Day; loser—Paige.
Attendance—48,400.

1943

East

	AB	R	H	E
Cool Papa Bell (Homestead Grays), lf	4	0	0	0
Henry Kimbro (Baltimore Elite Giants), cf	1	0	0	0
Juan Vargas (N.Y. Cubans), cf	2	0	0	0
Buck Leonard (Homestead Grays), 1b	4	1	1	0

	AB	R	H	E
Josh Gibson (Homestead Grays), c	3	0	1	0
Howard Easterling (Homestead Grays), 3b	4	0	1	0
Lennie Pearson (Newark Eagles), rf	3	0	0	0
Sam Bankhead (Homestead Grays), 2b	3	0	1	0
Horacio Martinez (N.Y. Cubans), ss	2	0	1	0
Dave Barnhill (N.Y. Cubans), p	1	0	0	0
John Wright (Homestead Grays), p	0	0	0	0
Bill Harvey (Baltimore Elite Giants), p	0	0	0	0
Leon Day (Newark Eagles), p	1	0	0	0
George Scales (Baltimore Elite Giants)	1	0	0	0
Jerry Benjamin (Homestead Grays)	1	0	0	0
Vic Harris (Homestead Grays)	1	0	0	0
	31	1	4	0

West

	AB	R	H	E
Jesse Williams (Kansas City Monarchs), ss	3	0	2	0
Lloyd Davenport (Chicago American Giants), rf	2	0	0	0
Alex Radcliffe (Chicago American Giants), 3b	4	0	1	0
Willard Brown (Kansas City Monarchs), cf	3	1	1	0
Neil Robinson (Memphis Red Sox), lf	2	1	0	0
Lester Lockett (Birmingham Black Barons), lf	0	0	0	0
John O'Neil (Kansas City Monarchs), 1b	2	0	0	0
Tommy Sampson (Birmingham Black Barons), 2b	3	0	1	0
Ted Radcliffe (Chicago American Giants), c	3	0	0	0
Satchel Paige (Kansas City Monarchs), p	1	0	1	0
Gread McKinnis (Birmingham Black Barons), p	1	0	0	0
Theolic Smith (Cleveland Buckeyes), p	1	0	0	0
Porter Moss (Memphis Red Sox), p	0	0	0	0
Bubber Hyde (Memphis Red Sox)	0	0	0	0
Fred Wilson (Cincinnati Clowns)	1	0	0	0
	26	2	6	0

EAST	000	000	001—1
WEST	010	100	00x—2

RBI—Leonard, Sampson. 2B—Paige. HR—Leonard. SB—Brown, Williams. LOB—East, 4; West, 6. DP—Bankhead and Leonard; Pearson, Gibson, and Easterling. SO—Paige, 4; McKinnis, 1; Wright, 2; Smith, 1. BB—off Paige, 1; Smith, 1; Barnhill, 1; Day, 1.

Winning pitcher—Paige; loser—Barnhill.

Attendance—51,723.

1944

East

	AB	R	H	E
Cool Papa Bell (Homestead Grays), lf	5	0	0	0
Ray Dandridge (Newark Eagles), 3b-2b	5	0	3	0
Al Coimbre (N.Y. Cubans), rf	5	0	0	0
Buck Leonard (Homestead Grays), 1b	3	1	1	1
Josh Gibson (Homestead Grays), c	3	1	2	0
John Davis (Newark Eagles), cf	3	0	2	0
Sam Bankhead (Homestead Grays), 2b-ss	3	1	1	1
Pee Wee Butts (Baltimore Elite Giants), ss	2	0	0	0
Horacio Martinez (N.Y. Cubans), ss	0	0	0	0
Terris McDuffie (Newark Eagles), p	1	0	1	0
Carranza Howard (N.Y. Cubans), p	1	0	0	0
Barney Morris (N.Y. Cubans), p	0	0	0	0
Bill Byrd (Baltimore Elite Giants), p	1	0	0	0
Marvin Williams (Philadelphia Stars)	1	0	0	0
Roy Campanella (Baltimore Elite Giants), 3b	1	1	1	0
Henry Kimbro (Baltimore Elite Giants), rf	1	0	0	0
	35	4	11	2

	AB	R	H	E
Sam Jethroe (Cleveland Buckeyes), cf	3	0	0	0
Neil Robinson (Memphis Red Sox), cf	2	0	0	0
Art Wilson (Birmingham Black Barons), ss	5	1	2	0
Lloyd Davenport (Chicago American Giants), rf	4	1	1	0
Buddy Armour (Cleveland Buckeyes), lf	4	2	2	0
Alex Radcliffe (Cincinnati Clowns), 3b	4	0	1	0
Bonnie Serrell (Kansas City Monarchs), 2b	3	1	2	0
Archie Ware (Cleveland Buckeyes), 1b	4	1	1	0
Ted Radcliffe (Birmingham Black Barons), c	4	1	2	0
Verdel Mathis (Memphis Red Sox), p	1	0	1	0
Gentry Jessup (Chicago American Giants), p	2	0	0	0
Gread McKinnis (Chicago American Giants), p	0	0	0	0
Gene Bremmer (Cleveland Buckeyes), p	0	0	0	0
	36	7	12	0

EAST	010	100	200—4
WEST	101	050	00x—7

RBI—Bankhead, A. Radcliffe (2), Serrell, Ware, T. Radcliffe (2), Campanella, Dandridge, Davis. 2B—Gibson, Dandridge, Ware. 3B—Leonard, McDuffie, A. Radcliffe. HR—T. Radcliffe. SB—Armour. LOB—East, 8; West, 7. DP—Jethroe and T. Radcliffe; Wilson, Serrell, and Ware. SO— by McDuffie, 2; Morris, 1; McKinnis, 1; Bremmer, 2. BB—off Jessup, 2; McKinnis, 1; McDuffie, 1. Hits—off Mathis, 3 in 3 innings; McDuffie, 5 in 3; Howard, 4 in 1⅔; Morris, 1 in 1⅓; Jessup, 3 in 3; McKinnis, 4 in 1; Bremmer, 1 in 1⅔; Byrd, 2 in 2. PB—T. Radcliffe.

Winning pitcher—Mathis; loser—Howard.

Attendance—46,247.

1945

East

	AB	R	H	E
Jerry Benjamin (Homestead Grays), cf	5	1	1	0
Frank Austin (Philadelphia Stars), ss	2	0	0	1
Horacio Martinez (N.Y. Cubans), ss	2	0	2	0
John Davis (Newark Eagles), lf	2	0	0	0
Gene Benson (Philadelphia Stars), lf	2	1	0	0
Buck Leonard (Homestead Grays), 1b	3	1	1	0
Roy Campanella (Baltimore Elite Giants), c	5	1	2	0
Willie Wells (Newark Eagles), 2b	5	0	1	0
Bill Wright (Baltimore Elite Giants), rf	1	0	0	0
Rogelio Linares (N.Y. Cubans), rf	3	1	0	0
Marvin Barker (N.Y. Black Yankees), 3b	2	0	1	0
Murray Watkins (Newark Eagles), 3b	2	0	2	0
Tom Glover (Baltimore Elite Giants), p	0	0	0	0
Bill Ricks (Philadelphia Stars), p	0	0	0	0
Martin Dihigo (N.Y. Cubans), p	1	0	0	0
Roy Welmaker (Homestead Grays), p	0	0	0	0
Lennie Pearson (Newark Eagles)	1	0	0	0
Bill Byrd (Baltimore Elite Giants)	1	1	0	0
	37	6	10	1

West

	AB	R	H	E
Jesse Williams (Kansas City Monarchs), 2b	5	0	2	0
Jackie Robinson (Kansas City Monarchs), ss	5	0	0	0
Lloyd Davenport (Cleveland Buckeyes), rf	4	1	1	0
Neil Robinson (Memphis Red Sox), cf	2	2	2	0

Alex Radcliffe (Cincinnati–Ind. Clowns), 3b	4	2	2	1
Lester Lockett (Birmingham Black Barons), lf	4	0	0	0
Archie Ware (Cleveland Buckeyes), 1b	4	1	2	0
Quincy Trouppe (Cleveland Buckeyes), c	1	2	1	0
Verdel Mathis (Memphis Red Sox), p	2	1	2	0
Gentry Jessup (Chicago American Giants), p	1	0	0	0
Booker McDaniels (Kansas City Monarchs), p	1	0	0	0
Gene Bremmer (Cleveland Buckeyes), p	0	0	0	0
	33	9	12	1

EAST	000	000	105—6
WEST	044	100	00x—9

RBI—Benjamin, Martinez (3), Wells (2), Williams (4), Radcliffe, Lock-ett, Ware (3). 2B—Wells, Davenport, Radcliffe. 3B—Williams. SH—N. Robinson. LOB—West, 5, East, 10. SO—by Mathis, 4; Jessup, 1; McDonald, 1. BB—off Mathis, 1; Jessup, 2; McDaniels, 2; Glover, 1; Ricks, 1; Welmaker, 1.

Winning pitcher—Mathis; loser—Glover.
Attendance—31,714.

1946

(At Griffith Stadium, Washington)

West

	AB	R	H	E
Art Wilson (Birmingham Black Barons), ss	3	1	1	0
Othello Renfroe (Kansas City Monarchs), ss	1	0	0	0
Archie Ware (Cleveland Buckeyes), 1b	4	0	0	0
Sam Jethroe (Cleveland Buckeyes), cf	4	1	0	0
Piper Davis (Birmingham Black Barons), 2b	4	1	2	0
Willie Grace (Cleveland Buckeyes), rf	4	0	1	0
Bubber Hyde (Memphis Red Sox), lf	3	0	1	0
John Scott (Kansas City Monarchs), lf	2	0	1	0
Alex Radcliffe (Memphis Red Sox), 3b	3	0	0	0
Quincy Trouppe (Cleveland Buckeyes), c	1	0	0	0
Buster Haywood (Cincinnati–Ind. Clowns), c	1	0	0	0
John Brown (Cleveland Buckeyes)	1	0	0	0
Dan Bankhead (Memphis Red Sox), p	1	0	0	0
Vibert Clarke (Cleveland Buckeyes), p	0	0	0	0

	AB	R	H	E
Gentry Jessup (Chicago American Giants), p	1	0	0	0
Clyde Nelson (Chicago American Giants), 3b	1	0	0	0
John Williams (Cincinnati–Ind. Clowns), p	2	0	0	0
	34	3	6	0

East

	AB	R	H	E
Henry Kimbro (Baltimore Elite Giants), cf	2	1	1	0
Larry Doby (Newark Eagles), 2b	4	2	2	0
Howard Easterling (Homestead Grays), 3b	4	2	3	0
Buck Leonard (Homestead Grays), 1b	3	0	0	0
Monte Irvin (Newark Eagles), lf	3	0	0	0
Josh Gibson (Homestead Grays), c	2	0	1	0
Leon Ruffin (Newark Eagles), c	1	0	0	0
Louis Louden (N.Y. Cubans), c	1	0	0	0
Murray Watkins (Philadelphia Stars)	0	0	0	0
Gene Benson (Philadelphia Stars), rf	1	0	1	0
Lennie Pearson (Newark Eagles), rf	3	0	1	0
Sam Bankhead (Homestead Grays), ss	2	0	0	0
Silvio Garcia (N.Y. Cubans), ss	2	0	0	0
Barney Brown (Philadelphia Stars), p	1	0	0	0
Frank Austin (Philadelphia Stars)	0	0	0	0
Pat Scantlebury (N.Y. Cubans), p	0	0	0	0
Bill Byrd (Baltimore Elite Giants), p	1	0	0	0
Pete Diaz (N.Y. Cubans)	1	0	0	0
Jonas Gaines (Baltimore Elite Giants), p	0	0	0	0
Leon Day (Newark Eagles), p	0	0	0	0
	31	5	9	0

WEST	000	300	000—3
EAST	200	300	00x—5

RBI—Davis, Grace, Hyde, Easterling, Leonard, Irvin, Pearson. SB—Doby, Irvin. SH—Leonard. DP—Wilson, Ware, and Davis; Bankhead and Leonard. SO—by Bankhead, 2; Jessup, 1; Byrd, 4. BB—off Bankhead, 1; Jessup, 1; Byrd, 1. Hits—off Bankhead, 3 in 3 innings; Clark, 3 in ⅓; Jessup, 2 in 2⅔; Williams, 1 in 2; Brown, 0 in 2; Scantlebury, 3 in ⅓; Byrd, 1 in 2⅔; Gaines, 1 in 2; Day, 1 in 1. PB—Trouppe, Haywood (2).

Winning pitcher—Byrd; loser—Clark.

Attendance—16,000.

(At Comiskey Park, Chicago)

East

	AB	R	H	E
Henry Kimbro (Baltimore Elite Giants), cf	4	0	0	0
Larry Doby (Newark Eagles), 2b	3	0	1	0
Howard Easterling (Homestead Grays), 3b	4	0	0	0
Buck Leonard (Homestead Grays), 1b	4	0	1	0
Monte Irvin (Newark Eagles), lf	4	0	1	0
Josh Gibson (Homestead Grays), c	3	0	0	0
Gene Benson (Philadelphia Stars), rf	3	0	0	1
Silvio Garcia (N.Y. Cubans), ss	1	0	0	2
Pat Scantlebury (N.Y. Cubans)	1	0	1	0
Peewee Butts (Baltimore Elite Giants), ss	0	0	0	0
Barney Brown (Philadelphia Stars), p	1	0	0	0
Bill Byrd (Baltimore Elite Giants), p	1	0	0	0
Jonas Gaines (Baltimore Elite Giants), p	0	0	0	0
Murray Watkins (Newark Eagles)	0	1	0	0
Leon Day (Newark Eagles), p	0	0	0	0
	29	1	4	3

West

	AB	R	H	E
Art Wilson (Birmingham Black Barons), ss	4	1	1	0
Archie Ware (Cleveland Buckeyes), 1b	2	0	0	0
Sam Jethroe (Cleveland Buckeyes), cf	3	1	0	0
Piper Davis (Birmingham Black Barons), 2b	3	1	1	0
Willie Grace (Cleveland Buckeyes), rf	4	1	3	0
Alex Radcliffe (Cincinnati Clowns), 3b	3	0	0	0
Bubber Hyde (Memphis Red Sox), lf	3	0	2	1
Quincy Trouppe (Cleveland Buckeyes), c	1	0	0	0
Felix Evans (Memphis Red Sox), p	1	0	0	0
Dan Bankhead (Memphis Red Sox), p	1	0	0	0
John Williams (Cincinnati–Ind. Clowns), p	1	0	0	0
	26	4	7	1

EAST	000	000	010—1
WEST	000	220	00x—4

RBI—Hyde, Davis, Doby. 2B—Hyde. SB—Wilson, Jethroe, Hyde. SH—Doby. DP—Davis, Wilson, and Ware. SO—by Brown, 3; Day, 1; Bankhead, 3; Gaines, 1; Evans, 1. BB—off Evans, 2; Brown, 1; Bankhead, 3; Byrd, 2. Hits—off Brown, 2 in 3 innings; Gaines, 0 in 2⅓; Byrd, 4 in 1⅓; Day,

1 in 1; Evans, 1 in 3; Williams, 2 in 3; Bankhead, 1 in 3. HP—by Bankhead (Garcia); Williams (Watkins); Brown (Jethroe).
    Winning pitcher—Evans; loser—Byrd.
    Attendance—45,474.

1947

East

	AB	R	H	E
Henry Kimbro (Baltimore Elite Giants), cf	4	0	0	0
Peewee Butts (Baltimore Elite Giants), ss	2	0	0	0
John Washington (Baltimore Elite Giants), 1b	4	0	0	0
Monte Irvin (Newark Eagles), lf	3	1	0	0
Silvio Garcia (N.Y. Cubans), 2b	3	0	0	0
Claro Duaney (N.Y. Cubans), rf	2	0	0	0
Orestes Minoso (N.Y. Cubans), 3b	3	0	0	0
John Hayes (N.Y. Black Yankees), c	1	0	0	0
Max Manning (Newark Eagles), p	2	0	1	0
Luis Tiant (N.Y. Cubans), p	1	0	0	0
Luis Marquez (Homestead Grays), rf	1	1	1	0
Louis Louden (N.Y. Cubans), c	1	0	1	0
Frank Austin (Philadelphia Stars), ss	2	0	0	0
Henry Miller (Philadelphia Stars), p	0	0	0	0
John Wright (Homestead Grays), p	0	0	0	0
Bob Romby (Baltimore Elite Giants)	1	0	0	0
Biz Mackey (Newark Eagles)	0	0	0	0
Vic Harris (Homestead Grays)	0	0	0	0
	30	2	3	0

West

	AB	R	H	E
Art Wilson (Birmingham Black Barons), ss	4	0	0	0
Herb Souell (Kansas City Monarchs), 3b	5	1	1	0
Sam Jethroe (Cleveland Buckeyes), rf	3	1	1	0
Piper Davis (Birmingham Black Barons), 2b	3	1	2	0
Quincy Trouppe (Cleveland Buckeyes), c	2	1	1	0
Jose Colas (Memphis Red Sox), lf	4	0	2	0
Goose Tatum (Indianapolis Clowns), 1b	4	0	2	0
Buddy Armour (Chicago American Giants), rf	4	1	2	0
Dan Bankhead (Memphis Red Sox), p	2	0	0	0

Gentry Jessup (Chicago American Giants), p	1	0	0	0
Chet Brewer (Cleveland Buckeyes), p	1	0	1	0
	33	5	12	0

EAST	010	000	010—2
WEST	211	000	01x—5

RBI—Davis, Colas (2), Duaney, Trouppe, Louden, Brewer. 2B—Davis, Armour (2), Marquez. 3B—Souell, Trouppe, Jethroe. SB—Jethroe, Davis. SH—Trouppe. DP—Wilson, Davis, and Tatum. SO—by Bankhead, 2; Manning, 3; Jessup, 1; Brewer, 1; Miller, 1. BB—off Manning, 2; Miller, 1; Brewer, 1. Hits—off Manning, 5 in 2⅓ innings; Tiant, 2 in 2⅔; Miller, 2 in 2; Wright, 3 in 1; Bankhead, 1 in 3; Jessup, 0 in 3; Brewer, 2 in 3. HP—by Bankhead (Irvin); Manning (Jethroe). PB—Louden.

Winning pitcher—Bankhead; loser—Manning.

Attendance—48,112.

1948

East

	AB	R	H	E
Luis Marquez (Homestead Grays), cf	4	0	0	0
Orestes Minoso (N.Y. Cubans), 3b	4	0	1	0
Luke Easter (Homestead Grays), lf	0	0	0	1
Lester Lockett (Baltimore Elite Giants), lf	2	0	0	0
Buck Leonard (Homestead Grays), 1b	4	0	1	0
Bob Harvey (Newark Eagles), rf	1	0	0	0
Monte Irvin (Newark Eagles), rf	2	0	0	0
Jim Gilliam (Baltimore Elite Giants), 2b	3	0	1	0
Louis Louden (N.Y. Cubans), c	3	0	0	0
Bill Cash (Philadelphia Stars), c	0	0	0	0
Peewee Butts (Baltimore Elite Giants), ss	2	0	0	1
Frank Austin (Philadelphia Stars), ss	1	0	0	0
Rufus Lewis (Newark Eagles), p	1	0	0	0
Wilbur Fields (Homestead Grays), p	1	0	0	0
Robert Griffith (N.Y. Black Yankees), p	1	0	0	0
	29	0	3	2

West

	AB	R	H	E
Art Wilson (Birmingham Black Barons), ss	3	0	0	0
Herb Souell (Kansas City Monarchs), 3b	4	0	0	0
Piper Davis (Birmingham Black Barons), 2b	3	1	1	0
Willard Brown (Kansas City Monarchs), cf	4	1	2	0
Robert Boyd (Memphis Red Sox), 1b	4	1	2	1
Neil Robinson (Memphis Red Sox), lf	3	0	1	0
Quincy Trouppe (Chicago American Giants), c	3	0	0	0
Sam Hill (Chicago American Giants), rf	3	0	0	0
Bill Powell (Birmingham Black Barons), p	1	0	0	0
Jim LaMarque (Kansas City Monarchs), p	1	0	0	0
Gentry Jessup (Chicago American Giants), p	1	0	1	0
	30	3	7	1

EAST	000	000	000—0	
WEST	020	000	01x—3	

RBI—Robinson, Hill, Boyd. 2B—Davis, Leonard. SB—Davis. DP—Gilliam, Louden, Minoso, Butts, and Minoso; Davis, Wilson, and Boyd. SO—by Powell, 2; Lewis, 4; LaMarque, 1; Fields, 2; Griffith, 2; Jessup, 1. BB—off Powell, 1; Lewis, 2; Fields, 1; Griffith, 1; Jessup, 1. Hits—off Powell, 1 in 3; Lewis, 3 in 3; LaMarque, 2 in 3; Fields, 1 in 3; Jessup, 0 in 3; Griffith, 3 in 2. WP—Powell.

Winning pitcher—Powell; loser—Lewis.

Attendance—42,000.

1949

East

	AB	R	H	E
Peewee Butts (Baltimore Elite Giants), ss	4	1	1	0
Pedro Diaz (N.Y. Cubans), cf	4	0	3	0
Lennie Pearson (Baltimore Elite Giants), 1b	5	0	0	0
Bus Clarkson (Philadelphia Stars), rf	2	0	1	0
Sherwood Brewer (Indianapolis Clowns), rf	2	1	1	1
Robert Davis (Baltimore Elite Giants), lf	4	1	1	1
Jim Gilliam (Baltimore Elite Giants), 2b	4	0	0	0
Howard Easterling (N.Y. Cubans), 3b	4	1	2	0
Bill Cash (Philadelphia Stars), c	4	0	1	0
Bob Griffith (Philadelphia Stars), p	1	0	1	0

Dave Hoskins (Cleveland Buckeyes)	1	0	0	0
Andy Porter (Indianapolis Clowns), p	0	0	0	0
Leon Kellman (Cleveland Buckeyes)	1	0	0	0
Pat Scantlebury (N.Y. Cubans), p	1	0	0	0
	37	4	11	1

West

	AB	R	H	E
Jose Burgos (Birmingham Black Barons), ss	2	0	0	0
Orlando Verona (Memphis Red Sox), ss	1	0	0	1
Herman Bell (Birmingham Black Barons)	1	0	0	0
Bob Boyd (Memphis Red Sox), 1b	4	0	0	0
Pedro Formenthal (Memphis Red Sox), cf	1	0	0	0
John Davis (Houston Eagles), cf	2	0	0	0
Piper Davis (Birmingham Black Barons), 2b	4	0	1	0
Willard Brown (Kansas City Monarchs), lf-3b	3	0	0	0
Lonnie Summers (Chicago American Giants), c	3	0	1	2
Robert Wilson (Houston Eagles), ss-3b	3	0	0	0
Gene Richardson (Kansas City Monarchs), p	1	0	0	0
Willie Greason (Birmingham Black Barons), p	0	0	0	0
John O'Neil (Kansas City Monarchs)	1	0	0	0
Gread McKinnis (Chicago American Giants), p	0	0	0	0
Willie Hutchinson (Memphis Red Sox), p	1	0	0	0
Jim LaMarque (Kansas City Monarchs), p	1	0	0	0
	28	0	2	3

EAST	110	000	020—4
WEST	000	000	000—0

RBI—Clarkson, Griffith, Gilliam, Easterling. 2B—P. Davis, Butts, Cash. SB—Easterling, Diaz, R. Davis. DP—Boyd and P. Davis; Easterling, Gilliam, and Pearson. SO—by Griffith, 1; Scantlebury, 1; Richardson, 2; Greason, 1. BB—off Richardson, 2; Griffith, 1; Porter, 1. Hits—off Griffith, 0 in 3; Porter, 0 in 3; Scantlebury, 2 in 3; Richardson, 4 in 3; Greason, 2 in 3; McKinnis, 4 in 1⅔; Hutchinson, 0 in ⅓; LaMarque, 1 in 1.

Winning pitcher—Griffith; loser—Richardson.

Attendance—26,697.

1950

East

	AB	R	H	E
Henry Merchant (Indianapolis Clowns), lf	5	0	0	0
Peewee Butts (Baltimore Elite Giants), ss	3	1	0	0
Rene Gonzalez (N.Y. Cubans), 1b	3	0	2	0
Pedro Diaz (N.Y. Cubans), cf	5	0	1	0
Louis Louden (N.Y. Cubans), c	5	1	1	0
Jim Gilliam (Baltimore Elite Giants), 2b	3	1	1	0
Ben Little (Philadelphia Stars), rf	3	0	2	0
Charles White (Philadelphia Stars), 3b	1	0	0	0
Sherwood Brewer (Indianapolis Clowns), 3b-rf	3	0	0	1
Joe Black (Baltimore Elite Giants), p	1	0	0	0
Raul Galata (N.Y. Cubans), p	2	0	0	0
Jonas Gaines (Philadelphia Stars), p	0	0	0	0
Pat Scantlebury (N.Y. Cubans), p	1	0	0	0
	35	3	7	1

West

	AB	R	H	E
Curley Williams (Houston Eagles), ss	1	1	0	0
Clyde McNeal (Chicago American Giants), ss	3	0	1	1
Herb Souell (Kansas City Monarchs), 3b	1	1	0	0
Leon Kellman (Memphis Red Sox), 3b	2	0	0	1
Jesse Douglas (Chicago American Giants), 3b	4	0	3	0
Alonzo Perry (Birmingham Black Barons), 1b	3	1	2	0
John Washington (Houston Eagles), 1b	2	0	0	1
Bob Harvey (Houston Eagles), rf	2	1	0	0
Pepper Bassett (Birmingham Black Barons), c	1	0	1	0
Art Pennington (Chicago American Giants), cf	3	1	1	0
Ed Steele (Birmingham Black Barons), lf	3	0	2	1
Casey Jones (Memphis Red Sox), c	2	0	0	0
Thomas Cooper (Kansas City Monarchs), c-rf	1	0	0	0
Vibert Clarke (Memphis Red Sox), p	1	0	0	0
Cliff Johnson (Kansas City Monarchs), p	2	0	1	0
Bill Powell (Birmingham Black Barons), p	1	0	0	0
	32	5	11	4

EAST	000	200	001—3
WEST	002	030	000—5

RBI—Diaz, Little, Douglas (2), Pennington (2), Steele. 2B—Little, Diaz, Washington. 3B—Johnson, Pennington. HR—Gilliam. SB—Douglas (2), Butts. SH—Souell, Gilliam. SO—Clark, 3; Johnson, 3; Powell, 4; Galata, 1; Gaines, 3; Scantlebury, 1. BB—off Clark, 2; Johnson, 2; Black, 1; Galata, 1. HP—by Galata (Steele).

Winning pitcher—Johnson; loser—Galata.

Attendance—24,614.

Index

Johnson, Jack, 9, 64
Johnson, James Weldon, 145
Johnson, Julius (Judy), 11, 66, 75,
    78, 91, 99, 134, 183, 201
Joseph, Newt, 11, 83, 188

Kansas City Monarchs, 19, 35, 55,
    62, 70–71
  creation of, 11
  in Denver Post Tournament,
    136–37
  effects of integration on, 19,
    188–89, 217–18
  minor league team of, 188
  in Negro World Series, 11
  and night games, 127–28
  reputation of, 17–18
  Robinson on, 201–2, 203
  on tour, 119, 123, 131–32
Kansas City Royals, 29–30, 184–
    85
Kincannon, Harry, 53
Knox, Elmer, 51

Lacy, Sam, 89
LaGuardia, Fiorello, 186
Landis, Kenesaw Mountain
    (Judge), 7, 114, 193
  on black vs white contests, 183–
    84
  racism of, 197–98
Lasorda, Tommy, 160
Latin American baseball
  integration of, 175–76
  Negro-league players in, 30–32,
    164–65, 169–74, 175, 176–
    177
  See also Specific countries
Leonard, Buck, 3–4, 20, 72, 76,
    78, 90, 98, 134, 186, 192,
    202, 219
  on Bingo Long film, 150
  discovery and recruitment of,
    43–44
Lincoln Giants, 11, 28, 182–83
Lloyd, John Henry, 9, 12, 40
Lowe, Nat, 185, 194
Lundy, Dick, 28
Luque, Adolph (Red), 157–58

McDonald, Webster, 8, 57–58, 79,
    80, 83, 219
McDuffie, Terris, 158
McGraw, John, 8, 158
Mack, Connie, 8, 183, 201

Mackey, Biz, 58, 83, 84, 109
MacPhail, Larry, 125, 186, 187
McQuery, Fred, 73
Madlock, Leroy, 140
major-league baseball
  integration of. See baseball
    integration
  and Mexican baseball, 170–71
  relations with Negro League,
    18–19
  games against 6–7, 31–32, 115,
    121–26, 179, 182–85
  numbers racketeers and, 113–
    14
  stadium rentals in, 24, 212–13
major-league players
  on integrated teams, 32, 135
  in California, 29
  in Caribbean, 30, 154, 155–
    56, 162
  in Dakota League, 139–40
  in Latin America, 175–76
  on Negro league ability, 181–82
Malarcher, Dave, 13, 78, 83, 189,
    219
  family background of, 42
  recruitment of, 42–43
Manley, Abe, 59, 77, 107, 109
Manley, Effa, 74, 77, 149
  baseball integration and, 186–
    87, 216, 217
  as civil rights activist, 109
  family background of, 108–9
  and Mexican league, 171
  and Newark Eagles, 109–10
  Rickey and, 212–13
  Stop Lynching campaign of, 94
Mann, Arthur, 210, 211–12
Marcelle, Ollie, 136
Marsans, Armando, 61, 153
Marshall, Jack, 219
Mathewson, Christy, 8
Mays, Willie, Jr., 76–77, 84
Mays, Willie, Sr., 51
Mendez, José, 11, 62, 155
Mexican baseball
  American tours by, 170
  Negro-league players in, 47,
    169–74
Miami Clowns, 146
Miami Giants, 28, 138
Midwest
  Negro American League of, 17–
    18
  tournament games in, 136–41

Tatum, Goose, 64, 142–43, 144
Taylor, Jim (Candy), 38
Tebbetts, Birdie, 82
Tennessee Rats, 55, 145–46
Texas Negro League, 46–47, 169
Thomas, Clint, 16, 70, 95–96, 219
Tiant, Luis, Jr., 156
Tiant, Luis, Sr., 156–57
Torrienti, Cristobel, 61–62, 155, 158
Trammell, Nat, 90
Trouppe, Quincy, 36, 47, 50, 69, 79–80, 133, 154, 158–59
in Dakota League, 139–40
in Mexico, 173–74
Trujillo, Rafael, 166, 167–68
Trujillo All-Stars, 140
Tut, King, 142
Twenty Years Too Soon (Trouppe), 36
twilight game, 23

umpires, 73–74
United States League, 207–8, 213

Vashon High School, St. Louis, 50
Veeck, Bill, 24, 215
integration attempt by, 196–97
on Rickey, 208, 209
Venezuela, Negro-league players in, 165
Vergez, Johnny, 194, 195

Waco Yellow Jackets, 7
Wallace, Bill, 41
Waller, Fats, 102
Washington, Kenny, 203
Washington, D.C., Negro-league baseball in, 93
Washington Senators, 159, 192
Welau, John, 122, 159

Wells, Willie, 24, 25, 59, 60, 70, 72, 73, 82, 85, 107, 109, 184 214–15, 218
barnstorming by, 127
baseball education of, 83, 84
batting helmet of, 74
in Cuba, 159
discovery and recruitment of, 40–42
in Mexico, 31, 169–70, 172
reputation of, 21
White, Sol, 86, 145
Wichita (Kansas), baseball tournament in, 138
Wilkinson, J.L. (Wilkie), 11, 17–18, 19, 61–62, 69, 132, 218
and baseball integration, 187, 188–89
Robinson and, 201, 202
Williams, Smokey Joe, 12, 13, 15, 43, 65, 78
against major league teams, 182–83
Williams, Ted, 176
winter baseball
in California, 28–29, 56
in Florida, 27–28
in Latin America and Caribbean, 155, 163–64, 165, 169
Wilson, Boojum, 101
Wilson, Rollo, 77
Wilson, Tom, 107
World War II, army teams in, 57
Wright, Bill, 172
Wynn, Early, 162

Yancey, Bill, 63, 164

Zorilla, Pete, 163, 164
Zulu Cannibals, 146–47

CPSIA information can be obtained
at www.ICGtesting.com
Printed in the USA
LVHW041654191118
597654LV00015B/362/P

9 780803 259690